PRAISE FOR THE INDISPENSABLE BRAND

Brand monotony—consumers' inability to distinguish between leading brands within most product categories—is something anyone involved in brand management should be concerned about. As this book points out, the digital revolution, changes in the commercial landscape, and a shift in the balance of power from manufacturer to consumer have all contributed to this condition. However, marketers themselves have also played a role. In The Indispensable Brand, Mitch Duckler proposes a number of significant changes to the ways we view and manage brands that can help combat brand monotony and achieve the goal of building brands our consumers truly cannot live without.

—REBECCA MESSINA, CHIEF MARKETING OFFICER, UBER

In this very readable and important book, Mitch Duckler takes us all the way back to the early days of marketing—and to the important foundational elements of the discipline that many of us have lost sight of. While the marketing landscape continues to change dramatically, the need for strong, differentiated brands remains constant. Mitch not only reminds us of this, but he also offers a clear road map for building powerful brands in today's crowded, fast-paced, and digitally-driven marketplace. It is a must-read for anyone managing brands in the twenty-first century.

—TIM MURPHY, SVP, DIGITAL MARKETING
LEAD, NORTH AMERICA, CHUBB

In his book, The Indispensable Brand, Duckler shows us, through numerous real-world examples, how to develop brand positioning in a way that is inherently more compelling and differentiated. Importantly, he also provides case studies of how strong brand positioning has been infused to inform and inspire virtually every other aspect of brand strategy and activation—from customer experience and brand extension to digital activation and measurement. This is an important read for anyone who is tasked with brand-building.

—ANN RUBIN, VICE PRESIDENT OF CORPORATE MARKETING, IBM

The environment and challenges impacting the world of marketing have changed dramatically in the past twenty-five years, and yet we continue to teach and practice this discipline as if that is not true. The Indispensable Brand offers an exciting new approach to brand strategy, starting with a significant advancement in how to think about brand positioning—a concept not reexamined since before the internet existed. Every marketer or, more accurately, every business leader must read this book to have a chance to survive and then thrive in this demanding age of the customer.

—JULIE FUSSNER, VICE PRESIDENT OF MARKETING,
CULVER FRANCHISING SYSTEM, LLC

For anyone looking to build a winning brand in today's complex consumer and retail landscape, The Indispensable Brand is a must-read. Mitch presents a compelling call to action and a practical, well-researched set of tools to help any modern marketer meaningfully differentiate their brands. His book is full of inspiration and ideas you can use immediately to set a better future direction for your brand.

—ANDREW GROSS, EXECUTIVE VICE PRESIDENT OF
MARKETING, SERTA SIMMONS BEDDING, LLC

The Indispensable Brand is a great guide for anyone who wants practical examples on how successful brands are conceived and brought to life. For big and small brands, B2C and B2B, and both product- and service-based businesses, Mitch provides great insights, examples, and suggestions for how to do this for your organization.

—STEVEN DOMINGUEZ, VICE PRESIDENT OF GLOBAL
BRANDS, HYATT HOTELS CORPORATION

In a world of short attention spans, skeptical consumers, insta-fads, and knock-offs, The Indispensable Brand offers the principles required to build brands and businesses that endure. Mitch's firsthand experiences and strategic insights serve as a must-read for the modern-day CMO.

—ADAM STOTSKY, PRESIDENT, E! ENTERTAINMENT,
NBCUNIVERSAL MEDIA, LLC

With The Indispensable Brand, Mitch successfully builds the case for making the ultimate pivot in how companies have to manage their brands to win in the twenty-first century. Chapter after chapter, Mitch lays out a virtual best practices road map for not only how to build an indispensable brand but how to sustain brand excellence over time.

—SCOTT DAVIS, SENIOR PARTNER, CHIEF
GROWTH OFFICER, PROPHET

Mitch Duckler reminds me why I fell in love with marketing, including all the nuances of attempting to understand ever-evolving consumer dynamics and translating that into emerging needs and opportunities. This book is a great read whether you are new to marketing or a seasoned veteran.

—YVETTE MORRISON, VICE PRESIDENT OF
MARKETING, SNAP-ON TOOLS

In The Indispensable Brand, Mitch Duckler proposes a road map for establishing and managing world-class brands—ones that first and foremost lead with a differentiated positioning strategy. He questions conventional wisdom around what it means to be meaningfully differentiated, and he urges brand leaders to reflect this unique positioning in every aspect of the brand experience. This is an important read I'd recommend for anyone charged with brand-building in today's challenging business environment.

—TODD TILLEMANS, PRESIDENT, THE HERSHEY COMPANY

The Indispensable Brand will help marketers get a grip on the overwhelming change around them. Importantly, this book is predicated on the irrefutable fact that the leading brands in the world got there and stay there not only because they performed better than their competition, but because they were different! The Indispensable Brand also makes the point that marketers had better become skilled in experience design if they intend to build a twenty-first-century brand.

—RUSS KLEIN, CHIEF EXECUTIVE OFFICER, THE
AMERICAN MARKETING ASSOCIATION

The Indispensable Brand is an eye-opening call to action for anyone who is tasked with brand-building and marketing in general. The evidence presented here about the relative indistinguishability between brands in most categories today is concerning. More importantly, Duckler proposes both the mindset changes and tangible actions required for marketers to combat this condition... and to transform brands from being indistinguishable to indispensable to the customers and other stakeholders they're intended to serve.

—ANDREW DAVIS, KEYNOTE SPEAKER, BESTSELLING AUTHOR

The fact that brands in most product and service categories are becoming indistinguishable from one another—which is clearly evidenced in The Indispensable Brand—should be a concern for anyone tasked with building strong, world-class brands. In this book, Mitch Duckler lays out the factors that have led us to this place and, more importantly, how changes to the way we approach brand strategy can reverse the current trend toward brand monotony.

—JARVIS BOWERS, VICE PRESIDENT OF DIGITAL
MARKETING, HOLLAND AMERICA

The Indispensable Brand is a wake-up call to brand leaders in every industry, from consumer packaged goods and retail to professional services and aerospace. We have to get back to the basics of branding. That means getting better at not only positioning our businesses with greater meaning and differentiation but also bringing them to life in ways that are consistent with that positioning. Duckler skillfully shows us how to do both. His how-to instructions will ensure that any business will keep its brand essence as the foundation of customer experience, brand extension, employee engagement, and brand storytelling.

—CARLA JOHNSON, INTERNATIONAL KEYNOTE
SPEAKER, BESTSELLING AUTHOR, STORYTELLER

The Indispensable Brand is a timely and relevant call to action for anyone involved in building brands. Brand monotony—the inability to distinguish meaningful differences between brands today—is indeed a crisis that needs our attention. Mitch Duckler provides a road map for how more thoughtful attention to brand strategy can accomplish this objective.

—CHRISTINE DAHM, VICE PRESIDENT OF
MARKETING, NOOSA YOGHURT

Mitch Duckler provides marketers with powerful reminders about brand strategy, stewardship, and activation that are all too easily lost or forgotten in today's digital, mobile, and omnichannel world.

—BARBARA BASNEY, VICE PRESIDENT OF GLOBAL
BRAND, ADVERTISING, AND MEDIA, XEROX

There are some key fundamentals of brand management, like clearly articulating what your brand stands for, particularly in a highly congested and competitive marketplace. But given the massively changing landscape of how to market to consumers and how quickly companies can effectively compete, the way in which we connect with consumers needs to be reinvented on a continuous basis. This book establishes that mindset, helping us to become stronger marketers.

—SANGITA WOERNER, VICE PRESIDENT OF
MARKETING, ALASKA AIRLINES

The
Indispensable
Brand

Move from Invisible to Invaluable

Mitch Duckler

RANDOLPH HOUSE
PRESS

THE INDISPENSABLE BRAND
Move from Invisible to Invaluable

ISBN   978-1-5445-0135-2 *Hardcover*
        978-1-5445-0134-5 *Paperback*
        978-1-5445-0133-8 *Ebook*

To Elaine, whose unwavering love, belief, and encouragement mean the world to me.

To Drew, whose pure goodness, sense of humor, and unconditional love make him not only my pride and joy, but my best friend for life.

Contents

Acknowledgments

Writing a book was an even more challenging endeavor than I had anticipated, and there is no way I could have accomplished it without a considerable amount of help along the way. There are many people to whom I owe thanks, as their encouragement and support were instrumental throughout the process.

This book is the culmination of twenty-five-plus years of work in the fields of brand management and management consulting. I would be remiss if I didn't acknowledge and thank the scores of clients over the years who gave me the opportunity to consult on some of the most esteemed and valuable brands in the world. I am truly humbled to have worked with them and their remarkable organizations, and I have benefited from the challenges and opportunities they entrusted me with.

I want to thank my wonderful wife, Elaine, and my son, Drew. They were patient and understanding from beginning to end, especially when deadlines and other commitments arose—and always at the most inconvenient times.

A very special thanks to Nancy Wulz and CJ Sultz—two reliable and insightful thought partners who helped me immensely at critical junctures of writing. I truly appreciate their dedication and hard work, as well as their ability to meticulously research highly nuanced topics and to help me support key premises and hypotheses with empirical data and real-world examples.

Importantly, there were dozens of brilliant marketing minds and prominent business leaders I sought out for perspectives and counsel. Through a combination of interviews and informal sparring sessions, they at times corroborated my hypotheses and at other times critically challenged my thinking. Both outcomes proved invaluable. Their individual and collective thinking is reflected—both implicitly and explicitly—throughout this book. The list of those who generously gave of their time in order to share their perspectives includes: Steven Dominguez, Tim Murphy, Todd Tillemans, Ann Rubin, Carolyn Tisch Blodgett, Rebecca Messina, Jeff Suttle, Jarvis Bowers, Julie Fussner, Ed Keller, Barbara Basney, Andrew Davis, Suzanne McCarron, Christine Dahm, Yvette Morrison, Carla Johnson, Andrew Gross, and Steve Wnuk.

I am also grateful to the team at Influence & Co.—Joanie Zinser, Elle Hammond, Seanna Tucker, and Carolina VonKampen. They provided much-needed project management, writing and publishing advice, and strategic counsel along the way. I especially appreciated their patience, consistent hand-holding, and flexible working style—attributes I appreciated more than they know.

Finally, thank you to the team at Scribe Media, including Zach Obront and publishing manager Diana Fitts. Their contributions were instrumental in helping me get this across the finish line.

Foreword

I wrote *Brand Asset Management* twenty years ago based upon the simple premise that brand is the most important asset a company owns, next to its talent, and should be managed as if it were on the balance sheet. Back then, I contended that brand, when built and managed like the best in the world, should become the face of your business strategy and your company. My book struck a chord for many companies, as brand was trapped in a marketing-led, discretionary spend, often marginalized world. Twenty years and four books later, having consulted with over half of the Fortune 200 companies on hundreds of brands, unfortunately, I would have to say we are still not there yet. Brand is still misunderstood at the most senior levels in companies today, too often thought of in tactical terms, and not embraced and fully leveraged to the extent it should be.

Mitch Duckler, someone I have both known and worked with for the better part of the past two decades, has taken the baton with *The Indispensable Brand*. Mitch truly has a rare killer combination. He is one of the strongest marketeering practitioners I have ever met—having worked at some of the most innovative and marketing-led companies in the world (Unilever and The Coca-Cola Company)—and he followed that up by becoming one of the most brilliant consultants I have worked with, period.

With *The Indispensable Brand*, Mitch successfully builds the case for making the ultimate pivot in how companies have to manage their brands to win in the twenty-first century. Chapter after chapter, Mitch lays out a virtual best practices road map for not only how to build an indispensable brand but how to sustain brand excellence over time.

Mitch shares his perspectives on why brand leaders have been blindly defaulting to so-called best practices, copying the strategies and tactics they see in their competitors, and following (as opposed to leading) consumers. Further, Mitch argues that the world of brand activation has changed dramatically in the past decade—driven first and foremost by the digital revolution—yet brand strategy has not kept pace with this transformation.

The Indispensable Brand proposes changes to both mindset as well as tools and frameworks. Mitch wisely recognizes there is no need to holistically discard current brand strategy frameworks, such as those for architecture, experience, extension, and measurement. The changes proposed in the book represent more of an evolution than revolution and present a success formula for the future with an appreciation for what has worked in the past.

One of the more substantial changes proposed in the book is in how marketers should approach brand positioning. Mitch appropriately calls into question the antiquated, overly simplistic, and advertising-centric brand positioning model that most companies continue to use, à la Ries and Trout. He smartly proposes several changes, including positioning brands around multiple target audiences (including noncustomer stakeholder groups) and allowing the promise—and therefore the brand's primary point of difference—to be something other than a customer end benefit.

This is just one example of many of how Mitch, with *The Indispensable Brand*, is shaping a new brand agenda, one absolutely needed to compete and win in today's hypercompetitive, dynamic, and consumer-led brand world. There is no one I would rather turn to for advice in brand-building today than Mitch Duckler. Short of getting him in person, *The Indispensable Brand* is a perfect alternative.

Scott Davis, senior partner and chief growth officer, Prophet
(Author: *Brand Asset Management, Building the Brand-Driven Business*, and *The Shift: The Transformation of Today's Marketers into Tomorrow's Growth Leaders*)

PART I

BRAND MONOTONY
AND THE CASE
FOR CHANGE

Chapter 1

———

What Is Brand Monotony?

In the mid to late twentieth century, a stroll down the oral hygiene aisle of your local grocery or drug store was amazingly clear, simple, and straight-forward. There were several brands that were differentiated around a meaningful consumer end benefit. You had Aquafresh and Close-Up for fresh breath. There was Crest for fighting cavities and reducing tooth decay. Ultra Brite was all about whiter teeth, and if you had sensitive teeth, you could always turn to Sensodyne. Additionally, there were a couple of brands whose primary point of difference was ingredient-based: Colgate was the brand with MFP fluoride, while Mentadent touted its baking soda and peroxide formula.[1]

Today, walking down that same oral hygiene aisle pulls you in every direction. You see toothpaste that whitens teeth, toothpaste for sensitive teeth and gums, toothpaste that's organic and "green," toothpaste for tartar control and enamel protection, toothpaste for kids...and the list goes on. In the 1970s, there were two Colgate toothpaste choices. Today, Colgate has approximately forty-seven different types of toothpaste. With forty-seven options for just one brand, it's no wonder consumers' heads are spinning.

What's most concerning is that it's often a single brand touting this veritable laundry list of features and benefits. And it's not just one brand—most of the leading brands in the category are promising virtually identical benefits. While technological advances and meaningful innovation—like some of the ones cited above—are certainly positive, they can quickly turn negative when companies resort to copycat new product introductions and "benefit loading" to the extent where brands become essentially indiscernible from one another.

Importantly, the business results speak for themselves. For example, despite years of launching new toothpaste twists such as tartar control, gum protection, and whitening, Crest saw its share in the United States decline from almost 50 percent with one product to 25 percent with fifty products.[2] Each introduction lacked differentiation from existing products and competed for the same usage without adding enough value to create incremental growth.

Let's face it—most toothpastes are homogeneous mixtures. They include fluoride and a mild abrasive, bound together with thickeners, sweeteners, humectants, and flavors. The role of toothpaste has always been to remove plaque and prevent cavities. Very few toothpastes in the marketplace with the ADA seal of approval would actually fail to perform these two tasks. So the challenge for brands in this category is regaining meaningful differentiation by refocusing on the singular point of differentiation that made them so distinct and successful in the first place.

To be clear, all brands need to have points of parity (i.e., attributes that are inherently undifferentiated) in order to compete effectively. However, this cannot be at the expense of establishing and maintaining relevant points of differentiation. It is these factors that give consumers reasons to buy their brand. This simple reality applies to not only oral care, but to virtually every product and service category today.

AN IDENTITY CRISIS: BRANDS ARE BECOMING INDISTINGUISHABLE

In general, brands today are suffering from a crisis of differentiation. Granted, the assertion that differentiation is important is not newsworthy—it's one of the oldest and most basic tenets of successful branding. Since the earliest days of brand management, the importance of differentiation has been well understood and documented. In fact, it could even be said that this is the very foundation upon which strong brands are built.

However, it remains a critical and often overlooked void in pursuit of other brand-related goals and objectives. The extent to which leading brands within many industries are indistinguishable from one another today is unprecedented. Professional services, insurance, retail, and wireless are just several examples of industries drowning in the proverbial sea of sameness. Take air travel, for example. To most consumers, American Airlines, Delta Air Lines, and United Airlines might as well be the same airline. When sitting on an airplane, how easy is it for frequent travelers to tell which airline they're flying that day? And if you ask travelers which airline is best, they will likely tell you "whichever one you have the highest status on."

When you look at a brand's product package, an advertisement, or any type of collateral, if you were to remove the brand name, would you be able to tell which brand it represents? In most cases, the answer to this question is a resounding no. This is just one simple way of demonstrating that brands in general are suffering from an identity crisis, the root cause of which is a lack of differentiation. When it comes to branding today—especially in the digital realm—companies are increasingly following a set of so-called best practices and, worse yet, copying one another when they see something they like in the competitive set.

But the news gets worse. Companies are not adequately differentiating their brands, and consumers have an unprecedented ability to compare brands and realize just how indistinguishable they are from one another. Any device with an internet connection allows anyone to compare prices, reviews, and functionality across products or services within seconds. Customers can quite literally stack options next to each other in a stripped-down, impersonal matrix designed specifically to allow for comparing and contrasting. These tools serve to further expose the lack of differentiation we see today among brands in most categories.

THE PROOF IS IN THE NUMBERS

Evidence of this identity crisis can be traced as far back as 2000, when Copernicus, a marketing research and consulting firm, studied consumer perceptions of brand differentiation in forty-six major product categories.[3] Copernicus fielded a survey resulting in 615 responses, which were weighted to be demographically representative of consumers nationwide. The research revealed that brands were becoming more distinct in only two of the forty-six categories: soft drinks and soap. Consumers said brands were "holding their own" in only four categories; in the other forty categories, brands were converging and becoming less distinct.

A subsequent Copernicus and Greenfield study conducted in 2006 revealed that an increasing number of categories were becoming more commodity-like in the eyes of consumers.[4] In forty-eight of fifty-one categories studied—everything from home improvement retail to water bottles to credit cards—brands were seen as becoming less differentiated.

This trend continued in the next decade. A 2012 Deloitte Insights article titled "A Crisis of the Similar" concluded that "consumers believe many product categories are relatively homogeneous; they think differences between national brands are insignificant, as are differences between national brands and private labels."[5] It also pointed out that the onslaught of incremental line extensions—often posing as meaningful innovation—has done little to increase perceived differentiation in most categories: "Despite an unending array of variations in supermarkets and mass merchandisers, the differences between brands are typically not significant enough for any single brand to stand out."

Market research firm Kantar Millward Brown also provides evidence for the lack of differentiation among brands today.[6] Its BrandZ database contains information on more than six thousand brands collected over ten years from category buyers around the world. It notes that, "On average, the proportion of people willing to endorse any brand as 'different from other brands of (a specific category)' is low." However, what's even more troubling is what they found for brands that are considered to be "acceptable" by consumers: "Among those that consider a brand acceptable, an average of 18 percent agreed that it was different from others." So even for brands that are considered to be relevant, fewer than one in five consumers see them as differentiated.

BRAND INDISTINGUISHABILITY: ANOTHER CASE STUDY

Findings like the ones above are perhaps nowhere more evident than in the wireless industry today. Now that all four major US wireless carriers offer unlimited data plans, picking a wireless provider has become even more complicated. Every provider claims they are the best in some respect—most reliable, fastest, cheapest, highest in customer satisfaction, etc. Not to mention, plans typically have a confusing array of features and pricing options, making an apples-to-apples comparison difficult. This begs the question: where does the industry go from here?

T-Mobile effectively repositioned itself back in 2013 as the "Un-Carrier," focused on eliminating consumer pain points. Given the nature of the industry, however, others quickly followed with their own no-contract plans, unlimited calling plans, and more. Thus, their differentiation no longer exists because it was based on a tangible feature that was easy for competitors to emulate.

The US market for wireless service is essentially saturated—the path to growth has become a "zero-sum game" where new customers can only be stolen from competitors. And it's not just customers who are being lured. Remember Verizon's iconic "Can you hear me now" pitch man? He defected to Sprint to tell consumers that "its network is almost as good as Verizon's, and its service costs half the price."

According to a study by PwC's global strategy consulting team, Strategy&, market shares in the wireless telecom industry are normalizing due to price competition, not differentiation.[7] As wireless markets mature, fierce competition over a finite number of subscribers is intensifying, and price cuts and promotions are the only means for winning over customers. Consequently, the average rate per user (ARPU) is falling and intense competition is leaving operators little room to grow in a meaningful way. Their products and services are essentially interchangeable. This is eroding profit margins while diminishing value and the opportunity to differentiate.

With no other meaningful point of difference on which to compete, Sprint has run major price promotions that have won it new customers from competitors. But that hasn't helped grow the top line. Although Sprint attracted additional customers, it's not able to hold on to them. Its postpaid subscriber churn rate is higher than all three of its main competitors.[8] Essentially, Sprint has been unable to make headway in differentiating its service from its competitors on anything other than price (if even that). And as most marketers realize, there are at least two big downsides to competing on cost: it generally yields lower product margins, and it is a "positioning" that is easily emulated and difficult to own and sustain over time.

WHY IS IT IMPORTANT FOR BRANDS TO DIFFERENTIATE?

The problems associated with brand indistinguishability are multidimensional, and they can be seen across three distinct categories of metrics. The first category of measurement affected by a lack of differentiation is core brand health metrics, such as decreases in levels of awareness, relevance, uniqueness, consideration, and purchase intent. These are the measurements many brand managers care most about, and although these are certainly troubling in their own right, they pale in importance when compared to other metrics.

The second category is broader business metrics, such as lower levels of sales, brand loyalty, and market share. These are even more problematic because they're not only attitudinal (like many of the brand metrics mentioned above), but they reflect actual customer behavior. Namely, customers are purchasing the brand less frequently.

But it doesn't end there. Ultimately, brand indistinguishability has a very direct and negative impact on a third, critical set of metrics: financial performance. Undifferentiated brands struggle to command a premium price point (including heavier reliance on discounting, aggressive promotion, etc.) and face slower revenue growth, lower margins and overall profit, and even decreased shareholder value.

According to Millward Brown's 2015 *BrandZ Top 100 Global Brands* report, a study that tracked brand value for the ten-year period between 2006 and 2015, differentiation was the single most important contributor to its Brand Value composite index.[9] Namely, the top fifty global brands had an average difference score of 139, compared with brands fifty-one to one hundred, which had an average difference score of 96. That 43-point swing in the top one hundred companies says a lot about the power of differentiation, especially in combination with the increases in value the brands saw during that stretch of nearly a decade. The top brands enjoyed a 124 percent boost in value, while the next fifty grew just 24 percent over the same period. (See figure 1.1.)

Figure 1.1
Differentiation & Brand Value

Brands consumers view as "Different" generally achieve a higher Brand Value than brands not viewed as different.

BRAND VALUE BRANDS 1 TO 50	BRAND VALUE BRANDS 51 TO 100
Average Difference Score	Average Difference Score
139	**96**
10-Year Value Change	10-Year Value Change
+124%	**+24%**

Based on the BrandZ™ Top 100 Most Valuable Global Brands 2006 and 2015
Source: BrandZ™ / Milward Brown

Similar results are seen with the Young & Rubicam (Y&R) BrandAsset Valuator model. This model is comprised of more than 350,000 consumer interviews conducted across the globe and measures more than fifty-five different consumer perceptions with regard to more than twenty thousand brands. It proposes that four measures (pillars)—differentiation, relevance, esteem, and knowledge—are consistently linked to a brand's ability to deliver revenue and profit, regardless of category, country, or age of the brand.

With regard to the differentiation pillar, Y&R had this to say: "The critical pillar is the first one, Differentiation, which represents the distinctiveness of the brand. To have a chance in today's marketing world, a brand must be perceived as different and unique. It must be seen as possessing a distinctive persona with a meaning all its own. While Differentiation, in general, is very strong among the successful brands, it is usually the first pillar to dissipate for those going bankrupt."[10] Y&R goes on to conclude that differentiation is the key margin driver; the higher a brand's differentiation, the higher its margin potential. Brands that increase their differentiation have around a 50 percent higher operating margin on average than those that have declining differentiation. (See figure 1.2.) And, as seen in figure 1.3, the results are even more dramatic for operating earnings.

Simply put, not only do consumers suffer the consequences of indistinguishable brands, but so do the companies that own them. It has a very direct and negative impact on bottom-line results.

Figure 1.2
Differentiation & Operating Margin

10-year Financial Performance

Source: Young & Rubicam. Brand Asset Valuator® Tool Kit, 2003

Figure 1.3
Differentiation & Operating Earnings

10-year Financial Performance

Differentiation
D Grew

▲ Operating Earnings = **128%**

▲ Operating Earnings = **289%**

D Declined

▲ Operating Earnings = **1%**

R Declined   R Grew

Relevance

Source: Young & Rubicam. Brand Asset Valuator® Tool Kit, 2003

Differentiation is still a relevant and worthy goal, and the good news is it's well within marketers' control to achieve this outcome. And as brands become more distinguishable, they also become more relevant to customers and more profitable for the companies that own them. Below are five themes that are essential to establishing (or reestablishing) differentiation, which will be referenced consistently throughout this book. Collectively, they are what enable brands to become indispensable to consumers.

1. IDENTIFY A COMPELLING POSITIONING

Every brand needs to have a positioning that is meaningful, compelling, unique, and credible to not only customers but to any stakeholder interacting with the brand. Brand positioning is the foundation of any brand strategy. Without a differentiated positioning, brands have little to no hope of being differentiated in the marketplace. This is because all expression and activation elements related to a brand should be consistent with—and informed by—the brand positioning. Traditional brand positioning frameworks feature a target audience, a frame of reference, a primary customer benefit, and proof points. While this basic framework still has some merit, a dramatically transformed brand activation environment necessitates revisiting brand positioning with an eye toward evolving some of these four components and adding completely new ones as well.

2. CRAFT A BRAND-INSPIRED EXPERIENCE

Crafting a brand-inspired experience is about touchpoints and a customer journey that are consistent with the brand positioning, as opposed to a hypothetical ideal experience. It is astonishing how many companies set out to identify what they characterize as the "optimal customer experience"—as if to imply there is only one. The fact is, customers are different and seek different types of experiences. As such, companies should seek to identify the optimal experience for customers that is inspired by—and consistent with—the brand positioning. This goes a long way toward ensuring brands achieve meaningful distinction within their respective categories. It requires evaluating every single touchpoint in the customer journey and determining how to shape it in a way that is consistent with the brand positioning.

3. PERSONALIZE THE OFFER

If delivering a brand-inspired customer experience is essential to achieving brand differentiation, personalization is one of the best ways to ensure an experience is distinctive and memorable. Personalizing an offer requires ensuring products and services avoid making customers feel as though they are being mass marketed to. Advances in technology and greater creativity and sophistication of marketing make it easier than ever to personalize the offerings of even the most mass-marketed brands. Tools and methodologies, such as customer relationship management (CRM), marketing automation, retargeting, social media, and more, can be used to make customers feel as though they are something more than a mere statistic or personal identification number.

4. FOSTER A BRAND-RELEVANT RELATIONSHIP

Beyond merely transacting, brands need to form an emotional connection with customers. Technological advances in general—and the internet and social media in particular—have made it easier than ever for brands to form meaningful relationships with customers. However, as is the case with experience, the type of relationship fostered should be consistent with the essence of the brand. Specifically, how brands interact with customers in person and online needs to reflect the brand positioning. Customers can easily detect disingenuous efforts on the part of companies when trying to develop a relationship that is inconsistent with how they view the brand. As such, these interactions need to be sensitive to common etiquette and social norms as well as the essence and persona of the brand.

5. PUSH BOUNDARIES ON GROWTH

Brands can no longer settle for only incremental innovation in the form of "flavor of the month" line extensions; instead, they must also seek transformational, brand-inspired growth. While there is a meaningful role for line extensions, it is breakthrough innovation that elevates and distinguishes brands from one another. However, many owners of brand strategy struggle with how far they can (and should) stretch their brand's bounds of extendibility. Play it too safe and the likely result will be close-in, ho-hum line extensions that underwhelm customers and are short-lived in the marketplace. Stray too far from the brand's core positioning and you risk diluting—or even irreversibly damaging—a brand's valuable equity. Striking the optimal balance between these two extremes can help brands become more indispensable to customers and consumers.

WHAT TO EXPECT FROM THIS BOOK

At a time in brand management when everyone is talking about and focused on marketing activation—particularly in the digital, mobile, content marketing, and social media realms—this book will take a step back and talk about the important role *brand strategy* plays in establishing and maintaining differentiation. After all, it is brand strategy that should help shape the activation activities that are often being executed without a solid basis for uniqueness and differentiation.

Specifically, the next two chapters will detail the factors that have contributed to the current state of brand indistinguishability and provide a high-level overview of the changes that need to occur in order to reverse this trend. Subsequent chapters will focus in more detail on key components of brand strategy that often serve as "make or break" points when it comes to developing and maintaining a differentiated brand. They will begin with arguably the most important component of all—brand positioning—and encourage readers to think about this topic more flexibly and liberally in pursuit of achieving differentiation. Chapters will then address other core aspects of brand strategy, such as customer experience, digital activation, brand extendibility, employee brand engagement, and brand measurement, and explore how they need to be thought about differently and more strategically.

Ultimately, this refreshed take on brand strategy should help brand and marketing leaders migrate their brands from indistinguishable to indispensable. And perhaps even more importantly, it will help them more consistently and reliably reap the benefits of more meaningfully differentiated brands referenced earlier, including premium pricing, superior revenue growth, increased market share, greater levels of customer loyalty, and improved profit margins.

Chapter 2

Seven Factors That Have Forever Changed Brands

It was far simpler in the early days of brand management to be distinctive and to be indispensable in customers' eyes. For starters, there were fewer competitors, brands, and product or service offerings in most categories and industries. For that matter, there were even fewer categories and industries. Not surprisingly, in a world with fewer alternatives, it was significantly easier for any single brand to be distinct from all others.

In order to position their brands, marketers conducted some market research and determined how they wanted to be perceived in the minds of consumers. Then they created their thirty-second ad—and ran it over and over—on one of only three broadcast networks. To get their products in the hands of consumers, manufacturers went through traditional brick-and-mortar retailers, who were basically at the mercy of manufacturers to sell what was provided to them. This was particularly the case before a number of factors (e.g., retail consolidation, access to scanner data, and private label growth, to name a few) began to change the dynamic between manufacturers and retailers.

The role of consumers was simple and limited, too. They bought and used the products manufacturers made. While it's true they "voted with their checkbooks," they had very little influence in the commercial equation. Clearly, it was a simpler time back in the golden age of brand management. In a nutshell, manufacturers produced, retailers sold, and consumers purchased. And in this admittedly oversimplified value chain, manufacturers held all the cards.

THE TURNING OF THE TIDE

Needless to say, a lot has changed between then and now in all corners of the world. New technologies emerged to upset the balance. Cheaper manufacturing and distribution options lowered the barriers to entry for many consumers and B2B industries. Personal computers and the internet gave customers access to more information. Smartphones took that information mobile, empowering customers to learn about products in real time. Social media allowed everyday people to create instant, permanent reviews of products for all their friends—not to mention complete strangers—to see.

Suddenly, manufacturers were under fire. Advanced technologies disrupted old businesses, and take-it-or-leave-it dynamics crumbled in an on-demand world. When big brands failed to deliver on consumer expectations, agile players entered the market to change the status quo. Brand managers no longer had the luxury of power and control; they had to work much harder in order to distinguish themselves from the pack and be more relevant to customers.

Today, consumer power permeates every industry. On-demand services provide digital platforms that offer immediate access to whatever people want. Uber delivers cars with a tap of an app, Airbnb lets property owners and renters communicate directly, and Amazon ships anything anywhere at a moment's notice. So again, a lot has changed. Let's take a closer look at seven distinct yet interrelated factors that have affected branding the most.

FACTOR 1: TECHNOLOGICAL ADVANCES

Consider for a moment how profoundly technology has impacted the brand landscape and how brands reach consumers since the *Mad Men* days of traditional marketing. Since the debut of the internet, marketing is no longer limited to billboards, television and print advertising, direct mail, or catalogs to reach global audiences. Today, virtually any brand, global or local, can reach customers and prospects around the world with minimal effort. The barriers to market entry have not just been lowered—they have been virtually eliminated.

The internet is undoubtedly one of the most influential innovations in recent history. Within thirty years of its widespread adoption, the tool we once referred to as the "information superhighway" now drives many of the world's most valuable companies. Brands are launched and flourish almost instantaneously. Consider that Facebook and Google, two of the most powerful and valuable brands in the world today, didn't even exist twenty-five years ago.

Beyond the internet, social media, digital streaming media, and mobile networks and smart devices have ushered in a new era of real-time, unfiltered, highly personalized, multichannel communications that are rewriting the rules of brand management and marketing in general. Today's consumers are digital explorers. Online ratings, peer reviews, videos, and in-depth product details are imperative as would-be customers move along the path to purchase.

In May 2015, mobile searches surpassed desktop searches, significantly shifting the way businesses engage consumers.[1] The proliferation of mobile devices as the go-to search-and-buying tool has unveiled myriad opportunities for brand-to-consumer interaction that just didn't exist before. In our new reality, apps like Snapchat, WeChat, and WhatsApp demonstrate everything happens in real time. From communication to coordination to purchase, marketers need to keep up with the dizzying pace of consumers. The points of engagement and transaction are converging; brands that can offer immediacy, personalization, authenticity, and accessibility will win out.

Tech has changed *everything*, and the ongoing debates continue: Is digital marketing replacing traditional marketing or merely supplementing its reach? And is there a balance to strike between the two? We're all familiar with traditional marketing methods. They're easy to understand, and we've used them for decades. Traditional marketing is based on an in-your-face "interruption" strategy—brands bring their message to consumers via television commercials, printed billboards, and print advertisements. Digital marketing, on the other hand, is relatively new and based on an inbound strategy. Companies publish their product and service information via corporate websites, blog posts and articles, pay-per-click ads, and posts on social media platforms for potential customers to find, all of which offer an opportunity for more targeted advertising.

FACTOR 2: THE PROLIFERATION OF CHOICE

In the early days of brand management, there were fewer options in the market across the board—fewer categories, fewer brands within those categories, and fewer alternatives within any given brand. Today there are more competitors going to market with more brands than ever before. A more crowded and competitive marketplace makes it infinitely harder for brands to stand out from the pack. This phenomenon has been exacerbated by the digital world. Namely, digital platforms offer great reach for brands. But a brand also runs a higher risk of becoming just another number when it is one of dozens of online search results, as opposed to one of only a handful of options on physical store shelves or, for a B2B company, on a tradeshow floor.

Proliferation of choice also affects customers. When faced with a staggering number of available options for virtually any given purchase decision, people prefer to walk away rather than make a difficult decision. In this sense, choice truly can be debilitating. A study conducted by researchers in California demonstrated this phenomenon using jars of jam.[2] The team set up a booth to sell jam, offering samples to passing customers. Sometimes, the stand offered twenty-four selections, other times, only six. Sixty percent of passersby visited the stand with twenty-four choices, but only 3 percent of those visitors made a purchase. While only 40 percent of visitors stopped to see the smaller stand, 30 percent of those people bought something.

Further research from Northwestern University found that, as the number of options goes up, the marginal value of each option goes down.[3] People faced with three products perceive distinct differences in quality, but when faced with three dozen, they see most of the products as interchangeable. Additional options don't create more value in customers' eyes, but they do create more stress, which leads to fewer sales.

FACTOR 3: CHANGES IN DISTRIBUTION

Choice is not expanded by abundance alone but also by accessibility. This can be clearly demonstrated through an abbreviated recap of the history of retail distribution. In the 1800s, railroads and urban centers made department stores possible. As cities grew, shopping options remained limited to stores within walking distance. The general store, tailor, and department stores couldn't be too far away, or visiting one became an all-day affair. People within a community relied on neighbors, shop owners, and local advertisements to discover new products.

Then, when the Sears catalog arrived in the early 1900s, people could for the first time order products they didn't see in person. For the consumer, that was thrilling—it felt like the world was at your fingertips (because, in a way, it was). Not long after that, shopping malls with specialty stores popped up to serve the blossoming suburbs, thanks in large part to the automobile. Instead of going to one of the few clothing boutiques in a town, people could suddenly shop at twenty or more apparel shops within an afternoon. And discount chains and big-box stores joined these malls during the 1960s and 1970s, transforming consumers' errands into quicker, more convenient items on their to-do lists.

Then the internet happened, dramatically shortening the distance between the customer and product once more. The giants that had been comfortable since the 1970s couldn't handle this new disruption, and by the year 2000, seven of the eight biggest brick-and-mortar retailers in the United States had either gone bankrupt, been acquired, or tumbled into obscurity.[4] Digital retailers like Amazon and Pets.com introduced online shopping, hit a snag during the dot-com bubble, but continued their universal takeover of distribution until digital retailers became the behemoth we know today.

We take the prevalence of online shopping for granted, but as recently as 2000, people remained wary of buying things over the internet. A study published by Pew Research Center in December 2016 found that around 80 percent of Americans bought at least one thing online that year, compared to just 22 percent in 2000.[5] In our new convenience economy, physical stores are just one of many distribution points for products. Omnichannel retail is on the rise, and retailers now focus more on empowering consumers to research, compare, return, and purchase products than they focus on bringing people into stores.

And this is not just a B2C phenomenon, either. New technology, in particular, has changed distribution dynamics in the world of B2B as well, especially for service-based businesses. Advances and innovations such as affordable air travel, virtual offices, teleconferencing, email, and video-conferencing make it easier than ever for a potential client in Paris, France, to hire a company that is based in Paris, Texas. As Thomas Friedman noted in his best-selling book by the same title, the world is flat.

FACTOR 4: CHANGES IN COMMUNICATION AND MEDIA

We've seen yet another seismic change in media and communication. Understanding this change is essential, as media outlets are the means by which consumers gather information and communicate with each other and with brands. Take television, for instance. Back in the day, three television networks (ABC, CBS, and NBC) ruled the airwaves. People didn't have cable TV, much less the internet. Because of this, branding was fairly straightforward: marketers bought ad time on a given network and were guaranteed to reach a hefty percentage of consumers within their target media demographic.

That all changed in the early 1980s, when cable turned three channels into three hundred, decimating the previous dominance of the Big Three and splitting consumer attention among many more options. The internet introduced even more to consider here, opening up an entirely new form of media on which consumers could spend time. Brands followed suit, tracking consumers to their favorite channels and selling ads to networks and websites their target demographics preferred, limiting breadth and only hoping for depth; the entire industry of programmatic advertising focuses on just this.

And it's not just the media outlets themselves that have affected branding; it's consumers' attitudes and behaviors toward media, too. Yes, we still watch TV today but not as much as we used to. Thanks to smartphones and computers, we consume content constantly, whether we're lying in bed, waiting in line somewhere, or even in front of the TV. Our appetites for movies, news, sports, pop culture, and politics continue to grow, and we have more options than ever to sate our thirst. And we haven't even mentioned DVR yet. For some time now, consumers have had the ability to record their favorite TV shows for viewing at a time more convenient for them and to fast-forward through the commercials that are so near and dear to us marketers but annoying to them.

These changes in media consumption and behavior apply to younger consumers especially. Millennials and members of Generation Z watch far less TV than preceding generations, and when they do, they often use their phones at the same time. The cable television industry that revolutionized the 1980s is failing in the face of streaming services, which provide a more personalized, on-demand experience and are even accessible in quick bursts wherever people have phones or tablets. This new form of consumption matches our shrinking attention spans, which spread to our buying habits. We want what we want, and we want it now.

FACTOR 5: A SPIKE IN THE AMOUNT OF INFORMATION AVAILABLE

Historically, brands enjoyed an advantage in part because of consumers' lack of sufficient information. Faced with a wide array of products and services, often seemingly similar, customers needed to spend tremendous time and energy to become fully informed and examine the alternatives before making their choice. To make matters worse, this painful process carried no guarantee that the ultimate choice from such a journey was the best. In a world of insufficient information, brands provided a trusted route (or seal of approval) to facilitate the decision-making process. Additionally, consumers didn't have the forums of today (like social media) to educate themselves and share their opinions, which now challenge the control companies enjoy in the market.

The dramatic changes in the media environment also increased the amount of information available in the world—and information is power. Thanks to the explosion of the internet and online technology, customers now have access to information that was once the exclusive domain of large companies, and more information becomes available every day. According to some estimates, we created more new information in the last ten years than in the rest of human history put together; smartphone users have access to all of it, with most users keeping their phones within arm's reach for most of the day. With this much information at buyers' fingertips, the influence and power shifts from producer to consumer.

Additionally, strategic advances among savvy retailers have helped change the power dynamic between manufacturers and retailers, thanks in large part to technology that delivers information to retailers and distributors. Nielsen and IRI leveled the playing field with scanner data, allowing companies to review detailed information on their sales by scanning barcodes and uploading the info into databases. This means manufacturers can no longer "strong-arm" retailers into stocking products they know may not sell. Put another way, increased access to information has resulted in manufacturers being squeezed in multiple ways, from both the retailers that distribute their products and the consumers who purchase them.

Of course, brands also can be the beneficiaries of increased information. Companies are able to acquire just as much information on customers as the customers are on them. Entirely new companies and business models have arisen because of the abundance of information and the ability to do very sophisticated analysis with it. Sharing economy businesses have reshaped the ways many Americans live their lives. Ride-sharing apps like Uber and Lyft have altered the transportation landscape, and Airbnb and other short-term rental networks have permanently transformed the vacation lodging industry. These companies represent an innovative way to use data effectively to provide services to people when and where they want them.

Finally, no conversation about the role of information and insights in the world of brand would be complete without discussing market research. Monumental leaps in the field of market research have made it easier than ever for manufacturers to analyze what buyers want and anticipate shifts in market demands. Companies are listening to what consumers say, sometimes before consumers even open their mouths. Advances in qualitative research techniques include ethnographic, observational, phenomenological, and co-creation. On the quantitative front, we've seen the likes of multidimensional segmentation, conjoint analysis, structural equation modeling, and big data—just to name a few.

This, of course, is mostly good news, but it carries with it implications for brands. The cost of market research has dropped dramatically over the years, taking capabilities that used to be an exclusive privilege for the most powerful companies and putting them in the hands of smaller entities. Small businesses no longer have to rely on gut instincts while corporations enjoy sophisticated insights. Everyone is on a level playing field. And with so many players collecting the same data and coming to the same conclusions, it is increasingly more difficult for brands to achieve meaningful differentiation through the use of data and analytics alone. Market information is no longer a competitive advantage for the privileged few, but a table stake for competing effectively in a crowded and cutthroat marketplace.

FACTOR 6: THE ENLIGHTENED AND EMPOWERED CONSUMER

One of the most significant changes in the marketing landscape in recent years has been the way consumers interact with companies and purchase their products and services. For starters, the traditional purchase funnel that existed during the early days of brand management is no longer relevant, as it no longer accurately depicts the purchase process. Gone are the days when consumers moved in a linear and sequential manner from awareness to consideration to trial to repeat purchase to loyalty.

Rather, the technological advancements detailed in this chapter have fundamentally changed consumers' decision-making processes. To build successful brands today, marketers need a solid understanding of this new path to purchase. For starters, consumers are increasingly rejecting what marketers tell them in favor of personal research. According to Search Engine Land, 73 percent of online purchases begin with a search on Google or Amazon, but few purchases remain within the bounds of those sites alone.[6] Multichannel journeys are on the rise as customers research products through third-party sites, manufacturer websites, and multiple retailers. It is now possible for any consumer, from the comfort of home, to compare brands and products. By the time a customer gets to the shopping cart, contacts a salesperson, or enters a physical store, most of the purchase decision is already complete.

And when they do seek input, it's not necessarily from the companies providing the products or services. At the heart of this issue is trust, and this is where social media comes into play. Interpersonal online connections have democratized commerce to the point where consumers trust other people—even people they've never met—more than they trust brands. Eighty-eight percent of buyers trust online reviews as much as personal recommendations from friends.[7]

Millennials are leading the way in not trusting companies. Eighty-four percent of them don't trust advertisements, and more than 50 percent of Millennial consumers feel they are "better connected" and able to find information more quickly than retail associates.[89] When customers turn to their mobile device instead of to employees or in-store technology, brands miss a valuable engagement opportunity. As a result, brands lose control of their messages, which become fragmented on social media until the original intent all but disappears. Brands need to create personalized digital experiences through the mobile devices that shoppers already carry with them if brands hope to reach this increasingly elusive demographic.

If taking greater control of the transactional relationship weren't enough, consumers are also becoming more demanding. People have higher expectations of speed, service quality, and personalization. They want instant gratification and real-time virtual dialogues with brands. Two-day shipping on Amazon Prime is now slow; same-day delivery services are the new expectation.

So what does this all mean? There has been a fundamental shift in power from companies to consumers. With this shift, brands no longer possess the means to control—much less dictate—how customers interact with them. The days of pushing out a finely tuned, carefully controlled marketing message and trusting it will be received in the manner intended are long gone. What's perhaps most concerning about this shift in how consumers make purchase decisions is that it's increasingly leaving brands out of the conversation altogether—and out of the minds of purchasing consumers.

FACTOR 7: CHANGES IN THE BEHAVIOR OF MARKETERS THEMSELVES

To be sure, much has changed in the world in the past few decades. And while these changes may have landed consumers more in charge than ever before, companies can't blame the indistinguishability of their brands on the masses. Marketers themselves must take responsibility for that.

In response to the aforementioned advancements in technology and accompanying behavioral shifts, marketers have played follow-the-leader, especially with regard to digital activation. Marketers are under constant pressure to create the next big idea, so companies are continually taking the safe (and lazy) road, opting to blindly follow an endless array of so-called best practices and copying the strategies of others rather than branching out with original ideas.

In digital marketing, there is a delicate balance between staying relevant and jumping on the bandwagon. One mistake many brands make is to assume an "I can do that, too" attitude—just because a platform or technology is trendy, they think they should automatically add it to their marketing mix. In reality, it's never a good idea to blindly follow the latest trends without first gaining an understanding of how implementing a new approach or technology will benefit your brand. Brand and marketing leaders certainly need to stay on top of the latest and greatest in digital marketing but not mindlessly jump on a trend before getting a sense of how it fits in with overall business and brand strategy, if at all.

Online brand activations, such as websites, blogs, online ads, and social media campaigns, are driven more by channel best practices than brand positioning alignment. When one brand figures out a best practice in SEO or another marketing discipline, other marketers jump on board without considering whether the new strategy works for their brands. It seems many marketers would rather be wrong in a group than risk trying something new (and potentially better).

When everyone creates the same content and distributes it to the same people in the same way, brand monotony eventually results. If every company blogs on the same topics, emails on the same day of the week, and tweets at the same time of day, people can scarcely tell which brand is which. As brands run out of interesting things to say and do, they fall back on commoditized factors like price, sealing their fate to struggle in a homogenous environment.

Social media provides all the tools marketers need to distribute content, but even the lines between these platforms are beginning to blur. Facebook and Instagram stole the Stories feature from Snapchat, and similar "thefts" happen all the time. Brand leaders need to more carefully scrutinize social media platforms to determine which audiences are most appropriate for their brands and the best way to represent themselves on these platforms. Even for socially savvy brands, that's not easy. When the brandgym surveyed one hundred marketing directors in multiple industries, "keeping up with the latest trends" emerged as the primary driver of social media use.[10] Even more concerning, under 25 percent of survey respondents claimed social media use drove tangible business results.

Companies are in such a hurry to connect to consumers that they forget the fundamentals of brand strategy that won over their audiences in the first place. Brand marketers must stop playing copycat and start pursuing meaningful differentiation—leading consumers rather than following them and the competition.

PROGRESS ISN'T THE PROBLEM; IT'S BAD CHOICES THAT MAKE BRANDS INDISTINGUISHABLE

Noting the above changes and the ripple effects they create is not to say that those factors were negative. To the contrary, innovation and progress are almost always positive, as are most of these shifts. Each of the advancements outlined in this chapter may have made differentiation more challenging, but they have all provided immense benefits to businesses, consumers, the economy, and society overall. Increased competition, greater choice, more information, and new technology make customers' lives easier and make businesses more productive and profitable. Progress is, after all, essential to a thriving economy and society, so this brief history recap shouldn't be misconstrued as a condemnation of advancement and innovation.

Rather, what this means is that brand leaders can't ignore the looming unintended consequence all these changes have brought; doing so will only leave marketers spinning their wheels and wondering how to reconnect with consumers without actually tackling the problem. To accept indistinguishability as inevitable and insurmountable is foolish—because neither is the case. Brand managers may no longer enjoy the power advantage they once had in the company-customer relationship, but the democratization of branding can be just as much of a benefit as it can be an obstacle. It is time for companies to resume their roles as leaders through more robust brand strategies based on differentiated brand positioning, not on copycat behaviors.

It is our responsibility as marketers and brand-builders to ensure that the ongoing pursuit of smarter activation—and adherence to standards and best practices—remains consistent with the essence of our brands. Traditional brand strategy components such as positioning, architecture, experience, and extendibility need to evolve in order to account for a radically different activation environment. Bottom line: to differentiate our brands without missing out on new opportunities, we must rethink some of the basics of brand strategy and the frameworks that accompany it. This also includes the very processes and procedures we use to manage them. We'll dive into these in the remainder of this book.

Chapter 3

———

From Indistinguishable to Indispensable

As is often the case regarding seismic shifts that occur over years (if not decades), the causes of brand monotony are numerous; its solutions, multidimensional. Reversing this disturbing trend will require changes to two key components of brand strategy: marketers' mindset and strategic frameworks. In other words, we need to change the way we think about brand strategy *and* the tools and models we use for developing and managing it. Addressing only one aspect of the problem without simultaneously tackling the other will do little to reverse the trend of brand monotony.

The mindset component of the solution refers to how marketers, as the primary stewards of brand-building, have become complacent in their responsibilities. Thanks to the confluence of factors we discussed in the previous chapter—massive changes in technology, market structure, distribution, information, communication, and consumer purchasing dynamics—marketers have become understandably overwhelmed. In the face of these challenges, many have thrown in the towel. These marketers have moved away from the leadership roles that characterized the early days of brand management, opting instead to react and respond to what they *think* customers want. What's worse, they've also taken to copying one another in the process.

The frameworks component of the solution refers to the brand strategy tools and models that exist today. Namely, few new models and frameworks for brand strategy have been proposed in recent years, and even fewer new models have found success. Traditional frameworks for brand positioning, brand architecture, brand experience, and brand extension from long ago still dominate the field of brand strategy. This is particularly problematic when compared to the relative pace of change in brand activation. Brands are conceived, launched, and activated in an entirely new, dynamic digital environment, yet the strategic frameworks and models for building brands have largely remained static, not evolving to keep pace with the new reality.

Unlike when many of the current brand strategy frameworks were developed, consumers today engage with media nearly every waking moment. They grab their phones before they eat breakfast, browse the web at work, watch television at night, and check their phones again during several small breaks throughout the day. As such, brand strategy must evolve to keep up with how brands are being activated and how consumers are experiencing and interacting with brands today.

Let's review how marketers have contributed to the current state of brand monotony, then focus more intently on what needs to change to build truly distinctive and indispensable brands. We'll start with the mindset component, then cover tools and frameworks.

BRAND MINDSET 1.0: "COMMAND AND CONTROL"

As referenced in chapter 2, the heyday of brand management years ago operated in a much simpler commercial environment that clearly favored manufacturers and brand owners. Companies were more easily able to exert leadership and influence relative to how their brands were positioned and marketed to consumers. Importantly, this pertained to virtually every element of the value chain from producer to consumer, permeating every component of the market mix.

Consider, for example, the role of brand positioning in this environment. Communication in these decades was almost always unidirectional. So when a company identified an attractive (and, yes, distinctive) positioning for its brand, it was far easier to control the dialogue and ensure all brand messaging remained on strategy. The same was true for the brand experience. With fewer touchpoints, more control over those touchpoints, and no online environment to worry about, architecting and delivering the desired brand experience was more attainable. Even pricing was easier back then, thanks to fewer competitors and distribution channels to manage.

All this contributed to an environment in which marketers were able to operate in more of a command-and-control manner than they can today. The command-and-control environment that characterized brand management decades ago isn't to suggest marketers had it easy, nor that they could do as they pleased with their brands. To be sure, they still needed to follow tried-and-true branding principles, such as customer centricity, single-minded focus, and consistency in execution. And they also faced traditional business and financial challenges, such as driving bottom-line performance. But in this environment, marketers who did their due diligence to establish meaningful differentiation and execute a thoughtful strategy were more certain of success than they would be in today's dramatically different and more challenging branding climate.

Today, heavy-handed command-and-control tactics can be a recipe for disaster. A few years ago, Nutella discovered that a fan of its products named Sara Rosso had, unbeknownst to the company, started World Nutella Day on social media.[1] Rosso shared her Nutella recipes, posted pictures, engaged with other fans, and encouraged them to spread the Nutella love as well. Did Nutella celebrate and encourage this fortunate gift that landed in its lap? Not exactly. In fact, the company actually sent Rosso a cease and desist letter, opting instead to retain tighter control of its brand. Eventually, the company wisely gave up on the power struggle, but not before losing some goodwill in the bargain. Conversely, more enlightened modern-day brand strategists love people like Rosso. She was acting as an unpaid marketer—and a highly effective one at that—by increasing engagement with Nutella fans and building valuable brand equity along the way.

The command-and-control approach, which worked well in the early days of brand management, now comes across as uninformed at best and heavy-handed at worst. Nutella tried to silence one of its biggest fans and, in the process, failed to recognize that brand fans like Sara Rosso are a blessing, not a curse. Savvy marketers realize consumers like her exert at least as much influence over the fate of brands as the companies that are marketing them.

BRAND MINDSET 2.0: EXECUTING, IMITATING, AND REACTING

If a command-and-control approach characterized the first phase of brand management, the pendulum has swung 180 degrees in the decades since. While multiple factors have contributed to this swing, as detailed in the first two chapters, the most profound has been the emergence and immediate dominance of the digital landscape. In a relatively short time, we have witnessed the proliferation of the internet. Online, we are bombarded by a dizzying array of related new concepts, such as e-commerce, search engine optimization (SEO), banner ads and pay-per-click advertising (PPC), social media, mobile marketing, and more.

While change and progress are typically positive—even when that progress is as profound and rapid as the advent of the internet—evolution does not come without a cost. Seemingly overnight, brand marketers needed to master these complex concepts, then deploy them effectively to their benefit. As soon as companies figured out one digital technology or marketing discipline, a new one became the flavor du jour. Overwhelmed marketers' response to these changes was to retreat, then execute, imitate, and react.

EXECUTING WITHOUT UNDERLYING STRATEGY

Marketers, many of whom were not digitally savvy, understandably struggled to master new tactics that required at least a base level of technological know-how. Unfortunately, many lost (or at least suppressed) their ability to think strategically in the process. There was so much to learn and only so many hours in the day.

Almost without realizing it—and with a healthy fear of being left behind—formerly disciplined strategic marketers evolved into tacticians. Strategic planning horizons began to shrink from years to months, then to weeks and days. According to *Taking Advantage of the Mobile Opportunity*, a report from Adobe, only 20 percent of companies have mobile marketing strategies that extend beyond one year.[2] Imagine telling marketers from thirty years ago that they would have no plan for their brands beyond the next twelve months.

When marketing plans become a laundry list of programs and activities with little thought as to how they work together and what they should collectively achieve, brands suffer. It might not be as interesting or trendy as adopting the latest ad platform or social media forum, but focusing on brand strategy remains as important as ever for building and nurturing meaningful and enduring economically viable brand assets.

Long-term equity and brand-building—both abstract and difficult to measure—have taken a back seat to much more immediate, quantifiable objectives, such as website traffic, page ranks, and click-through rates. Now, as content and social media have begun to dominate the marketing landscape, posts, likes, followers, and shares have become newly important key performance indicators. Ironically, when companies most desperately need strategic thinking to inform their approach to these new tactics, they no longer have time to "indulge" in strategic thinking.

IMITATING INSTEAD OF INNOVATING

When marketers focus more on activities and tactics rather than underlying strategy, two undesirable side effects emerge. First, marketers become overly fixated on best practices. Once again, the easy measurability of digital tactics (not to mention the real-time feedback they provide) has created a landscape where everyone now follows the same digital best practices. Digital agencies and other self-professed gurus began publishing the best time of day to tweet, the optimal layout for a company newsletter, and best practices for writing email headlines. Companies began blindly following these formulas, regardless of whether these tactics made sense for their brands.

Second, in addition to following so-called best practices, companies began following one another. In other words, playing copycat. Not only is this mentality *common* today; it is actually *encouraged* by reputable authorities. One article in *Harvard Business Review*, "When It's Smart to Copy Your Competitor's Brand Promise," praised the sameness, arguing that best tactics are best tactics regardless of individual goals or distinctions.[3] The piece used bottled water to emphasize its point, but how many consumers truly feel brand loyalty toward one bottle of water over another? These brands all focus on the purity of their water sources, and today, visitors at convenience stores pick the bottle that's easiest to reach, not one with a brand they care about.

Spotify, which seemingly mastered the digital landscape by creating a highly demanded music streaming platform, may be falling into the same trap. No longer limiting itself to music, Spotify wants to offer video streams, podcasts, and curated playlists for runners.[4] What was once its primary differentiator is quickly becoming just one of Spotify's offerings. To be fair, extension is a necessary and beneficial function of brand management, and it's the subject of an entire chapter later in this book. However, it must be approached in a very strategic and purposeful manner that is consistent with the essence of the brand. Time will tell whether Spotify's extensions are enhancing or denigrating its brand.

A more blatant example: when Samsung wanted to challenge Apple in smartphones, designers at the company didn't try to do anything differently. In fact, the company created a 132-page document to help designers copy the iPhone as closely as possible without breaking copyright laws.[5] Talk about perpetuating brand monotony!

Importantly, this copycat mentality applies to not only product and service offerings, as is the case in the examples above, but to online activity as well. The fear of missing out, or FOMO, is alive and well. Marketers think to themselves, "Our competitors have Facebook pages and Twitter accounts, so how can we not?" So they add these vehicles to their marketing mixes, executing in ways that are eerily similar to those of their direct competitors. With all these dynamics converging, is it any wonder we're drowning in brand monotony?

REACTING (TO CONSUMERS) INSTEAD OF LEADING

Finally, as detailed in the first two chapters, consumers have become more informed, skeptical, and savvy and have begun to wrestle away control over brands from manufacturers. In response, marketers have become complacent, rationalizing that it is no longer possible to control brand positioning. "The best we can hope for," they argue, "is to influence our brand positioning." In reality, however, most marketers are not even doing that, instead choosing to merely follow consumers and hoping they like where they take their brands.

So clearly, the net effect of Brand Mindset 2.0 has been largely negative. Marketers have gradually evolved from strategic thinkers into pure tacticians, from adhering to sound brand practices to blindly following so-called best practices; from innovating and striving for distinctness to copying one another; and from leading the consumer dialogue to merely following it. Needless to say, if we want to distinguish our brands and enjoy the business and financial benefits of doing so, this has to change.

BRAND MINDSET 3.0: TRUE INFLUENCE

So this means brand marketers should revert back to the command-and-control mindset to reclaim control, right? In a word, no. The days of command-and-control brand management are over, and that's not a bad thing. But, at the same time, the status quo of mindlessly following best practices and copying each other cannot continue if we want to resume brand leadership and reverse this trend of brand monotony.

It may be helpful to consider the three phases of brand mindset as a continuum. On one end of the continuum is the heavy-handed command-and-control approach that characterized the early days of brand management. On the other end is the far more passive and reactive approach of today. The ideal point on the continuum is probably what marketers originally had in mind in response to all these changes—a midpoint best characterized as "influencing." But once again, most brand marketers are not even attempting to influence their positioning anymore; instead, they resort to the easier paths of merely following a general set of best practices—and each other. In effect, marketers are unwittingly contributing to brand monotony by following each other or, at best, leaving differentiation to chance by allowing customers to position their brands for them.

Influence, on the other hand, assumes a higher degree of active participation and leadership in the shaping of brands' identities. As always, it involves listening to (and taking direction from) customers but not necessarily taking a back seat and leaving a brand's fate to chance. Influence involves less following and more leading. Above all, it requires us to revisit brand strategy from both a mindset and frameworks perspective.

Representing the ideal balance between a firm grip and an open hand, influence is a soft yet firm touch that guides consumers in the brand's preferred direction without making them feel like they are merely a pawn in the commercial equation. To achieve this balance, however, brands cannot improvise. Influence depends on a forward-looking, informed brand strategy. And informed brand strategy requires tools, frameworks, models, and methodologies that are relevant in a far more dynamic brand activation environment.

FROM MINDSET TO FRAMEWORKS: EVOLVING BRAND STRATEGY TOOLS AND MODELS

The first portion of this chapter has focused on marketers' mindset toward brand strategy. But what about the actual tools and frameworks that help marketers develop brand strategy? Surprisingly, despite the mind-boggling pace of change in the way brands are activated (especially digitally), brand strategy frameworks have largely remained unchanged. Many of the frameworks for brand strategy used today were created in the 1990s or earlier. Even the most creative and engaging brand activation is only as effective as the strategy that supports and informs it. Outdated strategic frameworks prevent marketing tactics from reaching their full potential— and brands from achieving and maintaining meaningful differentiation.

Perhaps the most vivid example of this is the framework typically used for brand positioning, the subject of the next chapter in this book. The framework is decades old and was designed to shape advertising development and other forms of mass communication. After all, it was developed during the aforementioned golden age of brand management. The model's four basic components consider a single target audience, frame of reference (often a category descriptor), primary benefit, and supporting proof points to lend credibility to the benefit.

Today, we live in a more complex environment, and our branding efforts need to apply to more marketing mix components than just advertising. For example, most brands (especially large global ones) have multiple and often equally important target audiences. Additionally, many brands are highly experiential in nature, and the above model is not necessarily well equipped to accommodate that.

Brand positioning isn't the only strategic framework that has not evolved, however. For decades, brand architecture has been defined essentially along a continuum of branded house (a portfolio built around a single master brand) and house of brands (a portfolio consisting of multiple, often unrelated brands). This, too, while still relevant, may be overly simplistic in a more complex world of multibillion-dollar global brand portfolios. In reality, most companies fall somewhere in the middle of this continuum, which is inherently more complex to manage.

Likewise, brand extendibility, employee engagement, and metrics have not evolved quickly enough. While some of these strategic areas have evolved in thinking slightly over the years, they are still unequipped to thrive in a significantly more demanding, complex marketplace environment. These components of brand strategy cannot remain rooted in the past if the brands utilizing them expect to succeed in the future.

SETTING THE STAGE FOR BETTER BRAND STRATEGY

The remainder of this book will address the key components of brand strategy, as well as some important internal and external issues that affect it. One recurring theme throughout many of the chapters (and already mentioned earlier in this one) is the need for marketers to shift mindsets—the very way we think about brand strategy—in addition to the frameworks and tools that comprise it. When it comes to the latter, many of the changes proposed represent more of an evolution than revolution. Here's what we will discuss throughout the remainder of this book:

CHAPTER 4: BRAND POSITIONING

Traditional and simplistic brand positioning frameworks that historically served an advertising function must be more holistic and versatile today. Modern brand positioning now serves and informs a more complex commercial ecosystem. Companies need to allow for multiple target audiences while still retaining an all-important single-minded focus.

Additionally, brand positioning today needs to allow for more types and forms of differentiation, not assuming the only thing that can differentiate a brand is a customer benefit. Namely, the audience a brand targets (the "who"), the way the brand delivers the benefit (the "how"), and the reason a brand exists (the "why") are all viable alternatives for a brand's promise and a legitimate basis for meaningful differentiation. Examples of highly successful brands that have achieved meaningful differentiation through each of these methods will be provided.

CHAPTER 5: BRAND PORTFOLIO STRATEGY

While the traditional framework of branded house and house of brands is still relevant today, the fact is most companies reside somewhere in between these two extremes. When this is the case, brand portfolio management becomes more complex and challenging, and more guidance is required to inform strategy development. Additionally, there has not been much written to date on the internal and external factors that should determine where on the spectrum a company should choose to reside.

Beyond the branded house and house of brands frameworks, this chapter will detail the components that comprise a comprehensive brand portfolio strategy and the questions that should be addressed through it. It will also propose a set of guiding principles for brand portfolio strategy that tends to be relatively universal in nature (i.e., equally applicable to B2B and B2C, product-based and service-based companies, as well as industry-agnostic).

CHAPTER 6: BRAND EXPERIENCES

Customer experience frameworks typically include things like touchpoint models (e.g., prepurchase, purchase, and postpurchase) and customer journey maps (visualizations of the path a customer takes, from first awareness through initial trial and beyond). While these are both valuable frameworks, their application is often suboptimal. Much has been written about "the" ideal customer experience, as if there is only one such experience shared by all, but that is not the case. Rather, companies should reframe this as the ideal *brand* experience, inspired first and foremost by the brand positioning and promise.

Unsurprisingly, the optimal experience for one target segment (and the brand best serving that segment) will differ from that of another target segment. This is why customer experience should be distinctive to a given brand, not uniform across brands. Multiple examples of brands whose experiences brilliantly reflect their brand positioning will illustrate the points.

CHAPTER 7: BRAND EXTENSION

The extremely high failure rate of new brand extensions has been well-documented for years. Some sources indicate that more than 85 percent of line extensions fail within three years of launch.[6] Although a multitude of reasons could explain this poor track record, much of the blame resides with a lack of inspiration when it comes to extending brands. While brand managers are wise to protect the valuable equity of their brands and not risk dilution or erosion by straying too far, an overly conservative approach to extension presents equally challenging obstacles.

Incremental and unimaginative line extensions must be replaced with transformational growth and innovation that are inspired by brands' intangible and emotional equities, not merely by tangible product features. To ensure success in a new marketplace, the brand needs to be a source of inspiration for growth, not merely guardrails that protect it from dilution. This chapter will provide examples of how companies have successfully leveraged their brands' strong equity to drive transformational and profitable growth.

CHAPTER 8: BRAND STORY

The transformative power of storytelling in society has been well documented. When carefully crafted and skillfully communicated, stories have the ability to influence and inspire in ways simple facts and raw data simply cannot. Importantly, storytelling is equally powerful in the world of business and brands. Research has proven that consumers are considerably more willing to purchase from brands that have a compelling story they can relate to than from brands that do not.

This chapter leverages seminal work in the art of storytelling from Christopher Booker to detail seven story archetypes and how they relate to the world of brands. It will also put forward several guiding principles that can help marketers craft compelling brand stories. Both the archetypes and guiding principles will be illustrated with real-world examples of brand stories that have deeply connected with consumers and customers, as well as other important brand stakeholders.

CHAPTER 9: BRANDS IN AN ERA OF DIGITAL ACTIVATION

As referenced earlier, the digital-first mentality of today should be replaced with a brand-first, digitally enhanced mentality. If there is one factor that is most responsible for the current state of brand monotony, it is the way companies have approached digital activation. Ironically, the transformative power of digital technology also represents the single most important factor that can help us break through and reverse the disturbing trend of brand monotony. Instead of striving to follow generic best practices—resulting in brand monotony—companies should strive to bring brands to life in a digital format consistent with the brand positioning.

Additionally, most consumers do not draw a distinction between their experiences with brands offline versus online, but companies often do. In extreme cases, the online platform of a company is sometimes an entirely separate entity that competes against its brick-and-mortar counterpart. Just as the brand needs to be delivered consistently across traditional offline touchpoints, it also needs to feel similar to consumers when experienced in an online environment. Examples of how companies have leveraged the essence of their brand positioning to drive digital activation will be provided throughout the chapter.

CHAPTER 10: BRAND-BUILDING IN THE WORLD OF B2B

As mentioned earlier, the roots of modern-day brand management can be traced back to the world of consumer packaged goods. As such, "brand" is sometimes mistakenly thought of as the domain of B2C businesses and considered less relevant in the world of B2B. However, it is interesting to note that some of the most valuable brands in the world today—according to trusted sources such as Interbrand and BrandZ—are either pure B2B brands or have a significant B2B component.

Many of the basic precepts of brand strategy discussed in this book transcend industries and business models, and they can apply equally to B2B and B2C. However, that is not to say that B2B companies do not face some unique challenges and nuances when it comes to brand management. This chapter will address a few myths and ongoing debates that pertain to branding in the world of B2B, such as the role of individuals versus companies when it comes to defining target audiences, as well as the pros and cons of rational and emotional motivations when it comes to brand promise.

CHAPTER 11: LONG LIVE THE CORPORATE BRAND

As is the case with powerful B2B brands, corporate brands such as Coca-Cola, Johnson & Johnson, and Harley-Davidson represent some of the world's most important brand assets today in terms of economic valuation. After a lull of several decades, there has been a renaissance for corporate brand-building in recent years. Procter & Gamble, SC Johnson, ExxonMobil, General Electric, and The Coca-Cola Company are just a few examples of companies that have recognized the importance of their corporate brand and company reputation, even though some of them go to market to a far greater extent with their product brands.

This chapter will make a strong case for investing in building the corporate brand, and it will explain its resurgence in recent years. It will also detail the numerous benefits a company gains by building a strong corporate brand. Importantly, these benefits are both tangible (e.g., risk mitigation and improved financial performance) and intangible (e.g., company purpose and internal esprit de corps).

CHAPTER 12: EMPLOYEE BRAND ENGAGEMENT

In a more complex relationship-driven brand world, employees' understanding of (and buy-in to) brand strategy is essential. They must know, feel, and act in accordance with brand strategy. This is especially true for service-based companies, where frontline employees are far and away the most important touchpoint for the brand. It is also true in many retail and hospitality industries, where experience is one of the most important contributors to brand preference and loyalty. However, successful employee brand engagement goes beyond the marketing department and frontline employees. To be effective, it needs to include the entire employee base.

What can make this even more challenging is that in many industries, once-removed employees such as franchisees and third-party representatives (whether branded or white-labeled) are often charged with delivering a genuine, on-brand experience. In these cases, employees become the literal face of the brand, and their ability to understand, embrace, and deliver the brand promise is essential. This chapter will provide guidance on how to ensure brand strategy is embraced throughout the organization, regardless of industry or business model.

CHAPTER 13: BRAND MEASUREMENT AND MARKETING ACCOUNTABILITY

Traditionally, brand metrics have been mostly backward-looking. They track historical data points over time and, at best, pinpoint or diagnose problems and opportunities after the fact. However, in our more complex, fast-moving business environment, measurements need to also look forward. In other words, brand measurement needs to evolve beyond the diagnostic (i.e., flagging an issue or opportunity) to become prescriptive (i.e., suggesting how to address the issue or opportunity).

Additionally, brand stewards must undergo a concentrated effort to better correlate traditional brand metrics more directly with broader business performance metrics, such as revenue, market share, and profitability. This will also go a long way toward elevating the stature of brands from a discretionary expense item to an invaluable revenue-and profit-generating asset. This chapter will suggest changes to the way we view brand measurement, and it will provide examples of how companies can use it as a means to establish competitive advantage.

THE HIGH PRICE OF FAILURE

Companies that fail to address these factors will face dire consequences. If brand strategy does not evolve and if activation continues to move forward in ways that may be harmful to long-term brand equity, the result will be even more monotony. Brands will increasingly lack distinction from one another. To consumers, they will be anything but indispensable. Companies with uninspiring, undifferentiated brands will have no choice but to resort to copycat strategies and compete on price. Key market metrics such as distribution, market share, and volume will suffer, as will financial metrics like revenue, unit margin, and profitability.

Undoubtedly, brands that wish to escape the cycle of monotony face challenges. However, the challenges are not insurmountable. The solution begins by recognizing that brand strategy, as it is defined today, has fundamental issues and that the necessary changes cover both mindset and frameworks. Brand strategy needs to evolve to keep up with rapid and dramatic changes in the world of activation—changes that have made the environment brands operate in almost unrecognizable from its previous form a decade or two ago.

The way we manage brands needs to change, too. The pendulum has swung too far in recent years, going from "command and control" to "sit back and watch." While we cannot and should not revert to the former mentality, we need to do more to influence the roles our brands play in the lives of customers.

PART 2

THE FIVE KEY COMPONENTS OF BRAND STRATEGY

Chapter 4

―――――

Brand Positioning

Brand positioning represents the very foundation of brand strategy. While many companies might not formally define and document other aspects of brand strategy (e.g., brand architecture or brand experience), most at least articulate a formal positioning statement for their brands.

By definition, positioning plays an instrumental role in achieving differentiation. It is the key to breaking the cycle of monotony. Without a unique positioning, a brand has little hope of establishing meaningful differentiation within its category.

What is brand positioning, and why is it so important? According to Philip Kotler, one of the great thought leaders in the field of brand strategy, brand positioning is "the act of designing the company's offering and image to occupy a distinctive place in the mind of the target market."[1] Elaborated, brand positioning is often defined as the promise a brand makes to its key stakeholders. However, as we will elaborate in subsequent sections, stakeholders are more than just customers, and a brand's promise does not necessarily need to center on a customer benefit.

A well-defined brand positioning provides many benefits to marketers. For starters, positioning informs every aspect of brand development, including the basic product or service offering from the brand; the visual and verbal communications and expressions that support it; and the experience it delivers to stakeholders. Positioning can also serve as a filter or screen for decision-making—for instance, to help a company determine whether a potential tactic under consideration is consistent with the essence of the brand.

A great brand positioning is single-minded, compelling, differentiated, and credible. That is, it should have one consistent theme woven throughout (single-minded) and motivate stakeholders to act a certain way or feel a particular emotion (compelling). It should also stand for something unique in stakeholders' minds (differentiated). Finally, its promise must be both realistic and believable for that brand (credible).

Unfortunately, most brands do not satisfy these core positioning requirements. Perhaps the most common shortcoming pertains to the uniqueness criteria—which explains why we are currently suffering from a crisis of brand differentiation.

BRAND POSITIONING BACK IN THE DAY

The origins of brand positioning go back at least as far as 1969, when Al Ries and Jack Trout proposed the concept in an article entitled "Positioning Is a Game People Play in Today's Me-Too Marketplace."[2] As suggested in the title, Ries and Trout were already referring to an environment characterized by excessive brand monotony. They later evolved this philosophy in their book *Positioning: The Battle for Your Mind*.[3] This work, along with several others published later, helped establish brand positioning as a legitimate business concept, further elevating the world of branding as a true strategic business discipline.

Some of the key tenets put forward by Ries and Trout in their seminal thinking on brand positioning included the notion that positioning happens in the minds of the target market (i.e., perception is reality), not solely in the mind of the marketer. Although we as marketers strive to define and achieve a particular positioning "space" for a brand, the aggregate perception of the market toward that brand defines its true positioning relative to its competitive set. Additionally, Ries and Trout argued that even if marketers foolishly choose not to proactively position a brand, positioning happens reactively by default, according to how customers consciously or unconsciously choose to perceive that brand.

At the risk of oversimplification, the essence of their work led to a positioning model that loosely consisted of four components: target audience, frame of reference (often, but not always, a product or service category), benefit, and proof points. Collectively, these components help marketers define who they intend their brand to serve, how they want customers to think about their brand, what the brand intends to provide its customers, and tangible evidence—reasons to believe that the brand can deliver on its stated promise.

Ries and Trout consistently expanded upon their thinking on brand positioning for many years following their initial book. Other great thinkers in strategic marketing, such as David Aaker, Philip Kotler, Kevin Keller, and others did the same. Different thought leaders in brand strategy have created derivations of the model outlined above, but by and large, this basic framework for brand positioning (or nuanced versions of it) is still used by the majority of companies in myriad industries today.

Models based on the work of Ries and Trout hinge upon two basic assumptions: First, they assume brands must discover what their consumers consider to be important. Second, they assume brands must provide an incentive to customers to choose one brand over the others in that market. To accomplish either of these goals, the pair argued, brands need a differentiator—a truth even more profound today than it was in the 1960s.

DRAWBACKS OF THE RIES AND TROUT MODEL

To be fair, this model and its derivations have many merits. Marketers have used it for decades with commendable success. By no means should the key takeaway be that modern brands should abandon this philosophy altogether. Rather, we believe there is an opportunity to maintain many of this model's positive elements while modifying some of those elements—and adding entirely new ones—to broaden its application and increase its effectiveness.

The origins of this model trace back fifty years, which, as we have established, was a much simpler time for brands. Companies targeted a single audience, focused on a single differentiator (usually a benefit), provided some evidence, and called it a day.[4] Most marketers would agree that when this model was proposed, it was largely intended to inform communications and creative development. More specifically, marketers used this model to shape advertising.

However, once again, much has changed in the world of branding since the 1960s. Consumers are more sophisticated and demanding.

Distribution channels are more numerous and convoluted. Advertising and promotion look nothing like they did in years past, and brands themselves are larger, intercultural, and more complex than ever. It's no wonder that we should now revisit how we think about the framework for brand positioning.

In subsequent sections, we will elaborate on a few of the drawbacks relative to the traditional advertising-based positioning model. The two most notable drawbacks include the target audience and the promise. Both of these elements deserve reconsideration and refinement so they can become more useful and expand the infinite possibilities for modern brands.

In short, the current definition of target audience is too limiting. It assumes there can only be one target for any given brand and that the target needs to be a customer (or customer segment). The promise component is also too narrowly defined.[5] Many marketers assume the brand promise must be a benefit—and a customer benefit at that—as opposed to another meaningful point of difference, such as a proof point, a purpose, or other factors.

The following sections suggest changes to these core components of brand positioning as it is understood today, as well as other components marketers should consider.

EVOLVING BEYOND THE ADVERTISING-BASED MODEL

The following represents a derivation of the traditional advertising-based model for brand positioning. It maintains many of the same components outlined above, yet modifies the definitions of some, while adding a few new components to the mix. This evolved framework addresses some of the shortcomings of the traditional brand positioning model—namely, it serves functions beyond advertising and communication—and provides the versatility and flexibility required to operate in a more complex brand ecosystem. (See figure 4.1.)

Figure 4.1
Brand Positioning Model

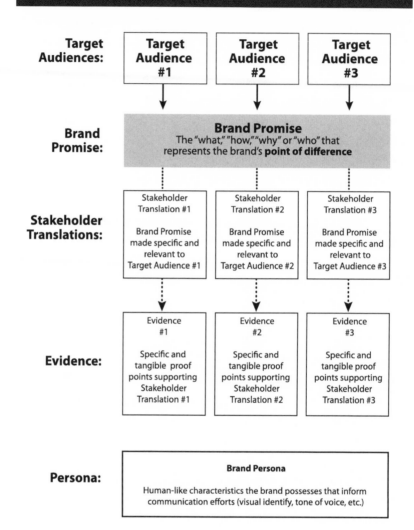

Target Audiences:

| Target Audience #1 | Target Audience #2 | Target Audience #3 |

Brand Promise:

Brand Promise
The "what," "how," "why" or "who" that represents the brand's **point of difference**

Stakeholder Translations:

Stakeholder Translation #1

Brand Promise made specific and relevant to Target Audience #1

Stakeholder Translation #2

Brand Promise made specific and relevant to Target Audience #2

Stakeholder Translation #3

Brand Promise made specific and relevant to Target Audience #3

Evidence:

Evidence #1

Specific and tangible proof points supporting Stakeholder Translation #1

Evidence #2

Specific and tangible proof points supporting Stakeholder Translation #2

Evidence #3

Specific and tangible proof points supporting Stakeholder Translation #3

Persona:

Brand Persona

Human-like characteristics the brand possesses that inform communication efforts (visual identify, tone of voice, etc.)

TARGET AUDIENCES

As the name implies, the target audiences component represents the "who," as in the stakeholders the brand is intended to serve. Target audience remains an essential part of the brand positioning model, but it needs to be considered more expansively. For starters, as referenced above, target audience need not be singular. In fact, it is almost naive to believe a brand today has only a single target audience. Additionally, a target audience need not necessarily be customers. Although customers remain a critically important target for virtually any brand, most companies have additional stakeholders who can dramatically affect the company's destiny and who should be considered when positioning brands.

Consider, for example, a professional services firm. To be sure, one of its most important targets is current and potential clients. However, the brand must also be relevant to other stakeholder groups, such as prospective employees, industry thought leaders, and the media. Each of these audiences has a slightly different relationship with the brand and seeks a slightly different experience from it. And each is important to consider when positioning the brand.

PROMISE (POINT OF DIFFERENCE)

Promise is the distinctive payoff a brand provides to its intended targets. It should also represent the brand's primary point of difference.

While the advertising-centric positioning model assumes the promise is a benefit (i.e., what the customer derives from purchasing the product or service), this need not be the case. Many successful brands offer promises that are about a purpose (a "why"), a process (a "how"), or relevance to a niche audience (a "who"), independent of (or in addition to) a benefit (a "what"). Regardless of which of these four types is chosen, the key is for the brand promise to represent something that is compelling about—and highly distinctive to—the brand.

Even though the promise needs to appeal to multiple stakeholder groups, as referenced above, it still needs to be single-minded. In other words, having multiple targets does not mean the marketer has permission to define multiple promises. Rather, the promise needs to be defined and articulated at a high enough level that it can be modified and applied (i.e., translated) for different target stakeholders—like an umbrella that covers multiple people.

For example, the hypothetical professional services company referenced above might broadly define its promise around "business impact." The concept of business impact can and should intentionally be defined broadly so the firm can make it relevant for multiple stakeholder targets, each of whom has different associations with—and expectations of—the brand. To understand how a brand promise is made relevant to different stakeholder groups, consider the next component of the model: stakeholder translations.

STAKEHOLDER TRANSLATIONS

Think of translations as a "reconciliation" component of sorts, given the tensions that sometimes arise when a single-minded brand promise must be made relevant to disparate stakeholder groups. As stated above, the existence of multiple targets does not give marketers permission to develop multiple, unrelated promises (targeted to different stakeholder groups). Doing so would result in a disjointed brand. Therefore, the high-level "umbrella" brand promise should be expressed in ways that can apply to the various target audiences—customers, employees, investors, etc.—all without changing the essence of the promise or overly diluting it.

Continuing with the professional services example from above, this firm might have clients across multiple business functions, such as accounting, financial advisory, and taxes. In addition, beyond clients, the brand might need to be highly relevant to prospective employees to ensure the company attracts the highest caliber talent—another stakeholder target. As mentioned earlier, this hypothetical professional service brand's promise is loosely defined around the concept of "business impact." It needs, therefore, to establish a translation for prospective clients that articulates the type of business impact its services provide to those clients. It also needs to develop a translation for potential and current employees that articulates the type of impact the brand can provide for the careers of those who work for the firm. This is an example of a single-minded brand promise (business impact) being translated in order to be relevant to two different stakeholder targets: clients and employees. (See figure 4.2.)

Figure 4.2
Brand Positioning Model — Professional Services Firm

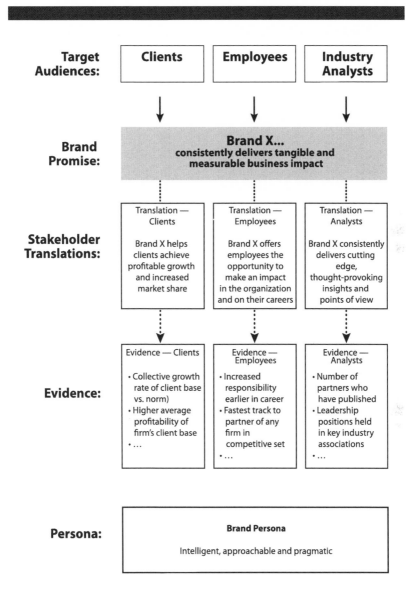

Target Audiences:

Clients	Employees	Industry Analysts

Brand Promise:

Brand X...
consistently delivers tangible and measurable business impact

Stakeholder Translations:

Translation — Clients	Translation — Employees	Translation — Analysts
Brand X helps clients achieve profitable growth and increased market share	Brand X offers employees the opportunity to make an impact in the organization and on their careers	Brand X consistently delivers cutting edge, thought-provoking insights and points of view

Evidence:

Evidence — Clients	Evidence — Employees	Evidence — Analysts
• Collective growth rate of client base vs. norm) • Higher average profitability of firm's client base • ...	• Increased responsibility earlier in career • Fastest track to partner of any firm in competitive set • ...	• Number of partners who have published • Leadership positions held in key industry associations • ...

Persona:

Brand Persona

Intelligent, approachable and pragmatic

EVIDENCE

Evidence is fairly analogous to the proof points component of the traditional advertising-based brand positioning model. Its objective in this model is the same as in the traditional model: to lend credibility and believability to the promise and corresponding translations. One subtle difference here is that, because of the multiple targets and translations, marketers must provide multiple sets of evidence—one for each stakeholder translation.

Continuing with the professional services firm, multiple sets of evidence would be required to lend credibility to the brand promise. For example, hypothetical evidence for the client stakeholder translation could include factors like average annual increase in profit for client companies, typical increases in client market share, and average growth rates of clients, compared to the competition. Evidence for the employee stakeholder translation could include the firm's faster upward mobility of its consultants, the challenging nature of assignments given to employees early in their careers, and the firm's extensive training curriculum and commitment to career development.

Once again, the important point here is continuity. A single brand promise, or payoff, is translated to be relevant for multiple stakeholder targets and is supported with relevant evidence for each translation.

PERSONA

As the name implies, the brand persona is the personification of the brand. This component of positioning gives the brand humanlike characteristics and is especially helpful when it comes to informing creative and communications efforts, both visual and verbal. Expression elements, such as logo, visual identity, and messaging, should draw their inspiration from the way brand persona is defined in brand positioning. As such, persona should be considered a standard component in any complete brand positioning model.

TAKING AIM AT MULTIPLE TARGET AUDIENCES

The first component considered during the establishment of a brand positioning should be target audience. This is for good reason. Because who you want to reach remains a vital component of any brand positioning model, it stands to reason that marketers need to know the people and entities their brands are intended to serve before addressing any other aspects of positioning. However, traditional considerations of this component often fall prey to two potential shortcomings.

First, as mentioned in the previous section, the current definition of target audience as it pertains to brand positioning assumes a brand operates in a world in which there can be only one target. To be sure, no brand should ever try to satisfy everyone. Sacrifice (including audience) is truly the essence of any good brand positioning. However, the notion that brands can only target a single group is unnecessarily limiting.

Years ago, Larry Light, former chief marketing officer for McDonald's, said, "We no longer live in a world where mass marketing to masses of consumers with a mass message delivered through mass media makes money. In fact, mass marketing as we know it is dead."[6] He went on to say that McDonald's has several consumer segments: each looks materially different regarding demographics, attitude, and behavior, yet all are strategically and financially attractive to the company. Light also noted that these segments think and act differently based on situational and environmental factors, such as the time of day, location, or urgency of need.

For example, McDonald's caters to mothers looking to feed, entertain, and perhaps treat their young children. But the fast-food chain is also highly relevant to business executives who only get a few minutes for lunch while racing through an airport to catch a flight. Interestingly, the business executive might entertain a client for dinner that night at a five-star restaurant. Here we have one consumer on two dramatically different occasions, each with different associated needs. For one of those needs, McDonald's is an ideal solution. For the other, it is irrelevant.

Second, beyond the ability to target multiple customer segments with a single brand, who says the only important audiences to whom brands have to be relevant is customers? There are many other categories of audience (or stakeholder groups) beyond customers that can directly impact—whether positively or negatively—a brand's marketplace performance.

Take, for example, the energy sector. Companies like ExxonMobil, BP, and Shell rely heavily on their ability to influence governments, opinion leaders, and policymakers—entities that enable them to gain all-important access to exploration and production rights.[7] These entities are not consumers, but they are clearly some of the most important stakeholders in these companies' ecosystems.

According to Suzanne McCarron, vice president of public and government affairs at ExxonMobil, "The world has changed in terms of how it views energy, and the energy industry in particular. There's a much broader conversation happening around energy now, and among a larger, more diverse target audience than ever before. As such, we've had to broaden who we are seeking to have a conversation with about our issues." McCarron continues by specifying the myriad stakeholders of the Exxon-Mobil brand: "Our brand touches consumers and business customers, to be sure, but it must also resonate with influencers, policymakers, foreign governments, and NGOs, just to name a few. It is important we are reaching out to them to ensure they understand our positions."[8]

Several examples from other industries exist as well. Think back to the professional services example referenced earlier. Big Four accounting firms like KPMG and Deloitte live and die based on their ability to attract and retain the highest caliber talent. When the difference between great talent and elite talent means the difference between winning a new client or losing it to a competitor, these brands must focus heavily on the target audience of current and prospective employees or risk becoming irrelevant.

For some brands, vendor relationships take the highest priority. Many sugar producers readily admit that their success depends as much upon sugarcane growers as the retailers and consumers who buy the end product. This dynamic has been exacerbated by the extent to which demand for sugar so frequently and dramatically exceeds supply. In other industries, such as financial services and health insurance, companies operate in highly regulated environments, and as such, regulators are important stakeholders in their ecosystems.

In each of these cases, people or entities other than customers make up at least one important target audience, if not more. For extreme cases, noncustomer audiences might even be the most important (i.e., primary) ones. It all depends on the unique needs of the brand—as does the following section, which covers the different types of promises brands can offer these audiences.

RECONSIDERING THE PROMISE

Once again, think of the promise as representing a brand's primary point of difference. In the traditional advertising-based model for brand positioning, conventional wisdom suggests the promise must be a customer benefit. This is essentially the "what" that the brand provides to customers. In fact, many positioning models actually refer to this component as "benefit," not "promise." However, this thinking is limiting and outdated for multiple reasons.

The first reason is that the customer is not necessarily the only relevant target for the brand. If that's true, why should the brand promise have to be a *customer* benefit? The second reason is that insisting the brand promise be a customer benefit is often what leads to brands becoming indistinguishable from one another. In some categories, the customer benefit is virtually universal (e.g., most everyone who uses shampoo wants beautiful hair), so the only way to differentiate is to emphasize some other aspect of the brand. Pantene Pro-V, for example, differentiates itself not so much on the benefit of beautiful hair, but rather its unique means for achieving it: vitamin-infused formulations. In this example, the point of difference is more in the "how" than the "what."

In addition to the "what," examples of other options for brand promise include focusing on the "how," the "why," and the "who." Let's look at examples of brands that have defined their promises and key points of differentiation through each of these four methods and discuss the reasons why each can be a viable alternative. (See figure 4.3.)

Figure 4.3
Four Types of Brand Promise

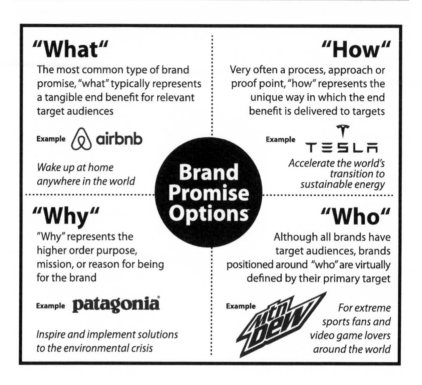

"What"

The most common type of brand promise, "what" typically represents a tangible end benefit for relevant target audiences

Example ⓐ airbnb

Wake up at home anywhere in the world

"How"

Very often a process, approach or proof point, "how" represents the unique way in which the end benefit is delivered to targets

Example T≡SLA

Accelerate the world's transition to sustainable energy

Brand Promise Options

"Why"

"Why" represents the higher order purpose, mission, or reason for being for the brand

Example patagonia

Inspire and implement solutions to the environmental crisis

"Who"

Although all brands have target audiences, brands positioned around "who" are virtually defined by their primary target

Example Mtn Dew

For extreme sports fans and video game lovers around the world

END BENEFIT ("WHAT")

As mentioned above, the most common method for defining a brand's promise is through a customer end benefit—the "what." As such, examples of brands following this route abound. You know your brand does this when its promise answers the question "What tangible benefit does the brand provide, presumably to its target customer?"

IBM offers one such example. Through "Smarter Planet," IBM leveraged and built a valuable space in customer minds. The "what" in this case is the empowerment of companies, cities, and communities around the globe to build a smarter planet. Commercials highlighting smart power grids, smart utilities, smart hospitals, and smart city roads drove this point home. By actively sharing its knowledge of technology, data, and systems, IBM inspired people to consider using the tools it offers to solve their unique problems. The important thing here is that "Smarter Planet" isn't just a catchy phrase. All of IBM's activity, from business operations to employee interactions with customers, ties into this core proposition.[9] When customers think of what benefit they get from IBM, the brand promise provides the answer.

Airbnb also offers a "what"-based brand promise. While some might argue that the essence of this brand lies in the "how"—namely, its sharing-economy business model for travel lodging—the brand has an even more powerful "what." Airbnb wants customers to "wake up at home anywhere in the world."[10] In 2014, the chief marketing officer for the startup, Jonathan Mildenhall, looked to some of the world's leading brands, such as Apple, Starbucks, Nike, Disney, and Virgin, as sources of inspiration to build a cultural ideology: belonging. Mildenhall convinced other executives to expand its "belong anywhere" internal mission statement to become the official tagline. One rebrand later, Airbnb prides itself on providing homes around the world, as evidenced by the four tenets represented in its logo: people, places, love, and Airbnb.[11]

According to the company's CEO, Brian Chesky, "For so long, people thought Airbnb was about renting houses. But really, we're about home. You see, a house is just a space, but a home is where you belong. And what makes this global community so special is that for the very first time, you can belong anywhere. That is the idea at the core of our company: belonging."[12] For Airbnb, that promise of belonging is a very powerful "what."

One last example of a "what"-based promise is global management consulting and professional services firm Accenture. Accenture has built a strong, differentiated brand on a simple yet powerful statement: "High performance. Delivered."[13] Importantly, although this is a market-facing tagline, it is far more than merely advertising copy. It is the brand's strategic positioning. It's a memorable statement that both makes a promise (high performance) and defines the category in which Accenture competes (implementation, not just pure strategy). Deloitte and PwC could undoubtedly make the same claim, but they have not.

Accenture has carved out a defensible brand territory by articulating to clients what it promises, as opposed to the services it provides. Chairman and CEO of Accenture Pierre Nanterme stated, "Our brand strengthens our unique positioning in the marketplace and drives significant competitive advantage. It reflects the trust our clients place in us and enables us to attract top talent."[14]

In 2011, Accenture initiated a campaign to embed this brand promise in the minds of all stakeholders that might interact with the company. From traditional advertising and social media to expert presentations, the company delivered its promise to more than two hundred cities on six continents, touting its unique benefit and communicating the value of its offering to every interested party.

This "what" definition of a brand's promise became commonplace for a reason. Not only is it effective, but it is also easy to identify and implement. As we have already specified, however, the "what" is only one of four potential definitions of a brand's promise. Next, let's look at the "how" and discuss the ways some brands use their unique processes or approaches to differentiate themselves from the competition.

PROCESS OR APPROACH ("HOW")

Sometimes, the brand's "what" might not be all that special, exciting, or unique. In some cases, it might even be a category ante, especially if the "what" is a highly functional benefit. When multiple brands in a category attempt to position around a common end benefit—especially a pedestrian category ante—brand monotony is the inevitable outcome.

Consider the airline industry. Getting you safely from point A to point B is just table stakes for any airline. If it can't do that, it won't remain in business for long. After all, when was the last time you chose one airline over another because it promised to "get you there"? But most people would agree that Southwest Airlines, Virgin Atlantic, and Emirates have discovered that *how* they get you from point A to point B can look and feel very different. Let's consider a few other brands in different industries that have made their mark and become distinctive based on the "how."

In 2012, Dollar Shave Club, a California-based subscription company for razors and other grooming essentials, became one of the most successful subscription services on the market. Dollar Shave Club is much more than just a razor and personal grooming company: it is a brand that provides an innovative way to make customers' lives easier and more enjoyable. It's also more than a good value, as is evident in the brand name. Dollar Shave Club defines itself through the intersection of convenience and cost. Customers save time by purchasing razors and other shaving supplies from the company and, thanks to monthly deliveries, they never run out.

In the transportation industry, Zipcar—a subsidiary of Avis Budget Group, Inc., a leading global provider of mobility services—offers urban dwellers a viable alternative to traditional car ownership. With hundreds of hubs around the globe, it is one of the world's largest car-sharing companies. Membership entitles you to use its vehicles anywhere, including Europe.

Zipcar is great for people who don't drive frequently. It's also beneficial for travelers who want the peace of mind of on-demand access to personal vehicles but don't want to pay for (and park) a rental car. Zipcar's focus on the "how" is reflected in its brand positioning statement: "To urban-dwelling, educated techno-savvy consumers, when you use Zipcar car-sharing service instead of owning a car, you save money while reducing your carbon footprint."[15] Dollar Shave Club and Zipcar both established new distribution channels or business models; however, differentiating on the "how" doesn't necessarily require a new business model or such dramatic transformation.

CA Technologies is a business software and services company based in New York City that creates software to run on a mainframe, distributed computing systems, virtual machines, and cloud environments. The customer promise at CA Technologies states, "To consistently deliver a superior customer experience by putting your organization at the center of all that we do."[16] Its mission, "Eliminating the barriers between ideas and outcomes," is completely focused on improving the customer experience and delivering the value customers are promised.

At this company, CX (customer experience) has become part of the lexicon. The new DNA at CA Technologies has "customer-centric" as one of its essential elements. As part of the CX transformation, many noncustomer-facing employees got involved in the Customer Engagement Program, directly interfacing with customers to solve a problem and help improve their experience. CA Technologies has been recognized and has won multiple awards for customer experience impact by Customer Experience Professionals Association (CXPA). The end benefit (i.e., tangible business results) customers receive from CA Technologies may or may not be differentiating, but how they receive and experience those benefits clearly is.

Similar to the airlines mentioned earlier, the essence of an automobile is to get you safely from point A to point B. Some manufacturers accomplish this with luxury and style, some through sportiness and high performance, and others through low cost and fuel efficiency. Tesla's current brand promise is to "accelerate the world's transition to sustainable energy."[17] Tesla's "how" traces back to its culture of technology, design, and innovation, fueled by a lofty ambition to eliminate polluting fossil fuels. The "how" Tesla created to accomplish this goal is a series of very cool electric vehicles, in addition to the infrastructure required to support them (a network of charging stations and a massive Gigafactory to make cost-efficient batteries).

For Tesla, the "how" permeates everything the company does. CEO Elon Musk's personal brand positioning of innovation is tied to public impressions of his company's process. Even as other car companies scramble to beat Tesla to market with electric vehicles or create more affordable options, Tesla's "how" has already made it the gold standard for electric vehicles in 2018.

A PURPOSE ("WHY")

In his now-famous TED Talk, Simon Sinek delivered a simple yet powerful message: start with why. Sinek says that strong leaders work with a sense of purpose from the beginning, which allows them to inspire loyal followings.[18]

"Why" is a purpose, cause, or belief. It's the very reason your organization exists—put simply, *why* it does what it does. When it's compelling and genuine, "why" can form the basis of an incredibly strong promise and a highly differentiated brand. Although this approach is often associated with corporate brands, it can filter down to product brands as well, as seen in Simon Sinek's popular concentric circle diagram. (See figure 4.4.)

Figure 4.4
Simon Sinek's "Start with Why"

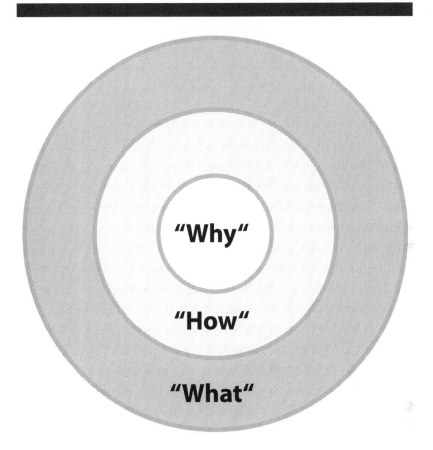

Why: The purpose. Represents the brand's cause. What it believes in

How: The process. How a brand goes about delivering the end result

What: The benefit. The end result that stakeholders derive from brand

Consumers are becoming increasingly interested in purchasing from purpose-driven brands, especially brands practicing sustainability: IRI and Boston Consulting Group found that brands prioritizing responsible consumption grew by 8.5 percent between 2013 and 2014.[19] These brands can even drive higher price points when leveraging their "why." Nielsen's 2015 report on global corporate sustainability found that about two-thirds of consumers in general (and almost three-quarters of Millennials specifically) are willing to pay more for a brand practicing sustainability.[20]

One such example is the outdoor apparel brand Patagonia. This company began as a novice manufacturer of rock climbing gear and hunting jackets, then soared to become a $750 million outdoor brand with an intensely loyal fan base. Patagonia aims to "inspire and implement solutions to the environmental crisis."[21] Everything Patagonia does (protesting Utah environmental policy, sourcing organic cotton, telling people not to buy shirts, and giving men extended paternity leave) supports this purpose. Clearly, it's not the product that sets this company apart as the choice for many outdoor enthusiasts. To be sure, the product is good, but Patagonia doesn't lean on the tangible aspects of its products alone. The company gets customers to explore, buy, and stay loyal because of its profound purpose and high-integrity actions.

While Patagonia's purpose focuses on adventure and conservation, software provider SAP's is more domestic. Founded over forty years ago, SAP is the world's largest provider of enterprise application software. SAP has always innovated and built technology to serve the agenda of its customers, fulfilling its mission to help the world run better and improve people's lives. Bill McDermott, CEO of SAP, refers to this purpose as the company's "enduring cause" and regularly discusses how important this stance is to the company, its employees, and its customers.

Julie Barrier, vice president of purpose-driven marketing at SAP, said, "This enduring cause is what we stand for. It's the 'why' behind what we do. It's championed from the top of our ranks and shows up in a variety of ways, including our initiatives in health, youth, and sports. It's through our enduring cause and these initiatives that we hope to contribute to solving some of the world's biggest problems and make a positive impact on people's lives around the globe."[22] SAP's commitment to communicate, educate, and inspire others about how to make an impact on global causes landed the company the twentieth position on Radley Yeldar's 2016 Fit for Purpose Index of the top one hundred most purposeful brands in the world—two spots higher than its 2015 ranking.[23]

One final brand that delivers its promise through its "why," PATOS Shoes, is a clothing company based in the United States. This brand sells indigenous-inspired sneakers for adventurous young people. Shoes are handcrafted by local Peruvian artists and delivered straight to customers' doors.

Without question, the space of socially conscious brands has become highly saturated. "Simply stating a charitable cause isn't enough anymore," explained PATOS CEO Fernando Rojo. "Your mission has to be central to your functions as a brand and not feel forced."[24] PATOS's social mission involved empowering Latin American artisans in impoverished communities by providing them with sustainable jobs. That mission isn't a short-term gimmick: it's a business model, steeped in a purpose, that differentiates the brand from its competitors. According to Rojo, PATOS's social mission leads customers to make repeat purchases and talk about the brand with their friends. That's why PATOS places a picture of the artisan who made the pair of shoes inside each shoebox to remind customers of the impact that buying PATOS shoes has.

Companies like these exemplify what it means to base a brand promise on "why." When purpose truly drives the brand, customers who share that purpose become fiercely loyal, to the point where their passion for the cause and their love for the brand become indistinguishable from each other. Not every company can boast an authentic "why," like Patagonia or PATOS, but for those that can, a powerful purpose makes for an exceptional brand promise.

THE INTENDED TARGET ("WHO")

A separate component of the positioning model, the target, can also provide inspiration for the brand promise. In this case, the point of difference is about the "who." The brand promise is crafted in a manner that is defined by—and can even help to define—the target audience for whom it is intended.

So-called lifestyle brands are often defined by the "who." Lifestyle brands embody the interests, attitudes, and opinions of a group or culture.

They inspire and motivate people with the goal of shaping consumers' way of life through their products or services. While it's true that every brand has targets, not every brand chooses to define its very essence (i.e., promise) around a target.

Mountain Dew is one such "who" brand. The favorite soft drink of a high-energy fan base, Mountain Dew is beloved by extreme sports fans and video game lovers around the world. Greg Lyons, Mountain Dew's vice president of marketing in 2015 (now chief marketing officer of PepsiCo), said, "The thing that really makes [Mountain Dew] different from a lot of other drinks, certainly from a lot of other carbonated soft drinks, is its incredibly loyal and passionate consumer base."[25]

In the same interview, Lyons talked about how one fan's grandmother made a tuxedo out of Mountain Dew cans for prom. He also mentioned a married couple with matching Mountain Dew tattoos. "I'm sure Mountain Dew is alienating to a part of the population of the US, and we're totally fine with that," he said.

Mountain Dew fans might not have their own distinguishing group name yet, but plenty of "who"-based brands do. That's exactly what singer-songwriter Jimmy Buffett has accomplished with his cult-like followers, self-proclaimed Parrot Heads. Most musicians focus their attention on making and selling albums and videos, but Buffett aimed higher, selling his fans the opportunity for a temporary escape to paradise—better known as Margaritaville. That lifestyle is what Parrot Heads around the world buy.

Buffett's rabid fans vicariously experience his lifestyle through his music and writing. That freedom allows them to escape the rat race to a private tropical paradise, if only for a short time. But Buffett didn't stop with his music. He extended paradise—and along with it, his personal brand—by opening his first Margaritaville restaurant and bar in Key West, Florida, in 1987.[26] The restaurant, bar, and store were so successful that Buffett opened several more in the United States, Mexico, and the Caribbean.[27] Today, Jimmy Buffett earns millions of dollars each year from his tours, restaurant sales, and albums.[28] The key to his success? Creating and embracing a lifestyle that legions of loyal fans love.

One last "who" brand, Warby Parker, arguably disrupted the eyewear industry with its business model, but its brand took the novel service and transformed it into a powerful company with a cult of loyal devotees.[29] As with all great brands, Warby Parker homed in on its precise audience—the young, hip urban crowd. The company sells fashionable glasses, often for as low as ninety-nine dollars, and lets potential buyers order up to five test frames before making a purchase. The order ships free, then users return the frames they don't want and pick the ones that look best. A smart business model, to be sure, but that's not why people love the brand.

Warby Parker was founded on the belief that a company should serve more than its customers and shareholders. With that in mind, the founders of Warby Parker cultivated a unique identity for customers to absorb. Wearing Warby Parker specs wasn't just respectable and fiscally smart—it became an identifier. Falling in love with Warby Parker's cultured, socially conscious, well-traveled customer base comes first; falling in love with its frames comes second. Young professionals, creatives, and digital natives all rallied around this smart, affordable service that disrupted the brick-and-mortar outlets Millennials had been forced to withstand for their vision needs.

That somewhat defiant tone adds to the brand persona, deepening the Warby Parker appeal. In addition, socially conscious young people love the brand's Buy a Pair, Give a Pair program, which provides one pair of free glasses to people in need for every purchase. Even if big brands manage to match Warby Parker's price and convenience, the brand's devotees won't shop anywhere else.

That's what makes "who" brands special. When the customers feel like they are part of the brand, it doesn't matter if someone else comes along with a cheaper alternative. The fans remain loyal because they see themselves reflected in the brand.

THE FUTURE OF BRAND POSITIONING

The traditional advertising-based model for brand positioning initially put forward by Ries and Trout was groundbreaking in the 1960s. It helped establish brand management as a strategic discipline, and it has served us very well over the years. In fact, it still represents a great foundation for thinking about brand strategy. Before the concept had a name, Ries called it "the rock"—the starting point upon which all branding depends.[30]

However, numerous changes to the commercial and consumer environments should prompt us to revisit this model and modify it accordingly so it can better serve us in these more complex times. In some cases, that means redefining or reframing the rock itself. In other cases, we need to add new components. Examples of this include translations (to increase relevance for individual target stakeholders) and a brand persona.

To be fair, these changes represent more of an evolution than a revolution. But, collectively, they make for a brand positioning model that is more relevant in addressing a more dynamic, digital world of activation; more widely applicable in serving all business functions, not just advertising and other communications-related functions; and more capable and versatile in serving larger, more sophisticated global brands.

Chapter 5

———

Brand Portfolio Strategy

The Procter & Gamble Company was established in 1837 when candle-maker William Procter and soapmaker James Gamble went into business together in Cincinnati, Ohio. More than 175 years ago, they never could have imagined how their business would grow into the multinational consumer products behemoth that it is today. And, as the concept of "brand portfolio" would not be birthed until more than a century later, they probably never thought about how to organize their business beyond product category lines. The whole concept of brand management, which was the brainchild of a young P&G employee in the 1930s, didn't help much with portfolio strategy. This early rendition centered on the notion that each brand was a winner—even at the expense of other brands in the portfolio. Therefore, managers had no incentive to care about their brand as it related to others within the company.

Fast-forward to modern day, and it's no surprise that a company like P&G used a combination of organic growth and acquisition to own more than two hundred brands around the world. However, that massive collection quickly proved unsustainable. In the early 2000s, P&G's portfolio optimization efforts shed brands that fell outside its primary product categories. Even though Cinch cleaners, Biz bleach, and Clearasil skincare brands were profitable, they resided in categories where P&G did not want to focus. Because of that, they were sold.[1]

As it turned out, those sales were just the beginning. In 2014, P&G was still bloated by too many brands. Investors were worried such a stretched company could not navigate an increasingly competitive landscape. To solve the issue, P&G announced that it would sell more than half its brands, keeping only those that generated 90 percent of its sales and 95 percent of its profits. The actual number culled was difficult to count—some brands had different names in different countries—but the final tally fell around one hundred brands.[2] Most of these brands had sales under $100 million, but not all big hitters were spared. P&G's pet food brands, with sales well over $1 billion, got the ax as well.

A range of diverse buyers lined up to take the brands P&G put on the chopping block. Coty picked up forty-three beauty brands. Rival company Unilever grabbed Camay and Zest soaps. Berkshire Hathaway acquired Duracell in a share transfer. P&G's CEO at the time, A. G. Lafley, told investors that if the company had removed these brands from its portfolio a few years ago, P&G would have beaten its organic sales growth over that period by 1 percent.

In addition to enhanced growth and profits, this breed of portfolio rationalization can also provide additional cash flow. Following the restructuring, P&G's Days Inventory Outstanding results decreased from seventy-eight days to fifty-eight days. This meant cash was no longer tied up in inventory and could be used for other purposes. As of 2018, P&G's portfolio has only sixty-five brands in ten product categories—a far cry from the two hundred plus at its peak.

This latest portfolio strategy was clearly a financial exercise to improve profitability and efficiency while maintaining market leadership for top-selling brands. Although P&G did not intend for the move to affect consumers directly, its divestment of so many brands empowered the company to focus on the needs of existing customers and bring new ones into the fold.

BREAKING DOWN BRAND PORTFOLIO STRATEGY

Brand portfolio strategy and architecture are critical components of a successful brand strategy. These are complex, highly nuanced topics, with entire books written about them. Although we will not cover all the nuances of these topics, no book on brand strategy would be complete without addressing these core concepts.

Additionally, unlike many other components of brand strategy in this book, most of the key tenets and premises of this topic are as relevant today as they were when they were initially developed. As such, this chapter will serve as more of an overview of existing thought than a call to action for changes or enhancements. But, that said, these concepts are important to the central theme of this book—achieving meaningful brand differentiation—and deserve the coverage provided below.

At its core, brand portfolio strategy dictates the number of brands that a company's portfolio should contain and how to deploy those brands within the business and in the market. It also provides a long-term approach to grow the business by establishing strategic roles for each brand, including what each should contribute to the company. Finally, brand portfolio strategy also dictates the relationships (if any) brands within a portfolio should have with one another. That final component, relationships between brands, is often referred to as brand architecture. While the terms "brand portfolio strategy" and "brand architecture" are often used interchangeably, we will refer to the latter as an important (but distinct) component of the former.

One of the reasons brand portfolio strategy has become so popular in recent years has been the elevated stature of brands in general. If brands truly represent a company's most intangible assets, it stands to reason that establishing the optimal mix is a high priority. The same is true of managing the brands to ensure maximum marketplace relevance and internal efficiencies.

The increasing prominence of merger and acquisition (M&A) activity has also played a role. As large multinational companies have acquired more companies, many have not taken the necessary steps to prune and optimize their brand portfolios post-M&A. The results have been bloated brand portfolios that confuse customers and other external stakeholders, limit internal efficiency, and increase costs. Perhaps the most high-profile example of remedying this situation occurred in the late 1990s and early 2000s when Unilever slashed its global portfolio from sixteen hundred brands to around four hundred, boosting financial performance across the board in the process.

On the academic front, two books by David Aaker—*Brand Leadership* and *Brand Portfolio Strategy*—did a wonderful job of proposing frameworks, structures, and guiding principles for management of large and complex brand portfolios.[3],[4] These books were instrumental in helping companies distinguish between different types of brands (e.g., sub-brands, co-brands, endorsed brands, descriptive brands) and their roles in driving competitive advantage and profitable growth. Perhaps most notably, Aaker's work produced a continuum framework for brand portfolios that is still widely embraced today. (See figure 5.1.)

Figure 5.1
Brand Architecture Continuum

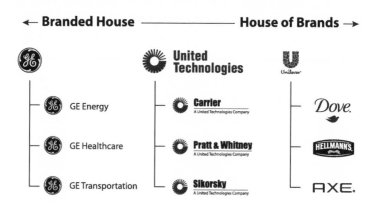

← **Branded House** ──────── **House of Brands** →

The master brand, typically a corporate brand, serves as the dominant (if not the only) brand within the portfolio

Standalone brands, each with little to no connection to the corporate brand, have the greatest equity

In *Brand Leadership*, Aaker refers to one end of the brand portfolio spectrum as "branded house." This is a portfolio in which the master brand (typically a corporate brand) acts as the dominant brand within the portfolio. Here, descriptive sub-brands have little to no role in establishing market-facing equity or driving business results. General Electric is the premier example of a branded house.

At the other end of the spectrum is what Aaker calls a "house of brands." In this scenario, independent, standalone brands—each with little to no connection to the corporate brand—have the greatest equity and represent the primary face to the market. P&G is an oft-used example of a house of brands, where brands like Tide, Dawn, Crest, and Febreze have greater consumer equity than the corporate brand. In a house of brands, independent brands in the portfolio are the primary conduit to customers. Later in this chapter, we will go into greater detail about the brand portfolio spectrum.

THE BUILDING BLOCKS OF BRAND PORTFOLIO STRATEGY

The exact components of a comprehensive brand portfolio strategy vary based on the company in question and the nature of its business. However, based on the definition above, most brand portfolios should (at minimum) address four key questions. Let's dive into each question in greater detail.

1. WHAT IS THE OPTIMAL NUMBER OF BRANDS?

One of the most basic questions regarding a brand portfolio is the optimal number of brands required to go to market. This is typically an outcome that follows the answers of the other three components detailed below, rather than a going-in goal or assumption on its own. However, companies should observe a few general rules regarding the optimal number of brands.

First, fewer is better than more, all other things being equal. There are many reasons for this, but the primary one is that brands are expensive assets to develop, launch, and maintain over time. In addition to hard costs, such as advertising, promotion, and digital activation, brands also require a great deal of time, effort, and oversight to manage. Without that effort, brands cannot maintain their relevance and points of difference. And, as was noted with the P&G example at the beginning of this chapter, even profitable brands have opportunity costs (e.g., cash tied up in inventory) that must be taken into consideration.

With these investments in mind, it makes sense that maintaining a portfolio of a few strong brands is a worthwhile objective. When new products or services enter the portfolio, whether organically or through an acquisition, the default response should always be to house the newcomers within an existing brand. If that is not possible, a separate brand is justified, but the new product or service must make a great case to deserve placement under a new brand.

2. WHAT IS THE STRATEGIC ROLE OF EACH BRAND WITHIN THE PORTFOLIO?

As assets in their own right, brands need to be managed strategically. Defining and continually reevaluating strategic roles for brands is of paramount importance. There are a variety of strategic roles to consider—some objective and quantifiable, others more subjective and qualitative. Three of the strategic roles that merit mention here include financial, customer, and competitive roles.

Financial roles are probably the most objective and straightforward of the three types. Examples include premium (or value) pricing, opening price point, loss leaders, and cash cows. Some of these pertain directly to pricing, while others are more about profitability and returns, but they all tie to financial goals and objectives. While brands may have individual offerings that are outliers or exceptions, they typically serve financial roles for their companies—implicitly or explicitly. For example, Hellmann's mayonnaise is a cash cow within the Unilever brand portfolio. It has high market share and low growth, and it can generate significant revenue for the company with minimal incremental investment.

Customer roles, as the name implies, pertain to the types of customers the brand serves. This is a common strategic role for B2C companies to define, as they often align their brands by target segment. The equivalent in B2B may be by industry or vertical, but the premise is the same. This role essentially charges a brand with the responsibility to serve (and win within) a particular market segment. As mentioned in chapter 4, Pepsi-Co's Mountain Dew is an example of a brand that serves an important consumer segment in the soft drink category—in this case, consumers who are young, primarily male, high-energy, and fans of video games or extreme sports.

Finally, there are competitive roles. In this case, brands are charged with taking on a competing brand and neutralizing its advantages or beating it in the market. A fighter brand, for example, is designed to undercut a specific competitor on price to undermine its success or steal market share. Intel's Celeron microprocessor is an example of a fighter brand.

Celeron is a cheaper, less powerful version of Intel's Pentium chips. This enables Intel to defend against lower-priced category competitors, such as AMD, while protecting valuable brand equity in the company's more premium Pentium brand.

3. WHAT IS THE SCOPE OF EACH BRAND IN TERMS OF HOW IT IS DEPLOYED IN THE MARKET?

The scope (or range) of a brand pertains to how the brand is deployed in the market. As we will see, this is closely tied to the customer and financial strategic roles mentioned above. Here, too, we have a number of different ways to define scope, which differs based on the company and nature of its business.

There are four common ways to think about a brand's scope: across customer segments, product categories, price or value tier, and geographies. Real-world examples of each of these four approaches will be provided in the next section, but let's take a moment to define them first. Consumer-oriented brands often define their range by customer segments. Conversely, many B2B companies define their brands' scope by the product categories they serve. Many businesses, both B2B and B2C, define that scope at least in part by their price or value tier. Global companies sometimes go to market with different brands (sometimes with nearly identical products) in different regions of the world.

Regardless of which approach (or approaches) a brand employs, the important point is that the brand portfolio strategy explicitly and purposefully dictates how brands should be deployed in the market.

4. WHAT TYPE OF RELATIONSHIPS SHOULD BRANDS WITHIN THE PORTFOLIO HAVE WITH ONE ANOTHER?

Another question marketers should consider when building a brand portfolio strategy is the type of relationships brands within the portfolio should have with one another. This question covers brand architecture, which defines the explicit relationships among brands in a portfolio. Very often, this involves the relationship between a product brand and a corporate brand. When an explicit relationship exists, it tends to be most evident in the company's visual identity system, specifically through logo locks and other overt linkages. Later in this chapter, we will detail how these links and relationships can be established to enhance the overall impact and effectiveness of a brand portfolio.

These questions cannot provide all the answers for every brand, but they do provide a solid foundation to build upon.

INS AND OUTS OF BRAND PORTFOLIO ORGANIZATION

With the above strategic roles in mind, we can start to think about how to construct (or realign) a brand portfolio.

Every portfolio has (or should have) an organizing principle. As the name implies, the organizing principle is the overarching framework or model to arrange brands within a portfolio. This principle is almost always the scope or range component of the brand portfolio strategy we covered earlier. Once the company settles on an organizing principle, it becomes easier to craft the optimal brand portfolio.

Let's take a look at examples of how each of the scope and range alternatives referenced earlier can translate into an organizing principle for a brand portfolio.

1. CUSTOMER SEGMENTS

Customer segmentation represents one of the most powerful ways to organize a brand portfolio. It is an approach that is, by definition, outward-looking rather than internally focused. As is hopefully evident by now, it's difficult to go wrong when brand strategy centers on the customer.

The concept of customer segmentation is, for the most part, well understood and embraced in marketing circles. Companies can segment customers across several dimensions: demographics, attitudes, needs, behaviors, or some combination of those factors. The key is that the branding revolves around the customer, not the company and its products.

For example, on its home page, PepsiCo—the parent company of Pepsi, Quaker Oats, Tropicana, Frito-Lay, and Gatorade—organizes its extensive portfolio by classifying its brands based on whether they are "Better for You," "Good for You," or "Fun for You," to tap into consumer attitudes related to food and drinks. Toyota structures its brand portfolio by consumer segment as well. The Prius serves "environmentally conscious early adopters," the Scion is for "hip-at-heart drivers on a budget," and the Camry is for "practical families who desire performance."

2. PRODUCT CATEGORIES OR VERTICALS

Companies can also organize brand portfolios around product categories or industry verticals. B2B companies do this more frequently than B2C companies. One of the attractions of this approach is that it is straightforward and simple. Categories and industries are easy to define and universally understood, which makes it tempting to structure a portfolio and position brands in this manner.

However, this organizing principle tends to be less sophisticated and effective than customer segmentation. For one thing, it inherently assumes that all customers that purchase from a category or within an industry have similar needs and other purchase drivers. More importantly, this approach can easily contribute to the problem of brand monotony we're trying to solve. When multiple companies with competing brands strive to position around a set of attitudes, motivations, and behaviors that are common to an entire category or industry, differentiation becomes a tall task. By definition, this organizing principle can clash with the goal of increased differentiation.

A successful example of organizing a brand portfolio by category is 3M. It structures its consumer brands by disparate product categories, such as cleaning and protecting; office; sports and recreation; and decorating, organizing, and crafts.[5] Within each category are strong brand names, like Post-it and Scotch, which are clearly specific to product category and generally not used across categories. Another company, Caterpillar, structures itself around function as well. Its Cat brand covers equipment like bulldozers and backhoes, while its Anchor brand covers engines.

3. PRICE AND VALUE TIERS

As the name suggests, organizing a brand portfolio by value tier is based first and foremost on price point. The tried-and-true retail approach of good, better, best is one such example.

While this approach does have its supporters, it's arguably an incomplete organizing principle at best. Most brand portfolios inherently have a value tier component, but this tends to be a secondary variable to something more compelling—like a customer need, want, benefit, or other component. As such, price/value in and of itself tends to be incomplete as an organizing principle for a brand portfolio.

On the surface, the thirty-plus brands under the Marriott corporate brand appear to be organized along the value continuum.[6] Fairfield Inn and Suites serves consumers in the mid-scale or moderate market, while The Ritz-Carlton brand caters to luxury. Another Marriott offering, the Moxy brand, targets young, hip consumers looking for an affordable option that doesn't sacrifice style or comfort.[7] However, price and value remains a secondary principle even here, as the different hotel brands (more importantly) also cater to different types of consumer segments and desired experiences.

4. GEOGRAPHIES OR REGIONS

Lastly, some global companies organize their portfolios by geography or region. In some cases, these companies market virtually the same product or service with different names and positioning in different places.

As is the case with price and value, geographies or regions are best used as an organizing principle when it's a secondary component to something more substantial and foundational. The primary reason a company would follow this approach to organize its portfolio would be if the needs and behaviors of its customers (i.e., our first organizing principle) differed meaningfully by region. So, like with price and value, this is a legitimate but incomplete way to structure a brand portfolio.

Alcohol giant AB InBev is a company that uses geography (in part) to structure its portfolio. The company has global brands in Budweiser, Beck's, and Stella Artois; multicountry brands like Leffe and Hoegaarden; and a host of brands to meet taste profiles within specific countries, such as Harbin Ice in China and Brahma in Brazil.

Of these four organizing principles, the first option—customer segments—remains the obvious choice for companies seeking increased differentiation. While the other principles serve their uses, they typically (at least on their own) are not sufficient to drive meaningful differentiation for the brands within any given company's portfolio.

WHOSE HOUSE IS IT? BRANDED HOUSE VERSUS HOUSE OF BRANDS

The terms "branded house" and "house of brands" were coined back in 2000 by David Aaker in his book *Brand Leadership*. Aaker did a great job of proposing a brand relationship spectrum to explain how offers in a portfolio relate to their corporate parent brand. The spectrum itself, along with those specific terms, is still used today by marketers who strive to identify the right approach to structure their brand portfolios.

Brand Leadership (and the subsequent *Brand Portfolio Strategy*) go into significant depth and detail on the brand architecture spectrum. Both books provide numerous examples of companies with portfolios on either end of the spectrum and at points in between. They also propose the pros and cons of each side. There is little need to repeat those details here, but it may be beneficial to discuss some of the considerations for companies deciding where to reside on that spectrum.

While factors vary by circumstances, several seem to be applicable to every company, regardless of size, industry, or other factors. (See figure 5.2.)

Figure 5.2
Factors Influencing Brand Architecture Continuum

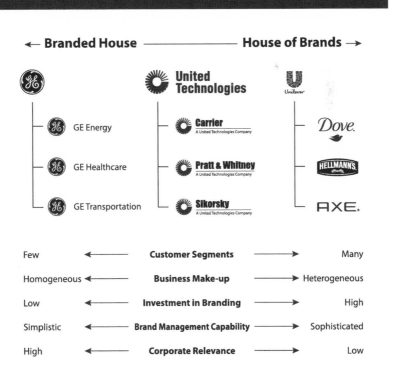

1. NUMBER OF CUSTOMER SEGMENTS

Companies should consider the number of distinct customer segments they serve and the number of segments they are attempting to target. For the most part, a well-positioned brand is targeted toward a single customer segment. That brand can serve only that segment—plus, at most, one or two others—exceedingly well. So it stands to reason that the more distinct customer segments in a market (and the greater number of those segments a company seeks to serve), the more brands required to do so effectively. In this scenario, companies tend to lean toward the house of brands side of the spectrum.

2. RANGE OR BREADTH OF OFFER

The range or breadth of offer is closely related to customer segments. Chapter 7 will go into detail on the concept of brand extension. One of the key premises of that chapter is how brands can (and should) be defined by something more than the product category or categories in which they compete. However, brands also have limitations in how far they can stretch across different categories.

Regardless of the strength of equity, there are some categories in which most brands simply won't make sense. Therefore, all other things equal, the greater the number of product categories in which a company competes, the more likely its portfolio will need to reside on the house of brands side of the spectrum.

As always, there are exceptions to the rule. Many exceptions in this category can be found in B2B organizations. General Electric is often cited as the quintessential branded house because its corporate master brand has demonstrated relevance across a diverse set of industries and product categories ranging from transportation and energy to healthcare and industrial.

3. CORPORATE BRAND RELEVANCE

Corporate brands, the subject of chapter 11, can have varying levels of market relevance based on several factors.

One is the nature of the business. In some businesses, the company behind the products and services is more important than it is in others. Professional services, as discussed earlier, is an industry in which the master brand is critical. Clients often buy the brand as much as the individual service offerings provided by the firm. In these cases, going to market with the corporate brand in a driving role is logical. Following this pattern of thought, firms such as McKinsey & Company, Boston Consulting Group, KPMG, and Ernst & Young are quintessential branded houses that trade heavily on the equity they've built in their master brands.

Another factor is the extent to which a company chooses to invest in the development of its corporate brand. Chapter 11 will showcase a number of companies across myriad industries that have taken steps to infuse equity into their corporate brands. Examples include SC Johnson, ExxonMobil, Procter & Gamble, and The Coca-Cola Company. Once again, all other things equal, the more established and relevant the corporate brand is, the greater its ability to reside on the branded house end of the spectrum (whether it chooses to do so or not).

4. INVESTMENT IN BRANDING

The extent to which a company is willing to invest in building brands—and not just its corporate brand—in part determines where on the brand portfolio spectrum it should reside. Brands are assets and require significant investment to develop, launch, and maintain. This includes expenses and ongoing investments, such as advertising, promotion, market research and insights, visual identity and assets, and digital activation. Because of these costs, a house of brands portfolio requires far more financial resources to support than a branded house portfolio.

5. COMMITMENT TO TALENT DEVELOPMENT (IN BRANDING)

In addition to financial resources, brand management takes human resources. Companies need human talent to build and maintain strong brand assets over time. Therefore, organizations must consider the extent to which they're willing to invest in developing and recruiting employees with the necessary skills to drive brand leadership.

Importantly, this applies to both the creative and strategic sides of brand-building. While some components can be outsourced to consultants and agencies, a house of brands portfolio almost always requires more internal brand and marketing talent than a branded house portfolio.

No matter where on the spectrum of house of brands versus branded house a company falls, differentiation remains essential to its success. If the brand is not individually compelling (or, in the case of a branded house, cannot rely upon a sufficiently compelling corporate brand), it will fail to break out of the increasingly common brand monotony of modern marketing.

BRAND ARCHITECTURE HIERARCHY AND EQUITY FLOW

Before we talk about the different types of brands and how they potentially can be associated with one another, let's take a brief look at two related subjects: brand architecture hierarchy and equity flow.

In addition to a portfolio's organizing principle, companies must also consider hierarchy. Brand hierarchy is a tiered structure that clarifies which entities, products, services, or other offerings are branded and their relative importance within the portfolio. This is a particularly important concept to address when dealing with complex B2B offerings, specifically when deciding how to name them and how to sequence their naming components.

Consider, for example, the B2B product offering ExxonMobil Chemical PE Exceed XP 6026. (See figure 5.3.) Here, we clearly see a product brand and a grade level (Exceed and XP 6026, respectively). However, we also see a corporate brand (ExxonMobil), a business unit brand (Chemical), and a category descriptor (Polyethylene, or PE).[8] Which of these entities are included in a product name, and in what order, is essentially a question of hierarchy.

Figure 5.3
Naming Architecture

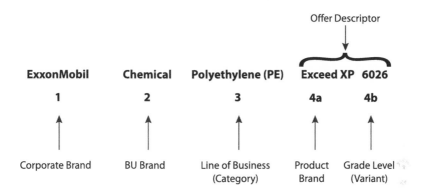

ExxonMobil Chemical PE Exceed XP 6026

As with organizing principle, the exercise to define hierarchy should be purposeful and strategic. This process should be driven more by external considerations (such as customer clarity) than by internal considerations. For example, many times an organization believes that a business unit brand is important to include in a product name, while its customers may not care as much. As a rule of thumb when naming, the sequencing of entities typically runs from macro to micro—usually beginning with the corporate brand and continuing down to the product grade or SKU.

As mentioned above, brand hierarchy and linkage should always be intentional, strategic decisions. If two or more brands are overtly associated with each other, there should be a compelling reason behind their pairing. Otherwise, they should remain separate.

Typically, the rationale for relating brands has something to do with equity flow—a desire for the association to transfer positive equity between the brands, whether in one direction or both. Equity flow tends to flow downstream in the brand hierarchy, usually from a corporate (parent) brand to a product (child) brand. In this case, the objective is usually for the more well-known, established corporate brand to lend the lesser-known product brand confidence or trust. It's essentially a form of endorsement or reassurance for the market that the lesser-known entity is a safe proposition. For example, when Amazon launched its voice-controlled assistant, Echo, it established an association between the product brand and the Amazon master brand. The goal was to transfer Amazon's valuable brand equity to the new child brand, and it worked.

However, there are exceptions to this rule. In some cases, brand equity moves upstream, from the child brand to the parent, when the smaller brand is either better known or more highly regarded than the larger one. One example of this is the reverse equity flow between Comcast and Xfinity.[9] Comcast, a global telecommunications company, has a less-than-stellar reputation for customer service issues. Xfinity, a provider of cable TV, internet, telephone, and wireless services, has a relatively more positive reputation. In this case, overt linkage with Xfinity is beneficial to the Comcast brand.

TYPES OF BRANDS AND HOW THEY FUNCTION

In his books about brand portfolio strategy and brand architecture, David Aaker presents myriad brands and the roles they typically serve within their respective brand portfolios. Master, sub-, co-, descriptive, endorsed, standalone, range, ingredient, and fighter are just some of the types of brands cited and illustrated in his work. Given his comprehensive and rigorous coverage of this topic area, there is little need for us to rehash his teachings in full.

However, after years of experience working with global clients on their brand portfolios, we have noticed a few types of brands that consistently rise to the top in terms of their importance and prominence of usage. They tend to form a continuum in terms of their closeness to the master brand. (See figure 5.4.) We will highlight each of these standouts below, including the typical reasons for their use and recognizable examples.

Figure 5.4
Brand Types

	Brand Type	Definition	Examples
Emphasis on **Master** Brand	Master	A brand that serves as the primary frame of reference, often carrying the corporate name	P&G U Unilever
	Descriptive	An equity that is purely functional/ descriptive in nature, with a logo lock to the master brand	FedEx Office. Google Analytics
	Sub-	A brand which establishes equity beyond a mere category descriptor, in conjunction with master	IBM Watson POLO RALPH LAUREN
	Endorsed	An equity that is endorsed by the master brand, deriving benefit from it by virtue of the association	COTG A Xerox Company careerbuilder.com A GANNETT COMPANY
Emphasis on **'Other'** Brand	Co-	An equity overtly linked to the master brand, receiving equal emphasis vis-à-vis the master (i.e., logo lock)	[Nike] Disney · PIXAR

1. MASTER BRANDS

A master brand serves as a primary point of reference. It is a dominant brand capable of standing independently within a portfolio. Depending on the type of portfolio (branded house or house of brands), the master brand exerts either a little or a lot of influence over other brands.

Most everyone is familiar with master brands. Popular examples include Amazon, FedEx, Tide, BMW, Crest, Virgin, Cheerios, Intel, Coca-Cola, Hershey, Google—the list goes on. In some cases, master brands are corporate brands. In other cases, they are product brands. Sometimes, they are both, but they share common characteristics of recognizability and dominance.

2. DESCRIPTIVE BRANDS

Descriptive brands have virtually no equity outside the master brands to which they attach. As the name suggests, this term merely describes the nature of the offer, which is typically a generic product or service category.

The idea is merely to signal the nature of the offer, then to trade entirely off the established equity of the master brand.

Examples of descriptive brands include NBC Sports, FedEx Office, and Google Analytics. In each case, the "sub" (in these instances, Sports, Office, Analytics) is little more than a generic category label, while the primary equity resides with the master brand.

3. ENDORSED BRANDS

The next two types of brands—endorsed brands and sub-brands—are fairly similar, but still distinct. These are brands that have some identity and equity on their own, but they borrow credibility through some form of association with a master brand. The key difference between endorsed brands and sub-brands is the extent to which the entity is in a subordinate versus a driving role through its relationship with the master brand.

In the first case, an endorsed brand, the role is more subordinate to the master brand. A company may use an endorsed brand to lend immediate credibility to a new entity or to establish or reinforce a new relationship (e.g., post-M&A). If the brand being endorsed is a new product offering, the master brand provides a "stamp of approval" that may eventually become unnecessary.

When the endorsed brand is the product of an acquisition, this relationship is intended to clarify a new ownership structure in the market. For example, when Xerox made Chicago Office Technology Group (COTG) a wholly owned subsidiary in 2007, the architecture adopted was "COTG - A Xerox Company," which is still in effect today.[10] However, in other cases, endorsed brand architectures are only temporary (e.g., eighteen to twenty-four months), until the association has been successfully established and overt linkage is no longer necessary.

4. SUB-BRANDS

As stated above, sub-brands are fairly similar in nature to endorsed brands. However, with a sub-brand, the role of the entity is slightly more substantial than it is for an endorsed brand.[11] The idea, in this case, is for the sub-brand to establish more of its own equity and independence from the master brand.

McDonald's brands—such as Egg McMuffin, McRib, and Chicken

McNuggets—don't have the full McDonald's name in front of them, but they still carry the identity of the McDonald's brand. Polo (Ralph Lauren) and PlayStation (Sony) are two other prominent examples of sub-brands.

5. CO-BRANDS

The most common definition of a co-brand is when two companies form a partnership to work together, creating a brand or marketing synergy in the process. However, this can also occur between two brands within a single company. In either case, there are two master brands paired together, each with meaningful emphasis. Two prime examples of co-brands are Apple Nike+ and Under Armour MyFitnessPal. Consumers know the co-brands individually, but their combinations give them even more power.

6. STANDALONE BRANDS

Standalone brands are special cases of master brands. This category is typically reserved for product brands, not corporate brands. The main idea here is a lack of desire to associate the standalone product brand with the master corporate brand. To do so would be irrelevant at best and detrimental at worst.

One of the most common reasons standalone brands remain autonomous from their master brands is tied to the price and value relationship. When a brand within a portfolio is either more luxurious or significantly cheaper than the master brand, an association between the two brands could harm one or both. Examples of standalone brands include Waldorf Astoria (Hilton) and any of the luxury car brands owned by Volkswagen (Porsche, Lamborghini, and Bentley).

WHICH BRAND TYPES AND ASSOCIATIONS TO CHOOSE?

As stated upfront, determining the type of brand to deploy in any given situation should be a highly strategic decision. During this process, a decision tree can help. Decision trees are simple tools that consist of a series of questions, each with a finite set of answers. The results of those questions lead to an outcome at the end of the tree that dictates the optimal branding option.

Needless to say, a decision tree is only as effective as the thought put into its development. Marketers must take considerable care to ensure they ask the right set of questions in the correct sequence—with the appropriate alternative answers and a logical path for those answers to follow. (See figure 5.5 for an example of one such brand decision tool.)

Figure 5.5
Brand Decision Tool—Illustrative Example

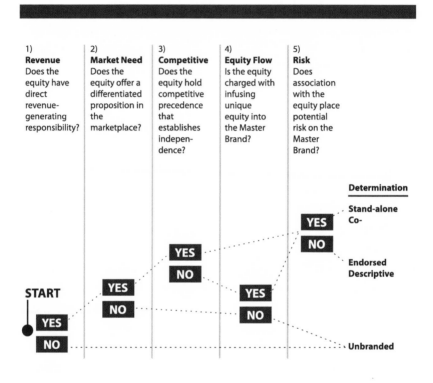

Decisions regarding how to best structure a brand portfolio are multidimensional and complex. Unfortunately, there are no ironclad rules to drive this decision, and each individual situation is unique. However, several guiding principles follow below:

GUIDING PRINCIPLE 1: BUILD AND LEVERAGE A STRONG CORPORATE BRAND

This principle recognizes the importance of the corporate brand in virtually any company's portfolio—not just a branded house. Building and leveraging a corporate brand that provides a clear and accepted frame of reference, as well as positive equity for other brands in the portfolio, should be the goal of every organization (except potentially for pure holding companies).[12] Chapter 11 will discuss the critical and unique role of corporate brands in greater detail.

For this principle, it's difficult to choose a single prime example. There are several great options, each for different reasons. IBM, Procter & Gamble, Microsoft, Apple, Cisco, Google, and Nike are just a few of the many strong corporate brands in operation today. Collectively, these corporate brands accomplish several goals: They provide a strong frame of reference and "reason to believe" for their respective offerings. They effectively extend their relevance across price and value tiers and product categories. And they instill significant confidence in important stakeholders other than customers, such as investors, media members, regulators, and industry analysts. Clearly, a strong corporate brand provides a level of power and influence that no other type of brand can match.

GUIDING PRINCIPLE 2: DEFINE STRATEGIC ROLES FOR BRANDS

As indicated earlier in this chapter, there are many strategic roles that any brand within a portfolio can play. The key is to identify the strategic needs and priorities of the business, then ensure the brand portfolio is aligned with those needs. In some cases, one look at a company's brand portfolio is all it takes to reverse engineer the strategic roles behind them.

American Express is a great example. Its portfolio features virtually every type of strategic role showcased in this chapter. The flagship Green Card is arguably the most versatile offering, given its broad mainstream appeal. However, the portfolio also features a brand targeted to a specific category—OPEN, a brand dedicated to small businesses. American Express uses co-brands to address specific consumer segments, such as Delta SkyMiles and Hilton Honors cards for frequent travelers who value miles, points, and other perks.

The Platinum brand addresses another consumer segment. Platinum caters to the higher end of the market, charging annual fees of hundreds of dollars in exchange for complimentary memberships, discounts, exclusive event access, and other privileges. American Express even has a brand defined largely by a competitive role: its Blue card. This product is essentially a fighter brand that competes against Discover, offering consumer-friendly perks, like no annual fees, zero percent interest, and cash back.

GUIDING PRINCIPLE 3: EMPLOY SIMPLE AND CLEAR BRAND ARCHITECTURE

We have already discussed how brand architecture is a central component of any brand portfolio strategy. It articulates the explicit, market-facing relationships that brands within a portfolio have with one another. Unlike some of the other principles, this one is almost entirely externally focused. This third principle is about establishing a brand architecture that makes it easy for outside stakeholders to view it quickly, understand it immediately, and know which offer works best for them.

A simple, clear brand architecture should feature a logical organizing principle and as few levels of hierarchy as possible. Great architectures also follow a rigorous set of standards and guidelines that ensure a consistent expression and execution in the marketplace. This includes, but is not limited to, the visual identity and verbal expression of brands, as well as the naming conventions for product and service offerings.

United Technologies employs a clear brand architecture. With a portfolio that includes diverse options like Otis, Carrier, and Pratt & Whitney, United Technologies could have made no attempt to tie its brand together— but then it would have missed an opportunity for leverage. Conversely, the company could have chosen (unwittingly, of course) to architect in a less thoughtful and strategic manner, which would have resulted in less market clarity than it enjoys today.

Instead, United Technologies found a way to organize and express its portfolio effectively. Despite taking advantage of natural synergies, this portfolio of brands still maintains important independence and distinction for its individual brands. As demonstrated in figure 5.1, United Technologies skillfully used its visual identity system and endorsement strategy to construct a brand architecture that is as internally efficient as it is externally clear and concise.

GUIDING PRINCIPLE 4: BUILD RELEVANCE ACROSS VALUE TIERS

Simply put, building relevance across value tiers means deliberately aligning individual brands to target segments within each value tier to maximize the company's reach. The key here—and in the following principle as well—is to push the boundaries for each brand's relevance (in this case, in terms of pricing) as far as possible. However, brands cannot push so far that they risk dilution or alienation. Even with skillful use of sub-branding, every brand has an inherent limit in terms of how far it can stretch up or dip down on price points. When a brand encounters those limits, it is essential that the company either find a different brand to house the offering at that price point or walk away.

The Whirlpool Corporation offers three distinct kitchen appliance brands.[13] Each targets a different value tier with benefits and price points appropriate to the price and value positioning. KitchenAid is an upscale brand (high-price tier) serving professional chefs and home enthusiasts and entertainers. Its products have innovative bells and whistles that are unnecessary for other users. The Whirlpool brand is a mass-market brand (mid-price tier) catering to families run by a "super mom." Whirlpool products are dependable, durable, and speedy. Roper is a value brand (low-price tier) that serves customers who buy based on price. Taglines from this brand include "sensible solutions for your family" and "simple, sturdy, affordable workhorse appliances."

GUIDING PRINCIPLE 5: MAXIMIZE EXTENDIBILITY OF BRANDS

This principle is similar in nature to the previous principle, as it is also about extendibility and stretch. However, instead of vertical extension across price tiers, this principle is about horizontal extension across categories. Despite the key difference, the primary takeaway is virtually identical.

The best practice, in either case, is to extend any given brand within a portfolio to the furthest extent possible without going so far as to dilute or damage its equity.[14] The result of this stretching is an improved ability to synergize, capitalize on economies of scale, and penetrate new categories and markets. Ideally, companies achieve this with a portfolio of as few master brands as possible, each with significant strength and equity. Chapter 7, on brand extension, will go into considerable detail on how to accomplish this objective.

A good example of maximizing extendibility within appropriate limits comes from the Clorox brand, which has its roots in bleach. The

Clorox Company learned that consumers were willing to allow the brand to extend itself into other categories where chemical cleaning solutions were acceptable, such as toilet bowl cleaner and bathroom cleaner product segments.[15] However, Clorox would not be accepted in places where bleach-based products would be detrimental to health, like in dishwashing detergent. Noncleaning categories, like salad dressing and charcoal, were firmly out of the question. In chapter 7, we will cover Clorox's brand extension strategy in greater detail.

Companies that follow these five guiding principles enjoy significant competitive advantages from their brand portfolio strategies and brand architecture. Upon this solid foundation, brands are able to achieve greater levels of differentiation, competitive advantage, and overall business success.

Chapter 6

———

Brand Experiences

In 2006, Hyatt Hotels Corporation launched the Hyatt Place sub-brand to compete in the rapidly expanding select-service segment of the lodging category. As the name implies, select-service properties offer limited degrees of services and amenities compared to full-service hotels, especially regarding meeting facilities and dining options. This segment of the lodging industry, which includes brands such as Hilton Garden Inn and Courtyard by Marriott, comprised an estimated 89 percent of total hotel projects under construction in the December 2016 *Pipeline Report* from STR.[1]

The Hyatt Place sub-brand was designed to appeal to a segment of travelers referred to as "smart self-reliants"—ambitious professionals who balance the demands of work and life on the road. These professionals are practical and value-oriented. They have a strong desire to be productive while traveling and seek laid-back, comfortable environments where they can be themselves.

With this target consumer in mind, the Hyatt Place brand team landed on a simple yet powerful brand promise: a stylish, comfortable, and seamless experience. According to Steven Dominguez, vice president of global brands at Hyatt Hotels Corporation, "Hyatt Place is a brand born out of the idea of making every aspect of the guest stay a frictionless experience. More than just convenience, it helps guests feel a greater sense of control over their environment."[2]

The team went on to develop a set of guiding principles to ensure its promise would ring true for its guests. Those promises are to yield experiences that are convenient and uncomplicated, to entail purposeful service that addresses individuals' unique plans and preferences, and to feature a business-casual environment that rejects unnecessary formalities.

Using the brand strategy as a solid foundation, Hyatt Place conducted consumer research to identify and optimize seven "signature experiences." These experiences are the interactions the brand team determined to be so central to a hotel stay that they make or break the overall experience and level of customer satisfaction. (See figure 6.1.)

Figure 6.1
Hyatt Place Signature Touchpoints

ARRIVAL
A friendly welcome

Our Porte-Cochère creates a sense of arrival that welcomes guests into the Gallery, which is a straightforward space where nothing is hidden and there is no guesswork. The multi-tasking Gallery Host extends a friendly greeting and warm welcome to all guests entering the hotel.

The Gallery Host engages with guests while efficiently checking them in. Conversations and interactions are natural, comfortable and meaningful to each guest's stay. The Host extends a gesture of our warm hospitality by stepping around the host stand to present each guest with a room key card. When possible, the Host offers a quick tour of the gallery, ensuring guests know where to find the essentials they'll need.

GUEST ROOM
Modern comforts they deserve

Our Roomy Rooms are spacious with a straightforward design that is not too stuffy. The Cozy Corner, free Wi-Fi and swivel TV give guests the ability to settle into our rooms in a way that is comfortable to them.

SOCIAL SPACES
Creating an easygoing atmosphere

The Gallery is a multi-functional space with a welcoming atmosphere where guests can flexibly transition from work to play. We offer comfortable, stylish and inviting lounge seating as well as dining tables where guests can enjoy freshly prepared meals from the 24/7 Gallery Menu or refreshing beverages from our Coffee to Cocktails Bar.

The Gallery also offers free Wi-Fi, wireless printing and public computers, so guests can either gather with friends or colleagues or work on their own. Our attentive and approachable Gallery host provides a familiar, friendly face to help with whatever guests need.

EVENTS
Perfectly flexible places for productivity

Our Meeting Places offer flexible spaces and support from our Gallery Host to make meetings and events a success. Whether it's a group of 20 or 50 attendees, our Gallery Hosts coordinate every last detail and provide ongoing support to organizers and attendees. We offer an all-inclusive package with food & beverage and audiovisual equipment options for a successful and productive meeting experience.

Figure 6.1 (page 2)
Hyatt Place Signature Touchpoints

DRINKING & DINING
Giving guests what they want at any time

We offer guests the convenience of freshly prepared meals any time, day or night. With the 24/7 Gallery Menu and a refreshing beverage selection from our Coffee to Cocktails Bar, guests can count on options being available regardless of their schedules. The Gallery Host offers guests the 24/7 Gallery Menu, sharing the details of the offerings. Whether they order food or a beverage, the multitasking Host is attentive to take orders, as well as prepare and serve all offerings from the menu.

Guests are able to start off the day with a free, hot breakfast. Our Gallery Kitchen serves our signature A.M. Kitchen Skillet™ and a plentiful variety of breakfast items for guest to choose from based on their individual preferences.

The 24/7 Gallery Market includes a Bakery Case with tasty pastries and other grab-'n-go items for guests to take with them or enjoy in the Gallery or guest room. The Gallery host is happy to warm pastries and sandwiches upon guest request.

ACTIVITIES & SERVICES
A friendly welcome

Our 24/7 Gym offers a clean and safe environment with quality equipment that's available 24 hours a day, 7 days a week, plus an Indoor or Outdoor Pool so guests can work out or take a swim when it's convenient for them.

The Gallery Host is available to provide guests with items from our Odds & Ends program, which includes must-have items guests may have forgotten or didn't have room to pack. If the guest is venturing outside the hotel, the Host provides local recommendations, per-printed maps of the area and transit schedules.

DEPARTURE
Making it easy from here to there

The Gallery Host warmly engages with the guest one last time, offering a friendly farewell along with an invitation back for future stays. From calling a taxi, to providing driving directions or airport shuttle details, the Gallery Host assists with any guest needs.

This is where the story of Hyatt Place gets interesting. The brand team resisted the temptation to overdeliver on these signature touchpoints by creating an experience more appropriate for a full-service hotel. Instead, the team remained true to the brand promise and guiding principles, using those factors to guide the development and design of every touchpoint.

For example, guest arrivals at Hyatt Place are all about a warm, friendly welcome. Their porte cochere creates a sense of arrival that welcomes guests into the gallery, which is a simple and straightforward space where nothing is hidden and there is no guesswork. The multitasking gallery host extends a friendly greeting and warm welcome to all guests entering the hotel and engages with guests while efficiently checking them in. Conversations and interactions are natural (not scripted), comfortable, and meaningful to each guest's stay.

The guest rooms, another signature experience, are spacious with a straightforward design that is not too stuffy. A space within each room, known as the "cozy corner," features a comfortable sofa sleeper and layout that creates a feeling of a distinct zone within the room. This zone helps guests feel the sense of control within their environment. Free Wi-Fi and swivel TVs give guests the ability to settle into their rooms in the style most comfortable to them. Every aspect of the room—the furniture, the floor plan, the layout, even the placement of the full-length mirror near the door—was carefully created with the brand in mind. Comfortable and seamless, once again.

"Social spaces" represent another critical signature experience for the brand. The gallery is a multifunctional space with a welcoming atmosphere where guests can flexibly transition from work to play. It offers comfortable, stylish, and inviting lounge seating, as well as dining tables where guests can enjoy freshly prepared meals from the 24/7 Gallery Menu or beverages from the Coffee to Cocktails Bar. The gallery can also transition into a comfortable, productive work environment. Thanks to free services such as Wi-Fi, wireless printing, and public computers, guests can either gather with colleagues or work on their own.

The brand promise is also clearly evident in the drinking and dining experience. Hyatt Place offers guests the convenience of freshly prepared meals at any time, day or night. With the 24/7 Gallery Menu, guests can count on available options regardless of their schedules. Hosts take orders for food and beverages, as well as preparing and serving all offerings from the menu.

What makes Hyatt Place such an interesting, powerful case study of brand experience is that every aspect of the experience is truly inspired by the brand promise. Clearly, the company could have designed a more luxurious and pampering experience—one that many travelers may find more appealing than the one described above—but that would not achieve the desired effect. Hyatt Place wisely chose to remain true to the needs and preferences of its target consumer segment, as well as the brand promise and guiding principles that underlie those needs.

CUSTOMER EXPERIENCE IN A WORLD OF BRAND MONOTONY

In 1999, B. Joseph Pine II and James Gilmore authored the groundbreaking book *The Experience Economy*.[3] The premise of the book is that, over the course of many decades, we have gradually evolved from an economy based on commodities to one based on goods, then services, then experiences, and ultimately transformation. As each shift occurred, the offerings from the preceding era became relatively undifferentiated, while those from the new era created differentiation, value, and competitive advantages. This evolution also underscored the importance of exceptional customer service over high-quality goods and services alone.

While the concept of the customer experience is not new, the dawn of the internet opened the world's eyes to the importance of the user experience. This spawned a new field with significant influence over how organizations deliver value and interact with customers. According to research conducted by the Keller Fay Group, a good customer experience is three times more likely to spark conversation compared to a traditional advertisement.[4] That same study also found that 50 percent of conversations triggered by in-person experiences resulted in purchases. In other words, interaction *really* matters.

As discussed previously, the experience behind the brand is sometimes its primary source of differentiation and the basis for its positioning. The Keller Fay Group found that 58 percent of consumers gave high credibility to information heard by word of mouth, with 50 percent reporting they were "very likely" to make a purchase as a result of a relevant conversation. In the companies studied, word of mouth drove more than 10 percent of sales volume. And nothing drives word-of-mouth advertising like great experiences.

In its simplest form, customer experience is the sum total of all interactions (touchpoints) that occur between a company and its customers over the duration of their relationship. Marketers commonly think about the customer experience across three distinct phases—prepurchase, purchase, and postpurchase. (See figure 6.2.)

Figure 6.2
Touchpoint Wheel

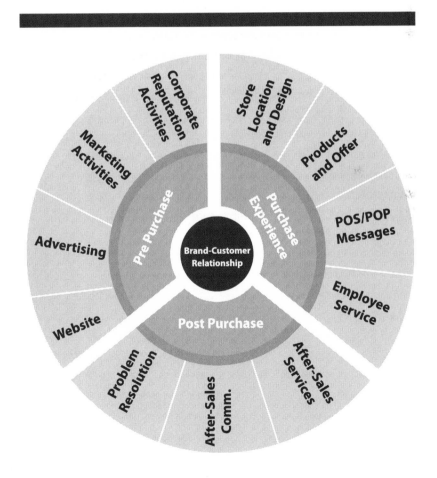

Prepurchase touchpoints create awareness of and familiarity with the brand. These include advertising, websites, public relations, sales collateral, and word of mouth. As one would expect, these touchpoints serve to educate consumers, create a sense of interest and preference, and ultimately lead to purchases for the brand's products or services.

Purchase touchpoints vary significantly by industry and transaction type. For consumer products, these touchpoints may take place in a retail store and include things such as point-of-purchase collateral and other merchandising vehicles. In B2B, purchase touchpoints could be sales meetings with customers to approve or sign contracts. No matter what the format, however, the goal is the same: to facilitate a smooth transaction, reinforce the choice the buyer made, and pave the way for ongoing satisfaction.

As in the purchase phase, postpurchase touchpoints vary widely by industry. These typically involve factors such as customer support, repairs, warranties, ongoing maintenance and service, and follow-up communications. Postpurchase touchpoints aspire to reinforce customers' ongoing satisfaction with a purchase, encourage additional purchases (i.e., remain loyal), and encourage favorable word-of-mouth marketing.

Marketers sometimes depict the customer experience using a customer journey map. This type of map serves as a visual tool that puts the customers front and center in the organization's conception of experience. When done effectively, maps highlight potential gaps and shortcomings in the experience, especially when compared to the brand promise the experience is supposed to deliver.

The customer experience touchpoint wheel and journey map are just two examples of tools to guide the design and development of customer experience. Both options are great, and for brands that prefer a different approach, several other options are equally effective. What's most important is how these tools are used. As we will cover in the next section, marketers often forget (or deliberately decline) to use brand positioning as the foundation and guidepost to develop the customer experience. Those marketers instead opt to follow customer research conducted outside the context of their brands and adopt generic industry norms and best practices. This is yet another explanation for why brands become indistinguishable from one another.

INTRODUCING THE BRAND EXPERIENCE

Had the Hyatt Place brand team set out to define the "ideal" customer experience for a hotel stay, even within the context of select-service markets, the team would have come up with a different experience than the one described earlier. That experience might have been adequate (and potentially more extravagant), but it also would have felt inconsistent with the brand promise and the needs of its target audience of smart self-reliants. Instead, Hyatt Place wisely chose to research and define its experience within the context of its brand promise. That decision ensured an on-brand customer experience and differentiated the Hyatt Place experience from others within the select-service segment.

To overcome monotony, brands must follow Hyatt Place's example to design a customer experience consistent with brand positioning. Rather than endlessly research and pursue the mythical ideal customer experience, marketers should strive to identify the unique customer experience that naturally emanates from their brand's positioning or promise.

Here, once again, market research supports the notion that a customer experience is best when inspired by the brand. According to studies by McKinsey, brand experience (called "experiential marketing" in the study) is the most powerful driver of word of mouth. This all-important prepurchase touchpoint accounts for 50 to 80 percent of word-of-mouth marketing in any given category.[5]

As detailed earlier, the world is growing increasingly complex and fast-paced. Technological improvements enable more and more companies to get the basics right. Copying is becoming increasingly easy as the sameness of more products and services makes differentiation more difficult. Fortunately, brand-inspired customer experiences can help mitigate these effects.

"BEST OF" BRAND EXPERIENCES

What exactly is a brand experience? Brand experiences are interactions so impactful and uniquely identifiable to a particular company that they essentially define the brand in consumers' minds, distinguish it from competitors, and favorably influence future behaviors. The remainder of this chapter will provide examples across various categories and industries of brand-inspired experiences. It will also suggest a set of core tenets to follow to ensure that brand experiences are as impactful as they can be and that they inspire customers to purchase from and remain loyal to a company's brand.

WHOLE FOODS MARKET

Whole Foods positions itself as the best source for the healthiest natural and organic foods. It is the first US grocery store to be certified organic.[6] Whole Foods procures its products from local and global producers, while ensuring products are manufactured without violating labor laws, human rights, or animal rights.

A cursory look at the Whole Foods brand experience suggests that it embodies its brand positioning throughout multiple critical touchpoints. For starters, consumers' increased appetite for diverse shopping options has led many brands to adopt a multichannel approach that combines a variety of platforms. Modern customers can shop online and through mobile apps for in-store pickup, curbside pickup, or home deliveries. Whole Foods is no exception to this trend. Since joining the growing list of companies acquired by Amazon, Whole Foods is poised to ramp up customer choice options to provide an enhanced grocery shopping experience for today's consumers who want to buy anytime, anywhere.

Whole Foods also focuses on Millennials with a special emphasis on wellness. The brand champions its commitment to fair business practices and environmentally friendly packaging. As part of this "greener" lifestyle promotion, Whole Foods ditched plastic bags in 2008.[7]

Amazon recognized the importance of Millennial targeting and the integration of physical stores with e-commerce technology.[8] The latest Whole Foods tools provide an "endless aisle" that integrates warehoused goods consumers can access online, at stores, and pickup kiosks. Once again, the point is to enhance the customer experience in a way that is consistent with the brand.

Acknowledging the reason people shop there in the first place (nutritious, wholesome food), Whole Foods uses a mix of tech-savvy and traditional marketing and branding. The brand leverages its website, offering consumers an entirely new experience both offline and online to share ideas and generate content that isn't boastful or sales-driven. Whole Foods understands what its customers look for and responds with hosted events (like its partnership with *Top Chef*, Whole Foods' blog publications, and its proprietary app). The grocery company has even embraced self-serve kiosks to merchandise specialty foods and ingredients, in pursuit of Millennial shoppers.

Additionally, Amazon extended its Amazon Prime subscription service, the world's largest loyalty program, to Whole Foods. This partnership provides consumers with access to Amazon rewards while shopping at Whole Foods, including members-only deals on products. Consumers can even pick up Amazon online orders at lockers located within Whole Foods stores. In 2018, Amazon Prime members living near a Whole Foods Market gained access to free two-hour delivery for purchases over thirty-five dollars. Whether customers shop online via desktop or through the Prime Now app, they have access to both modern amenities and socially conscious Whole Foods products—an exceptional brand experience.

PELOTON

New York City–based fitness company Peloton is another example. When it came time to position its brand, the marketing team at Peloton wisely resisted the temptation to focus on the obvious benefit of convenience. After all, what possibly could be more convenient for at-home exercise enthusiasts than a studio-like fitness experience in the comfort of their own home? But Peloton realized that, while true, this was a highly functional and uninspiring positioning that would not do the brand justice. Instead, through customer research and intensive discovery, it realized it had a much bigger idea on its hands. Namely, Peloton is a brand that makes you "show up." Show up not just on the bike, but off the bike. And not just in terms of working out, but in life.

According to Peloton's senior vice president of brand marketing, Carolyn Tisch Blodgett, "You are more confident in a meeting because you spent 45 minutes on a bike. You're more patient with your kids. Your mind is clear to come up with creative ideas for an organization you're involved in. It's all about how you show up...not just on the bike, but how you show up in the rest of your life."[9]

She goes on to provide inspirational, real-life accounts that support this notion: "We hear many amazing stories of how Peloton helped someone deal with the loss of a parent, helped them keep going through chemotherapy treatment, or gave them a sense of peace while going through a difficult divorce. And it's not just bad times, either. It also includes people who used it as motivation to look and feel their best for an upcoming wedding."

With this incredibly powerful and emotional positioning in place, Peloton set out to create a user experience that would credibly deliver this lofty brand promise. The company carefully examined every aspect of the customer experience, including the touchpoints that it deemed most central to fulfilling the brand promise. This includes the bike itself, obviously, but also content (e.g., live sessions, on-demand videos), knowledgeable and inspiring instructors, service and support teams, social media presence, and, very importantly, the members that form its avid user and devoted fan base. What resulted from this impeccable attention to detail around the experience—and steadfast determination to ensure it remained true to the brand positioning—is an experience that truly does make you "show up."

According to Blodgett, "We have a big, beautiful HD tablet, and there's also great sound quality. It's all interconnected with metrics, which make you want to work harder to get better. There is the Leaderboard if you want to compete with others, or you can hide it and race against your own personal record. This makes you constantly want to get back on the bike because you want to beat the score that you achieved the day before. These are the parts of our experience that are all in the name of making you want to show up."

NOOSA YOGHURT

In some ways, traditional consumer packaged goods companies are arguably at a slight disadvantage when it comes to customer experience. For starters, many are sold exclusively through conventional retail channels like grocery and drug stores, mass merchandisers, and big box retailers. This inherently places an intermediary between the company and the consumer—one that can weigh heavily on whether a purchase experience is positive or negative.

However, this challenge has not deterred Noosa Yoghurt from crafting an amazing brand experience. Based in Bellvue, Colorado, Noosa is not your typical food brand. It is an example of a company that has identified a differentiated and intriguing brand positioning, and it has found ways to infuse it into multiple aspects of its experience. And not just the consumer experience, but that of the entire value chain.

The essence of the Noosa Yoghurt brand positioning is a simple but powerful idea: "irresistible indulgence." The company's website claims that "ordinary is the enemy of awesome," and Noosa Yoghurt is a brand that surprises and smiles back at you.

According to Noosa Yoghurt vice president of marketing, Christine Dahm, the functional benefit of the brand is about providing a "taste revelation and an unexpected surprise." Every aspect of the brand feels like something you haven't experienced before. Even the inclusion of an "h" in the name is unexpected. According to Dahm, this functional benefit ladders-up to an even more powerful emotional benefit of "a refreshing break from convention."[10]

Even a cursory review of the customer experience reveals examples of how the brand essence is brought to life. Noosa Yoghurt was one of the first brands in the category to print on the package's foil, with pithy sayings such as "udder brilliance" and "you look moo-villous," in obvious reference to the brand's signature cow icon. But this doesn't just apply to the product packaging. Even the cardboard used for shipping is designed to amuse in-store stockers. It encourages the stockers to collect all six pieces in a set and put it together to form a cow to place on the backroom wall.

Unsurprisingly, social media is a pivotal touchpoint for the brand experience. In fact, the company has a "chief of fan love," whose entire job is to comb through social media looking for problems, opportunities, and reasons for outreach. The company uses social media to fuel its fan club and to give away free trips to see its farm. Those are just a few of the surprising delights for people who interact with the brand on social media. According to Dahm, "Every lunch hour of every day, I spend time looking at the conversations happening around the brand over the past 24 hours. It's my favorite part of the day. It's that kind of intimacy that is such a powerful example of how dedicated we are to making sure we give consumers the absolute best experience."

But what's perhaps most interesting is the company doesn't just think in terms of consumer experience, but a broader value chain experience. As Dahm points out, "With our retail customers and all our vendors, we always want to be a first-choice partner. We want to deliver that same amazing experience a consumer gets from our products when a partner deals with us as a company. It's been interesting to watch how this has essentially been a product...turning into a brand...turning into an experience...turning into a company value in recent years."

CINÉPOLIS

Cinépolis Luxury Cinemas positions its chain of theaters as a first-class movie destination. Cinépolis USA is a leading cinema exhibitor that offers guests enhanced moviegoing experiences through luxury cinema and theater concepts. Cinépolis CEO Alejandro Ramirez stresses that the Cinépolis brand strategy depends on the company's ability to stay relevant in a digitally driven world. To this end, his company emphasizes innovation and developing new concepts. "Placing the customer experience at the center of our concerns is part of our success," he said. "We are always trying to innovate and enrich the moviegoing experience."[11]

Cinépolis's growth strategy banks on the premise that some consumers want a more high-end moviegoing experience. At twenty dollars a ticket, including service charge, Cinépolis is eight to ten dollars more expensive than regular theaters, but includes online reservations for seats, eliminating the need to wait in line or show up early.

Cinépolis theaters offer tiers of service, including "premium" or "luxury" experiences not found at traditional movie houses. Luxury theaters have reserved seating, oversized reclining leather seats, and in-theater waitstaff. Servers take food and drink orders before the movie, and if guests want more, they can order additional items with the push of a button. Menus offer everything from chicken wings to lobster rolls, plus specialty cocktails, beer, and wine.

Large dining areas in Cinépolis lobbies include full bars where customers can spend time before and after their movies. This offers a more enriching experience for friends than a traditional theater, which limits interaction to whispers in the dark. Comfortable lounge areas include large digital screens to relax and watch TV. Patrons can order food and drinks outside the theater as well, including unusual theater fare like edamame and garden truffle flatbread pizzas. These luxury amenities, on top of standard offerings like popcorn and candy, contribute to a unique experience that is consistent with Cinépolis's brand positioning.

Cinépolis theaters aren't just for grownups, though. The theater chain recognized that families with young children wanted a better experience, too, so in 2017, the chain debuted Cinépolis Junior to offer a more family-friendly option. Cinépolis Junior offers unique spaces that combine theaters and playrooms, allowing children to play for twenty minutes before each film and for fifteen minutes during intermissions. The theater shows only G and PG films, so families can enjoy the Cinépolis experience (and reserved seating) together.[12]

Each of these brands creates a unique experience that fulfills the brand promise and differentiates the company—both to the target audience and the larger market. Cinépolis didn't poll moviegoers on their ideal movie experience: it promised luxury and made good on its word. Marketers who wish to separate their brands from the monotonous crowds would do well to learn from these examples.

DESIGNING THE OPTIMAL BRAND EXPERIENCE

The best brand experiences are unique to the brands that inspire and design them. An experience that works well for one brand might miss the mark with another. To design a great brand experience that effectively fulfills your brand's promise, seek first to understand the factors common to the best consumer experiences, then consider how those factors are best expressed distinctly through your brand.

1. BRAND FIRST, TRANSACT SECOND

The best customer experiences balance long-term equity building with near-term transaction driving. Most companies think of the customer experience as a series of events that ends in a sale, but many customer experiences don't end in a transaction (at least not immediately), especially for more complex or involved purchases.

Customer experiences build brands with individuals so that, when they are ready to purchase, they preferentially consider the brand behind the initial experience. As stated by Angela Ahrendts, former CEO of Burberry, regarding the Burberry in-store experience: "I don't want to be sold to when I walk into a store. The job is to be a brilliant brand ambassador.

Don't sell! No! Because that's a turnoff. Build an amazing brand experience, and then it will just naturally happen."[13]

Scandinavian-based furniture retailer IKEA, ranked twenty-fifth on Interbrand's Best Global Brands 2017 Rankings, focuses intensely on customer experience and value.[14] This brand has successfully created a unique in-store experience that gets customers excited about design, while satisfying their need for self-expression. IKEA makes customizing interiors easy by enabling customers to pick and choose among a wide variety of furnishing styles. When consumers browse IKEA stores, they receive two parts of inspiration and one part of sales—a good mix that balances brand and transaction.

2. DISTINGUISH BETWEEN CUSTOMER SEGMENTS

Big data, technology, and smart analytics enable increasing degrees of personalization. Modern companies can now tailor different experiences for different customers. When viewed through the stages of awareness, consideration, trial, purchase, and beyond, companies today can group segments into experience categories to guide a more strategic approach to brand experience design and management. Not all segments are of equal importance to a brand, and not all segments seek similar brand experiences.

To deliver a highly personalized customer experience, UK cosmetics retailer LUSH trains its workforce to recognize different customer types. By truly understanding customer behaviors and expectations, LUSH employees provide a tailored, enhanced customer experience.[15]

LUSH finds that assertive customers, for example, move more when they talk, often leaning in closer to speak with employees. They expect immediate customer service and enough information to make fast, informed decisions. Analytical customers probe deeper to assess their options before deciding what to buy. They tend to be more interested in personal touches and small details than basic product information, which they already know. Amiable customers like to talk. They expect LUSH employees to act like their friends, which means remembering who they are and what they like. These customers often form long-term brand relationships when they feel understood, so LUSH employees seek to make them feel welcome.

Recognizing different customer types provides LUSH employees with a deeper understanding of how their activities affect the customer journey and experience. Customers receive a friendly and personalized experience, which encourages them to visit more often and recommend LUSH to their friends.

3. PRIORITIZE DEFINING MOMENTS

Customer experience can be a complex and overwhelming subject to model, let alone manage. A multitude of moving parts interact with one another to create a mosaic that looks more like a Jackson Pollock painting than a definite plan. To create solutions for complex challenges, break down the whole into its essential components. After that, assess those smaller pieces to determine which ones to focus on to improve the overall effect. This is more than a decision of financial allocation: it's a return-on-effort decision. Any single touchpoint can take considerable time, money, and human capital to get right, so selection is paramount.

While several points of interaction and the interchange among them are important, careful analysis can reveal which touchpoints have the greatest impact on customers' impressions of the business and other important metrics. From a branding perspective, these touchpoints are "defining moments." These moments seed the brand in customers' minds and leave them with either a favorable or unfavorable perception for future considerations.

Nespresso's Business Solutions, which provides coffee to hospitality companies like hotels, recently decided to improve its postinstallation customer experience. When Nespresso coffee machines became inoperable, the downtime created a negative defining moment. No matter how quickly a service engineer arrived to solve the issue, broken machines still created bad experiences for would-be customers. Companies that depended on Nespresso for their coffee needs were upset about the negative impact the issue had on their hospitality, and customers who wanted drinks were left dissatisfied.[16]

To fix the problem and create a better defining moment, Nespresso implemented remote diagnostics to ensure every machine kept working as intended. After the upgrade, Nespresso machines were able to provide real-time information about factors like pressure and consumption rate. Service technicians no longer needed to wait for angry phone calls because the machines alerted them about potential problems before they occurred, allowing Nespresso to fix breakdowns before they led to downtime. Thanks to this move to preventative maintenance, Nespresso now creates more positive defining moments and enjoys better relationships with its clients.

4. MAKE PEOPLE FEEL SPECIAL

More than personalization, making people feel special further differentiates a brand and creates an enduring bond with the target audience. Unique, personal bonds will become increasingly important as global brands expand to standardize high-quality experiences around the world.

While operationally pragmatic, oversystemized experiences leave customers feeling cold and detached. Special touches can go a long way, even within processes that include mechanized or routine parts. Those small touches bring back the feeling of humanity, allowing companies and brands to connect with people on a deeper level while still saving money and providing convenience.

Zappos, an online shoe and clothing company based in Las Vegas, views every customer engagement as a personalized experience, which allows the brand to build stronger relationships. The company's CEO, Tony Hsieh, famously ignores common customer service metrics like time per call. He doesn't want his customer service agents to treat callers like numbers in a queue; rather, callers should be treated like real people who deserve personal attention to their issues.

According to Hsieh, this continued reliance on human contact creates positive defining moments in a way that not even the best online experiences can. He once said, "Too many companies think of their call centers as an expense to minimize. We believe that it's a huge untapped opportunity for most companies, not only because it can result in word-of-mouth marketing, but because of its potential to increase the lifetime value of the customer."[17]

The numbers back up Hsieh's theory on personal attention. Seventy-five percent of Zappos purchases come from repeat customers, and those customers order multiple times per year. Because Zappos makes its customers feel special during customer service touchpoints, those customers reward the company with their continued loyalty.

5. MAINTAIN CONTINUITY ACROSS CHANNELS AND PLATFORMS

Today, people gather information and experience brands in a multitude of ways. Television and print media still form their share of impressions, whereas dynamic digital channels, social sharing, and on-the-go mobile platforms are more impactful than ever.

Harmonizing expressions and information-sharing across these channels is important, but so is the way a company interacts with customers through two-way means. Part of experiencing a company is getting to know the brand: what it has to offer, its positioning relative to other choices, and its distinct identity. It is in a company's best interest to help customers (especially new ones) get to know the brand as quickly as possible to establish it as their preferred choice. During this "getting to know you" phase, there are few things more disruptive and damaging than inconsistencies, awkward transitions, and fragmented messages. Such discontinuities not only make for a frustrating overall experience, but they can discredit a company and diminish consumer confidence.

Pharmacy chain Walgreens has transformed itself into a model leader of modern multichannel convergence. This brand uses both mobile and social channels to drive loyalty and sales by connecting with consumers across web, mobile, and in-store platforms. Shoppers at Walgreens acquire and use points across channels, use mobile devices to upload photos for in-store printing, and receive coupons that work both online and offline. This approach is paying off for Walgreens, which has discovered that shoppers who shop both online and in stores spend three and a half times more than store-only customers, on average.[18]

6. MEASURE, MANAGE, AND MAKE CONTINUOUS IMPROVEMENTS

As customer experience becomes more professionally managed, metrics and measurement become increasingly important. Companies are adding new capabilities to capture critical data along customers' paths to purchase that enable continuous improvement and optimization.

Like any metrics-tracking effort, assessing the customer experience begins with establishing baselines across a host of attributes. Customer experience dashboards allow brands to highlight gaps and progress at regular intervals. These dashboards also provide useful tools to experiment with different elements, such as advertising, demos, and sales processes. This extra visibility allows companies to determine which factors impact the experience the most, whether positively or negatively.

As part of its customer-centric strategy, Zurich Insurance Group implemented a series of SMART (specific, measurable, achievable, relevant, time-bound) metrics to measure performance tied to its customer experience. For example, the company uses a TRI*M index to measure customer satisfaction in regional markets. This allows Zurich to understand how different components of the offer impact customer touchpoints. Combined with research from third-party companies, Zurich uses its data to identify opportunities to create more meaningful experiences. These measurements empower the executive team to plan high-level strategies and create action plans for local teams.

7. REMAIN FOCUSED ON OPERATIONS AND THE BOTTOM LINE

The essence of this chapter is focused on the intersection between brand positioning and customer experience. However, internal factors can be equally important when designing a brand experience.

Financial considerations are at the top of this list. In a world of finite resources, the expense associated with implementing various experience alternatives cannot be ignored. A close second to financial considerations, operational considerations can also affect the brand experience. How can the experience be streamlined from an internal perspective to make implementation as seamless as possible? Finally, technical considerations must be weighed. All other things equal, the brand experience should integrate well with any informational and technological systems in place.

For a great example of how to account for internal considerations while designing the brand experience, let's return to our discussion of Hyatt Place. In some ways, Hyatt Place is a B2B play, in that it franchises its brand to large hotel ownership groups. This consideration weighs heavily into the decisions the company makes when defining its brand experience.

According to Hyatt's Dominguez, "Every step of the way, we're constantly asking ourselves questions like, 'How would our owners feel about this? Is this solution too costly? What's the return on investment? Is there a more durable option? Is this easier to clean, and therefore a lower operational cost?'"[19]

As with any business decision, designing the brand experience requires companies to consider multiple factors. Only by weighing the pros and cons of various alternatives can a company arrive at a solution that combines the optimal brand experience with the practical limitations of reality.

A TRULY UNIQUE BRAND EXPERIENCE

Customer experience continues to increase in importance. Within some categories, experience is arguably as central to the brand as the product and service offering. In many ways, experience has become a greater potential source of differentiation than either of those two components.

However, to create a truly differentiated experience, marketers must change their approach. Brand positioning offers better inspiration for designing customer experiences than industry best practices or tactics copied from successful competitors. When positioning does not dictate customer experience, brands run a greater risk of becoming indistinguishable from other category brands.

Chapter 7

———

Brand Extension

Despite its late arrival to a stationery market facing a challenging future, Moleskine needed only a decade to dominate mindshare and lead the premium notebook space. This Italian company's brand management and extension strategy have been skillful. Despite rapid growth, new Moleskine products consistently echo and reinforce the aesthetic principles established by its original hit pocket notebook.

Moleskine made one of its first bold extension moves when it launched bags and pens in 2011. CEO Arrigo Berni said, "I [learned] a lot about brand extensions in my years with Procter & Gamble and Bulgari. Since the beginning of my association with Moleskine in 2006, I believed in the possibility to extend the brand into new categories, like Montblanc has done."[1]

Moleskine's extensions don't just maintain the brand—they take it to new heights. The young company's choices are frequently original and entertaining. Not many notebook companies line up to collaborate with LEGO, but Moleskine did just that, blending adult utility and childlike creativity to develop products both wonderful and practical. Thanks to this partnership, Moleskine further established itself as the go-to stationery company for anyone with a flair for fun.

For example, Moleskine's Smart Writing Set exemplifies the brand's ability to stay consistent during extensions. Through a combination of analog tools (pen and paper) and app integrations, the set creates a unique experience for Moleskine's users. The smart pen tracks users' writing through a hidden camera, and the app allows users to sync their work automatically with Google Calendar, Apple iCal, and other services. These modern touches add another layer of flair to an already hip product.[2] Intended for people who want to get creative digitizing or sharing their notes (like students and artists), Moleskine's Smart Writing Set enables users to act like serious nerds—but the emphasis is on fun, not meticulous function. Professionals who depend on reliable, highly accurate notes are better off with more traditional options.

Notepads and pens, while central to Moleskine's brand, represent only one part of a greater, evolving whole. Moleskine's extensions have allowed the brand to keep pace with new technology and take advantage of new market opportunities. Collaborations with Evernote and Creative Cloud add new layers to Moleskine's product offerings—and that's just the beginning.[3] The company recently opened its first standalone café in Milan, Italy, after a successful pilot concept at Geneva Airport in 2015.

How does this latest brand extension look? About like what you would expect. The café is a Moleskine notebook come to life. Part art gallery, part store, and part coffee shop, the café is a space for people to live and breathe the aesthetic that has given Moleskine so much success within its creative-minded target audience.[4] These extensions didn't end in Milan; they've extended to Hamburg, Germany, and Beijing, China, as well. Moleskine's cafés represent a contemporary version of café littéraire, where philosophers and scholars used to gather to discuss grand ideas.

Moleskine's cafés skillfully create links between customers and the brand. These are creative, inspiring spaces that highlight Moleskine's core values—to embrace and foster creativity in all its facets. The sales areas of the cafés allow visitors to browse through their favorite Moleskine products, further reinforcing the connection between Moleskine and creative life.

In his interview, Berni outlined the rationale behind the unique brand extension: "The founders' vision from the beginning was to leverage the incredible story behind Moleskine. Being associated with great artists and thinkers identifies the brand with a certain lifestyle and values: culture, memory, and exploration. The café is a way for us to provide a physical experience of the intangible dimension of the lifestyle brand we've been defining."[5]

Berni also said, "Interestingly, we find that we do better whenever we are closest to an Apple retail store. This may come as a surprise, but it makes perfect sense when one considers that the profile of a Moleskine user is very similar to that of an Apple user."[6] Beyond having a quality product, it's about selling a brand and a sense of belonging to a community, which is exactly what Apple does. If Moleskine manages to match Apple's culture-building success, the brand will have creative extensions like these to thank for it.

BRAND EXTENSION AND TRANSFORMATION

Brands must continually grow to flourish and maintain relevance. However, achieving and sustaining profitable growth is a constant challenge.

One of the most common ways for an established brand to achieve meaningful growth is through brand extensions, but many owners of brand strategy struggle with how far they can (or should) stretch their brands' boundaries. Play it too safe and ho-hum line extensions will underwhelm customers and fail to impact the marketplace. Stray too far from the brand's core positioning and you risk diluting or causing irreversible damage to the brand's valuable equity.

Profitable growth is the lifeblood of brands, though, and launching new products and services is one of the most popular ways to achieve it. According to PwC, American CEOs consider product and service information to be a key driver of growth, but those same CEOs also believe that they need to make substantial changes to their product development and innovation capabilities.[7] (See figure 7.1.) Essentially, some of the most influential business leaders in the world believe this critical driver of business growth needs an overhaul (or at least a modification). Their concerns are valid, as recent research regularly names innovation as both a key growth driver and top challenge.[8]

Figure 7.1
Sources for Growth

% of U.S. CEOs Citing Area as a Source for Growth

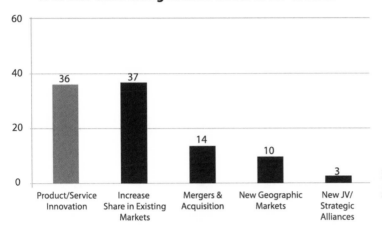

% of U.S. CEOs Citing Their Product Development & Innovation Capabilities as Follows

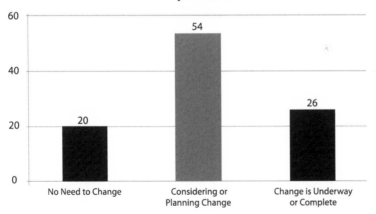

Source: PwC 17th Annual Global CEO Survey (2014)

Let's look at growth across two dimensions: brand extension and products and services. (See figure 7.2.) In this framework, brand extendibility offers a lucrative path to achieving growth. It has the potential to drive faster, more dramatic business results than simple efforts to increase market penetration. When done correctly and responsibly, brand extension carries less risk (and certainly less expense) than new brand launches to house new products and services.

Figure 7.2
Business Growth Matrix

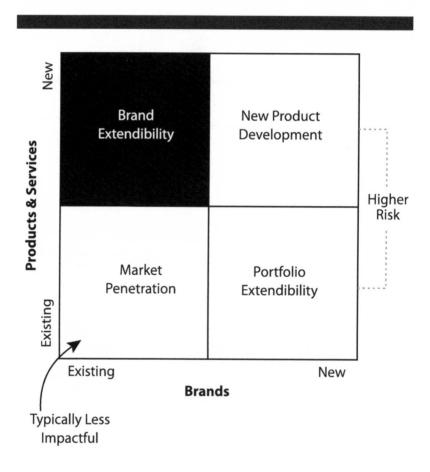

To further break down this relationship, brand growth is achieved at the extremes in two ways: incremental line extensions and transformational new products and services. All too often, especially in the world of packaged goods, brand leaders choose the former. Historically, incremental line extensions do not have a very good track record, especially in the world of consumer packaged goods. The failure rate of brand extensions is persistent and well-documented; research from EY reveals that brand extensions fail at an astonishing rate of 84 percent.[9]

So why is it that something that appears so straightforward has such a dismal success rate? Explanations for this poor track record abound, but most trace back to one or more of three primary reasons. Some failures occur because there is no demand (i.e., need or desire) for the extension. If it doesn't solve a problem or improve an existing process, the extension will likely fail. Another reason is that, although there may be demand, the solution offered by the brand is uninspiring or inadequate. In yet other situations, where the need is real and the solution adequately addresses it, the brand itself is either irrelevant or a poor fit for the solution. (See figure 7.3.) When all three factors are met—demand, solution, and brand relevance—the potential for success is high.

Figure 7.3
Brand Extendibility — Success Factors

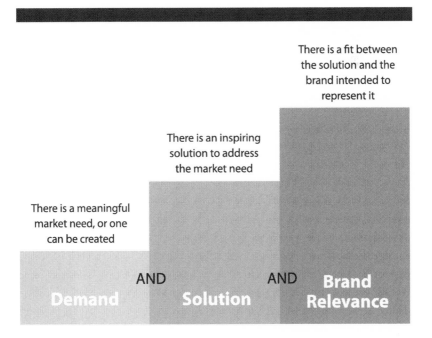

There is a meaningful market need, or one can be created

There is an inspiring solution to address the market need

There is a fit between the solution and the brand intended to represent it

Demand AND **Solution** AND **Brand Relevance**

Before we examine these three factors and their collective contributions to successful brand extensions, we should first distinguish between two definitions: line extension and brand extension. While both contribute to brand growth, line extensions are typically categorized as launches in which the company introduces additional items under the same brand name (typically in the same product category). New flavors, forms, colors, package sizes, and other minor additions fall into this category. Brand extensions, on the other hand, cover instances in which a new product, representing an entirely new category for that brand, is launched. An apparel company launching a new line of perfumes and colognes—under the same brand—would be an example of brand extension. As one would expect, brand extension represents a greater opportunity for dramatic revenue growth and brand transformation, which we will address later in this chapter.

THE FIRST FACTOR: DEMAND

Suffice it to say, no brand extension (or any new product in general) can be successful if this first condition is not met. There must be a need or desire for the new product or service. Or, if one does not exist, the brand must first find a way to create the need or want; this is more difficult, but it is still a viable path.

Need and want form the basis of underlying demand. It is surprising how often new products or services launch into the marketplace with no clear problem to solve or need to address. Google Glass, a pair of glasses that could take pictures and record videos, became a notorious flop for this reason. Not only did it hit the market for $1,500, but the product answered a question no one was asking. Google axed the project in 2015.[10]

PlantCam offers another example of a product that didn't meet a demand. The tool, a weatherproof camera that took photos of plants or gardens at regular intervals, met a confused market upon launch.[11] PlantCam claimed to help users create time-lapse photos of their gardens over the season. Users could also use the cameras to record slow-moving weather events, parties, or construction—but the market for this product proved nonexistent, and it became a dud. Turns out, watching grass grow is not an exciting sales pitch.

Sometimes there is a need, but it's being adequately met by existing solutions. Do we really need another toothpaste? Probably not. Clearly, it is not enough to know there is a problem or a need. The extent to which that need is met by current solutions is equally important. Ignorance of this condition partly explains the presence of so many me-too offerings in the market.

Even when a need exists and lacks satisfactory solutions, however, the market must be large enough to justify the business opportunity. In other words, the opportunity may be too niche. Consider the rise and fall of 3-D TVs as a perfect example. To be fair, this is less of a brand extension than it is an addition to multiple TV manufacturers' offerings, but the point still holds true.

When *Avatar* was raking in the money back in 2009, TV manufacturers decided that Americans were ready to upgrade their televisions to 3-D sets. They poured money into research and development, then flooded the market with new models. Each company hoped to be the first to get the technology right, and manufacturers waited eagerly for their innovations to fly off the shelves—but they never did.

Why? First, 3-D TV is a pain to watch. Viewers need special glasses, and some people even get headaches. When consumers realized what a pain it would be to join the 3-D revolution, they decided they were fine with one fewer dimension. Second—and more significantly—content creators never adopted the medium. *Avatar* was hugely popular, but James Cameron only makes so many movies. Options for 3-D entertainment dwindled quickly, and, with limited content, the technology faded from history.[12]

When it comes to consumer wants and needs (i.e., potential demand), a few other rules apply. Customers often don't know they have an unmet need, or even if they do, they may struggle to articulate it. Post-it Notes, laptops, ATMs, Wi-Fi, and even cars all showed people what they were missing and eased them into a better life. But clearly, these were not things consumers were asking for. That is why it is so important to not stop with asking consumers what they want when seeking to identify growth opportunities.

Finally, solving problems represents only part of the demand landscape. Some of the most successful new products address no discernible need. When Apple launched the iPad, Steve Jobs proudly proclaimed that he had no idea how the product would or should be used. However, he saw the incredible utility and potential of the device, and he trusted consumers to make it useful. He was right. They did, and today, iPads and similar tablets are in homes around the world. Apple, in effect, created a need that didn't exist before it launched a new product.

THE SECOND FACTOR: SOLUTION

Identifying a meaningful unmet need or want is a critical first step, but it is not sufficient to achieve successful brand extension. An appealing solution to address the need or want is also required. Several factors can go wrong during this step in the process, and each factor has the potential to singlehandedly derail an otherwise successful brand extension.

The first (and most obvious) mistake is if the solution does not squarely address the want or need in question, including solutions that simply fail to work altogether.

Nokia's N-Gage fell into this category.[13] As a hybrid mobile phone and handheld gaming device, the N-Gage made a lot of sense as a product, considering high demand for the concept and Nokia's positioning in the market in 2003. Despite the obvious fulfillment of a need, though, the solution itself was a mess. Users had to disassemble the device to change games. To use the N-Gage as a phone, people had to hold it sideways, thin edge against the temple. The N-Gage simply wasn't intuitive—and the few games it offered weren't much fun to play.

But even if the solution is spot-on, creative, and inspiring, the side effects (or unappealing attributes) of an offer sometimes can sink the whole proposition. One of the most infamous examples of this was the R. J. Reynolds Tobacco Company's smokeless cigarette.[14] The product worked by heating and aerosolizing tobacco flavor. It was intended to reduce or eliminate the unhealthy side effects of smoking both for the user and surrounding parties. On the surface, it appeared to be a home run: an intense and unmet need with a creative and appealing solution.

Unfortunately, the flavor and smell of the smokeless cigarettes were so foul, they left users retching. People complained about tasting charcoal, and even though the company insisted people could acquire the taste after a pack or two, most users smoked just one before giving away the rest. The product left shelves less than a year after its debut.

Solutions—and the extension efforts behind them—can also fail due to cannibalization. In this situation, the solution itself might be fine, but its revenue and market share come at the expense of another product or service from the same company or brand. Remember the beginning of this book? We discussed how Crest used to own 50 percent of the market with a single product, but now owns just a quarter of the market with fifty products.[15]

The Crest example, although extreme, is not unique. According to Catalina, existing brand buyers typically account for 42 percent of new product sales.[16] To avoid cannibalization, brands must not only ensure that they develop high-quality solutions that fulfill an unmet need, but they must also avoid merely moving revenue from one internal column into another.

THE THIRD FACTOR: BRAND RELEVANCE

While the preceding two factors arguably apply to innovation and product development in general, the third factor pertains specifically to brand extendibility. Brand relevance is the extent to which a new product or service idea fits the brand's existing positioning. Even when the need is significant and the solution is perfect, every extension depends on whether the solution in question makes sense for the brand behind it. When the fit is not strong, a new offering can dilute the brand's valuable equity. In some cases, bad extensions can destroy that equity altogether.

In 2006, eBay opened its eBay Express site, which aspired to operate like a regular e-commerce site. The site failed badly—eBay's brand was inextricably linked with auctions, and selling goods at fixed prices made no sense for the brand or to its consumers.

When determining brand relevance—the extent to which a new opportunity fits the brand positioning—we must first consider two important concepts: The first concept covers the multiple dimensions (tangible and intangible) that comprise a brand. The second is the degree to which different ideas along each of those dimensions fit the brand. (See figure 7.4.)

Figure 7.4
Brand Extendibility Footprint

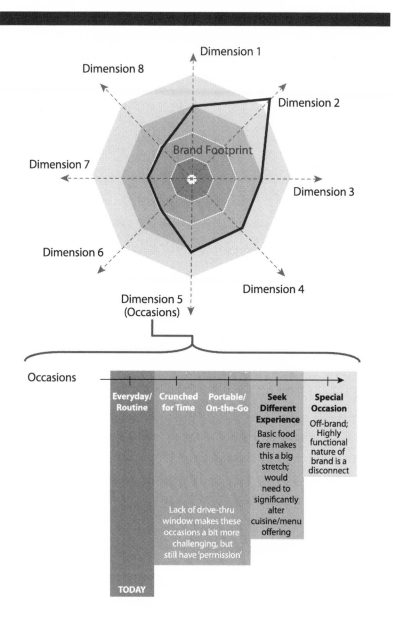

As demonstrated in this Brand Extendibility Footprint, the closer any potential idea is to the center of the diagram, the closer its fit with the brand positioning. The farther an idea extends into the periphery, the greater the stretch it represents and the more questionable its adoption becomes. It is important to note that ideas farther from the center can still work for the brand. When implementing those ideas, brands will need to connect the dots for customers to help them understand how this new offering fits the brand.

When determining the Brand Extendibility Footprint, think about the brand across many different dimensions: functional and emotional, tangible and intangible. In the food example in figure 7.4, some dimensions are highly tangible in nature (e.g., temperate state, cuisine, consumer segments) while other dimensions are more intangible (e.g., emotional payoff and persona). Intangible dimensions often give the brand permission to stretch into territories that may seem (on the surface) disconnected from the brand. In the next section, we'll explore examples of how brands have successfully extended into completely unrelated product categories by leveraging intrinsic aspects of positioning.

For example, The Clorox Company was traditionally known for laundry bleach but successfully extended its flagship brand into other categories, like wipes, sprays, and toilet cleaners. The brand managed to reach beyond the laundry room by tapping into the higher meaning of its mission to help consumers maintain cleanliness and health. Importantly, Clorox does recognize the limitations of the brand's reach. The company also has in its portfolio brands like Burt's Bees, Hidden Valley, Kingsford, and Liquid-Plumr (among others), which cover offerings the Clorox product brand would be unwise to house under its umbrella.

It is important to note that the dimensional exercise above should not be conducted entirely behind company walls. Like virtually all other aspects of brand strategy, the "outside-in" voice of the customer is essential during brand extendibility efforts. Consumer research helps brand leaders determine both the optimal dimensions in the Brand Extendibility Footprint and the extent to which new ideas fit the brand.

Finally, be cautious of the chicken-and-egg conundrum during this process. Customers tend to be fairly literal in their interpretations of brands, and they may be less willing to approve a potential brand extension in theory (i.e., in market research) than they would be to purchase a new product once it's in the market. Should the brand wait for consumer permission or proactively establish it? The answer often depends on whether the brand extension has the power to inspire consumer interest on its own.

AVOIDING STAGNATION THROUGH EXTENSION

As discussed above, some of the most meaningful, transformational brand extensions came to fruition as a result of companies tapping into intangible yet salient aspects of their brand positioning. Like many other components of brand strategy referenced before, successful extensions first require a shift in mindset. In this case, the shift pertains to the role brand positioning serves in the context of brand extension.

Marketers can turn to numerous sources of inspiration when it comes to brand extendibility. (See figure 7.5.) Surprisingly, few look inward to their brand positioning for inspiration. Most brand managers think of positioning as the guardrails that protect the brand from extending off the path. To be clear, this is a valid function of brand positioning and should never be compromised. However, brand positioning can and should also serve as inspiration for extendibility and new product development. The intangible—often more emotional—aspects of brand positioning pave the way for this inspiration.

Figure 7.5
Brand Extendibility — Sources of Inspiration

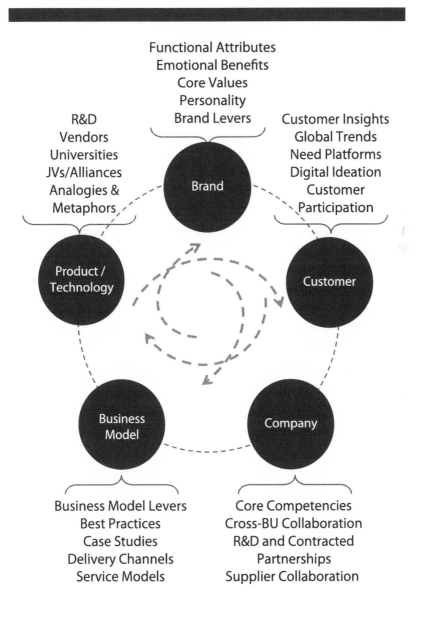

Functional Attributes
Emotional Benefits
Core Values
Personality
Brand Levers

R&D
Vendors
Universities
JVs/Alliances
Analogies &
Metaphors

Customer Insights
Global Trends
Need Platforms
Digital Ideation
Customer
Participation

Brand

Product /
Technology

Customer

Business
Model

Company

Business Model Levers
Best Practices
Case Studies
Delivery Channels
Service Models

Core Competencies
Cross-BU Collaboration
R&D and Contracted
Partnerships
Supplier Collaboration

For most people, the Caterpillar brand likely conjures up images of large, earth-moving equipment made for construction. Those people might be surprised to learn that Caterpillar also sells footwear—namely, work boots. According to the company, "At Caterpillar, we build the machines that help our customers build a better world. The boots and shoes we build are made with the same commitment."[17] Clearly, an idea beyond product category inspired that brand extension, as earth-moving equipment and footwear are not exactly adjacent categories.

Caterpillar isn't the only brand succeeding in this arena. Can you imagine if one brand became equally relevant across financial services, automobiles, power, communications, and food products? That's exactly what Indian multinational conglomerate Tata Group has accomplished. While most holding groups downplay (or completely ignore) their corporate brand, Tata has chosen the opposite direction. This holding group embraces its valuable brand, leveraging it to extend successfully into highly disparate businesses and product categories. The company states, "Excellence is a continual quest at the Tata Group, and Tata companies are supported in their efforts to achieve world-class standards in all aspects of operations."[18] Clearly, Tata Group knows a thing or two about using its brand positioning to inspire and guide extensions.

For a more thorough example, consider the fashion brand Giorgio Armani, one of Italy's premier names in luxury. When consumers hear the name "Armani," they think of concepts including style, sexiness, expertise, and sophistication. Armani's brand personality is a reflection of its founder's own personality, which guides consumers' perceptions of the brand and all products or services that bear its name.

As its inclusion in this section suggests, the Giorgio Armani brand extends far beyond the world of fashion. Armani's fashion portfolio consists of everything from haute couture to children's apparel to fragrances, but the brand has also diversified into several nonfashion product categories.[19] The Armani brand is attached to cafés, restaurants, hotels, nightclubs, flowers, and even chocolates—and not all of them cater exclusively to the elite. Even Armani's fashion brand extends into seven sub-brand categories, ranging from high-end to medium-priced men's and women's fashion goods, children's fashion, and home products.[20]

Armani has been criticized for its extension into mass-market offerings, such as jeans. However, the Armani brand extension strategy has successfully transcended fashion by maintaining its high-quality standards across every offering, regardless of audience or niche. Armani also uses a uniform marketing mix strategy for all its sub-brands, ensuring every representation of Armani provides the same impression of expertise and skill.

The key to Armani's effective brand extension strategy has been the brand's early understanding of the vital role the luxury consumer plays in its success. While many luxury brands focus on their products as their key selling factor, Armani concentrates first and foremost on its consumers and crafts its brand based on the needs and characteristics of the audience. While other personality-based brands struggle to escape the personality of their founders, Armani has evolved from a brand representing one man to a brand reflective of an entire customer segment.[21]

Armani identified different luxury consumer segments and designed products that would appeal to them. By understanding distinct consumer groups and their compelling needs, Armani adopted the brand extension strategy of sub-brands and the brand diversification strategy into nonfashion categories. As a result, Armani has successfully created a brand that has revolutionized the branding strategy of the luxury goods sector. So long as Armani maintains its mystique, especially in the world of fashion, its brand positioning will continue to empower its extension efforts.[22]

PROGRESSIVE EVOLUTION VERSUS "SWING FOR THE FENCES"

When developing a long-term brand extension strategy, it's wise to think in terms of time horizons, taking progressively bolder steps for departures from your core offering. Referring back to figure 7.4, the ideal way to extend is to begin close to the bull's-eye and gradually move outward along the various axes. This helps the brand build credibility and momentum over time, priming the market for more peripheral departures. For example, Moleskine's first foray into brand extendibility was not a café, but once the company made smaller extensions, the café became a logical and credible next step.

Procter & Gamble's Mr. Clean brand is a perfect example. The brand and its now-iconic bald mascot debuted in the 1950s, and the brand occupies a distinct and enviable positioning today. P&G says, "Mr. Clean embodies everything that makes his products so special. He's tough, fearless, inventive, helpful, and has the muscle to knock out dirt, grease, and grime no matter where it's hiding."[23] The brand aspires to be the hardest-working cleaner in history, and its charming mascot furthers that mission.

Mr. Clean first made its mark in the kitchen, offering consumers an unmatched solution for cleaning floors and walls. In the 1990s, the company set out to own more than just one room of the house. Mr. Clean debuted a toilet cleaner and liquid bathroom cleaner in 1992, and in 1993, it expanded further with its glass and surface cleaner.

The next decade saw progressively bolder moves as the brand moved beyond the interior of the home. In 2003, P&G introduced the Magic Eraser surface cleaning pad, which extended the brand's application and relevance to include exterior surfaces (e.g., vinyl siding and garage doors), patio furniture, and grills. Mr. Clean even reached outside the home to clean everything from car wheel rims to sports equipment.[24]

The brand's boldest move arguably came in 2007 when it ventured beyond household products to open a line of car washes. Customers who visit a Mr. Clean Car Wash can enjoy gourmet coffee and shop while they wait. The car wash offers a membership program, smartphone app, and VIP club for loyal customers. Not bad for a brand that started out scrubbing the kitchen floor. All of this was possible because Mr. Clean evolved gradually and progressively while remaining true to the brand's essence. Had the brand attempted to open a car wash immediately after achieving success with its first new product extension, ensuing initiatives likely would not have been as successful.

Another example comes from west elm, a division of Williams-Sonoma, Inc. After its launch in 2002, west elm quickly became a leader in sustainably produced home furnishings. However, the furniture and home décor company was determined to become much more than a residential furniture brand. Known for its chic and not-so-cheap home furnishings, west elm understands that the intricacies of modern life demand highly relevant customer experiences at work, at home, and away. Evolving from home furnishings into a purpose-driven brand, entry into office furniture—and then hotels—was a natural next step for west elm.

In 2015, west elm Workspace was launched out of an immediate need to furnish west elm's corporate offices in Brooklyn, New York. It's a modern office furniture line without the institutional look of mismatched desks and file cabinets.[25] By providing products that meet the changing needs of workplace design, the company skillfully channeled the design aesthetics of residential products (e.g., materials, finishes, and silhouettes) into office equipment. "People are looking to move away from commoditized, white, techy products in offices…They're figuring out how to retain staff, attract Millennials, and get people excited about their workspaces in new ways," said Peter Fowler, VP of Workspace and Hospitality at west elm.[26]

In 2016, west elm announced plans to open a fleet of hotels. Beginning in 2019, the brand will open properties in Detroit, Michigan; Indianapolis, Indiana; Minneapolis, Minnesota; Savannah, Georgia; Portland, Oregon; and Oakland, California.[27], [28] These boutique west elm Hotels will be furnished with pieces from west elm's contract line—furniture specifically constructed to withstand the wear and tear of high-traffic environments like hotels, offices, and commercial spaces. Betting that people who buy their products will stay at their hotels, this move into hospitality is a logical progression for the brand's growth.

David Bowd, cofounder of DDK (west elm's partner in the hotel extension) said, "Our entry into the hotel industry is a natural next step, as we are evolving from home furnishings to a purpose-driven brand. We knew that we had to expand beyond physical retail locations. Entering into hospitality…isn't a marketing aspect for us; it's about creating a new platform and creating a sustainable model for a unique boutique hotel."[29]

Will west elm's foray into hospitality succeed? That remains to be seen. However, the brand has put itself in a good position by taking a gradual, progressive path toward this brand extension. If west elm Hotels resonate with consumers, don't be surprised if this brand makes another bold move in the future.

BRAND POSITIONING: MORE THAN A SAFETY NET

These examples prove that brand positioning plays a vital role in extendibility. While positioning should continue to serve as the guardrails that protect valuable brand equity from harmful dilution or destruction, it can also serve as inspiration for new product and service ideas. This utility arises from a mindset that sees brands as more than the tangible, functional components that surround them. Marketers must consider the intangible, emotional qualities their brands represent and use those as inspiration for extendibility and growth efforts. With the power of brand positioning, marketers can break the cycle of safe, ho-hum line extensions that drop out of the market after a few years and pave the way for meaningful, transformational brand growth.

Chapter 8

———

Brand Story

The story that inspired the sports beverage brand Gatorade began on the hot and steamy football fields of the University of Florida.[1] In 1965, assistant football coach Dewayne Douglas reached out to Dr. Robert Cade, a University of Florida kidney disease specialist, to help him understand why players lost so much weight during games but rarely needed to urinate. Drinking more water wasn't the answer, as that caused nausea and cramps. What was the coach to do?

Cade determined that players' copious sweating left no fluids to urinate. Thinking further about Douglas's question motivated him to look deeply into the physiological components of sweat and the effects of heat on the human body. Cade engaged fellow researchers Dana Shires, Jim Free, and Alejandro de Quesada, and together they hypothesized that electrolytes lost through sweat—primarily sodium and potassium—were responsible for the upheaval of the body's chemical balance. To test their theory, the researchers asked head football coach Ray Graves if they could test their invention on some of his players.

Coach Graves gladly offered his freshmen as guinea pigs. Testing on these players revealed that during practices and games, their electrolytes were out of whack, their blood sugar was low, and their total blood volume was low. Each of those factors could cause trouble alone. Put together, they could easily cause the kinds of heat-related illnesses plaguing the team.

Cade's team's first solution was water with salt and sugar in it. The goal was to replace the salt lost through sweat and keep the blood sugar up without upsetting the athletes' stomachs. Cade's wife suggested the addition of lemon juice, because the initial batch tasted so awful that not even the researchers could drink it.

The freshman team tried a sample batch for the first time during a scrimmage with the varsity B team. The freshmen were down two touchdowns after the first half, but they came back to pummel the varsity squad in the second half, ultimately winning by more than four touchdowns. Florida's coaches attributed the victory to the scientific concoction and requested a larger supply for the team's game against Louisiana State the next day—a game in which the Gators were underdogs. Thanks to their superior stamina, the Gators went on to defeat LSU in the 102-degree heat.

By the start of the 1966 season, the powerful drink—dubbed "Gatorade"—could always be found on the sidelines of the University of Florida football team. When the Gators defeated the favored Georgia Tech in the Orange Bowl later that season in 1967, Georgia Tech's coach attributed his team's loss to Florida's secret weapon. "We didn't have Gatorade," he said. "That made the difference."[2]

In the late 1960s, the Stokely-Van Camp Company secured the rights to market Gatorade nationwide. The rest, as they say, is history. That company was acquired by Quaker Oats in 1983, which became part of PepsiCo in the early 2000s. Those are the humble origins of a powerful brand. Gatorade, born in a University of Florida lab, spawned an entirely new category of beverage.

As we will discuss in this chapter, a great brand story tells the narrative of a brand, including where it comes from and where it's going. The story invites users to connect to the brand through creative and emotional relevance. What makes Gatorade's brand story one of the greatest of all time is how it has inspired other aspects of managing the brand.

For example, the story drives Gatorade's positioning (for serious athletes and improved performance) and how it communicates in advertising campaigns through slogans like "Win from Within" and "Is It in You?" Brand ambassadors such as Michael Jordan, Mia Hamm, and Usain Bolt live the Gatorade story, inspiring athletes to use their inner drive to overcome physical and mental barriers.[3] The launch of the G Series line shows us how a new product development can leverage a brand story. This line—with its o1 Prime, o2 Perform, and o3 Recover products—takes the science of rehydration to a new level by focusing on the phases of the workout experience.

While consumers often try a brand because of its perceived benefits, they continue to buy when they become emotionally connected to the brand's story. Gatorade provides a classic example of an authentic story, rooted in science and innovation. That story continues to evolve, but it remains relevant to the brand and true to its history, as all the best brand stories do.

THE SIGNIFICANCE OF STORY

Many historians and psychologists believe that storytelling is one of the defining characteristics of our species. Stories, by definition, are accounts of imaginary or real people and events told for the purpose of entertainment or teaching lessons. Great stories create strong connections between people. The better the story, the stronger that emotional connection becomes. Stories often build tension through conflict and obstacles, then offer relief through problem resolution. The best stories have immense power to transform.

Humans might be the only animals that can create and tell stories. Evidence of human storytelling traces back to the Upper Paleolithic period (beginning about forty thousand years ago), when Cro-Magnon cave dwellers without the power of written language used cave paintings to convey what we now consider to be some of the first stories in recorded histories.[4] The culture of storytelling became even more powerful in seventh and eighth centuries BC when the Mesopotamian epic of Gilgamesh was carved into stone tablets.[5]

Today, of course, examples of stories are all around us. We see them in children's books and adult novels, textbooks, magazine articles, political speeches, and business presentations. Stories are fascinating because no matter what the context, they compel and motivate us. Whether housed in a fairy tale intended for a toddler or in the State of the Union address from the president, stories provide effective vehicles to improve recollection (remembrance over time) and motivation (persuasion toward a new belief or action).

Why do stories impact us so deeply? According to psychologists, we spend about a third of our time awake creating stories and the rest of our time consuming the stories of others.[6] Our lives and relationships flow through the stories we and others tell. For brands, that means a great story is essential to connect with a target audience.

Simply put, people remember stories far more easily than facts or figures. Whether we realize it or not, human beings tend to be persuaded to make decisions more by emotional factors than rational arguments. For these reasons, storytelling is a time-tested form of communication that is every bit as relevant in business settings as it is in our personal lives.

STORYTELLING IN THE WORLD OF BUSINESS

Storytelling is an equally compelling form of communication in business as it is in other contexts, but that fact is not always intuitive. We think of business as being driven by rational arguments and evidence, not emotional pleas. Statistics and data rule the day in most business environments. Despite this, it is important to remember that business executives are still human beings—and still subject to the same powerful, transformative properties of storytelling as the rest of us.

Consider the popularity of TED Talks as proof. If these were simple recitals of facts and statistics, they would be nowhere near as popular as they are today. We care less about the research than we do about the stories behind it. With great storytellers like Bill Gates, Elon Musk, and Jane Goodall on stage, those stories—and the lessons within them—take root in our minds.[7]

The format of TED Talks helps, too. Speakers get a maximum of eighteen minutes to present their ideas in the most innovative, engaging fashions possible. More often than not, storytelling makes the difference between a captivating speech and a ho-hum presentation. In 2016, Forbes Agency Council named "humanized storytelling" as one of the most important factors for a TED Talk. According to Brandon Stapper, who was interviewed in the article, "The more compelling approach is to focus on an individual. The audience can then either relate to that person or they cannot, but they should be compelled to some kind of buy-in, emotionally or on a humanistic level. We humans are suckers for human stories."[8]

The success of TED Talks is obvious, but even more powerful evidence of storytelling's benefits in business can be found in a report from Headstream, *The Power of Brand Storytelling: How Brand Storytelling Can Meet Marketing Objectives.*[9] For this report, Headstream commissioned researchers to survey two thousand UK adults in April 2015. The report and the research results that inspired it underscore the importance consumers place on good brand stories—and the economic benefits for companies that tell those stories. With regard to the importance of good brand stories and their bottom-line impact, Headstream's research offered four key findings:

1. YOUNG PEOPLE LIKE STORIES

Headstream found that 79 percent of its respondents preferred brands that told stories. People from the ages of eighteen to thirty-four were particularly interested in stories, indicating that Millennial consumers are less interested in sales pitches and more responsive to brands they can identify with on a personal level.

2. STORIES TIE TO EMOTIONS

According to Headstream, the most impactful types of stories are "humorous, dramatic, or heartwarming." (See figure 8.1.) We like it when a story makes us feel something. When brands deliver high-quality stories that affect our emotional state, we're more inclined to listen.

Figure 8.1
Interest Drivers for Brands

Q: What would make you more interested in any brand?

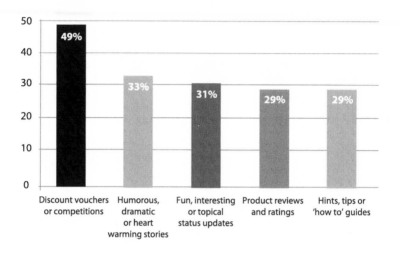

Source: Headstream

3. CONSUMERS LISTEN TO BRANDED STORIES

Fortunately, 64 percent of Headstream's surveyed population said brands tell good stories. That's great news for brands because it means that consumers don't automatically assume they want to sell something. If the brand tells a good story, people are willing to hear it.

4. STORIES TRANSLATE TO REVENUE

Even if stories themselves aren't sales vehicles, brands with better stories sell more. Headstream found that great stories created purchase intent in 55 percent of surveyed consumers. (See figure 8.2.) Stories are highly effective brand assets, but brands can't make up any old story and expect audiences to respond. They need stories that resonate—stories that feel both familiar and exciting. To create powerful narratives, brands must understand the building blocks of all great stories.

Figure 8.2
Impact of a Strong Brand Story

Q: If you really love a brand's story, what are you likely to do?

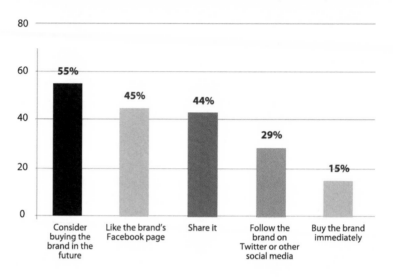

Source: Headstream

THE SEVEN STORY ARCHETYPES (AND WHAT THEY MEAN TO BRANDS)

In 2004, Christopher Booker published *The Seven Basic Plots: Why We Tell Stories*. This analysis of stories and their psychological meanings is the product of Booker's thirty years of research.[10] Booker argues that all stories in the world fall into one of seven basic categories. From sci-fi adventures to religious parables, every story that exists is simply a retelling of an existing narrative. The characters, setting, and motivations may change, but the arc of the story remains consistent.

Booker's work goes into great detail about each story type, so we won't cover all of that information here. Instead, we will review the central components of each story type, then discuss how brands use those story archetypes to engage their audiences.

1. OVERCOMING THE MONSTER

Overcoming the monster is one of the most common story themes. From "David and Goliath" to *Star Wars*, we love a tale about success against all odds.

In this type of story, the hero faces a challenge that appears to be insurmountable. Sometimes, it's a literal monster, like a dragon; other times, the monster is more figurative, like a big corporation. To defeat the monster, the hero must find inner strength.

Brands that use this type of story should make the customer—not the company—the hero of the tale.[11] Consider home cleaning and health categories. The role of the brand is to help consumers overcome the "monster" of dirt or sickness. In these stories, the product is not the hero—it's the weapon the consumer wields to conquer the foe. Let's look at two examples of this narrative in action.

Amazing storytelling lies at the heart of the Nike brand, which has successfully depicted the hero's journey for decades. In this case, the hero conquers the monster of laziness and apathy.[12] What's interesting here is how Nike paints the consumer as both hero and villain. The inner voice says, "I can't, because I'm too out of shape, too tired, and would rather sleep in." Nike knows that not everyone can relate to a fight against an external adversary, but everyone can relate to a battle against an inner monster. Nike products, from Air Max sneakers to the Apple Watch Nike+, help heroes (customers) emerge triumphant by challenging them to "Just Do It."

GEICO offers another great example. Long before the days of the talking gecko, GEICO—which stands for Government Employees Insurance Company—provided auto insurance to federal government employees. In the 1950s, the company shifted to offer traditional insurance policies to the general public, but it was never a major player in the insurance industry. Then everything changed.

In the 1990s, when Warren Buffett's Berkshire Hathaway conglomerate took over the company, GEICO began to leverage its underdog story to acquire new customers. The insurance company started to offer lower prices to challenge consumers to rethink their insurance-buying habits—"Fifteen minutes could save you 15 percent or more on car insurance!"—without directly mentioning its Goliath competitors, like Allstate and State Farm.[13]

For decades, the traditional insurance model had revolved around agents in local offices. Now, consumers were willing to trade that expensive face-to-face relationship for a better value proposition, which primarily did business via telephone and the internet. This strategy propelled GEICO into a new position of market leadership.

2. RAGS TO RICHES

Everyone loves an underdog story, whether it's against a monster or against life itself. Rags to riches stories begin with a hero who has almost nothing. People don't believe in this hero because the hero doesn't look the part and doesn't have the resources necessary to become one. It's through hard work, ingenuity, or another positive characteristic that the hero overcomes immense odds to rise above.

"The Ugly Duckling" and "Aladdin" are prime examples of this archetype. Beauty products love this story because it allows them to help consumers create riches for themselves (often through transformation). Education, training, and design companies typically follow a similar path.

The Johnnie Walker brand story harkens back to the hardships experienced by its founder.[14] John Walker was born a simple Scottish farm boy, but subsequent generations of Walkers worked hard to turn those humble beginnings into the biggest whisky brand in the world. Walker was a grocer who decided to improve upon the quality and consistency issues of single-malt whisky by creating a blended version, which proved to be both more popular and more consistent in taste. With the advent of the Industrial Revolution, Walker's son used trains to take his whisky to ships, which carried it to the ends of the earth. By the end of the 1920s, Walker's product could be found in 120 countries.

The "Walking Man" logo was created around the turn of the twentieth century to capture the forward motion of the brand and inspire others to keep pushing onward. According to the company, the brand's slogan, "Keep Walking," is "a rallying cry of progress, a joyful expression of optimism, and the best piece of advice you're ever likely to hear."

On an even grander scale, Walmart's story is one of moderate rags to ultimate riches. From its start as Walton's 5&10 Store on the town square in Bentonville, Arkansas, in 1950 to the behemoth it is today, Walmart's brand narrative is rooted deeply in the story of "Mr. Sam" and his goal to offer great value and customer service.[15]

Long before he opened his store, the boy Sam Walton sold milk from the family cow door-to-door. After college and a stint in the military, Walton bought a Ben Franklin store in Newport, Arkansas, with a $20,000 loan from his father-in-law and $5,000 he had saved from his time in the army.[16] He focused on high-volume sales of lower-priced products, portraying his sales strategy as a "crusade for the customer." When he couldn't negotiate an acceptable lease rate for his store, he opened his own.

Over the next sixty-plus years, the Walmart brand became the largest company in the world by revenue, serving 265 million customers per week, and the largest private employer.[17] The no-nonsense persona of Sam Walton lives on in the brand through everything from his promise for great value and customer service to Walmart's rigid requirements of its vendors. Walton famously said once, "There is only one boss: the customer. And he can fire everybody in the company, from the chairman on down, simply by spending his money somewhere else."[18]

3. THE QUEST

The quest is a linear story about progression from point A to point B. The protagonist stumbles across obstacles or challenges that must be overcome to progress the journey (and story). Famous examples include *The Lord of the Rings* and *The Wizard of Oz*. Travel and education brands are all about the journey into the unknown, as are many brands in the customer service and entertainment sectors.

Eyewear company Warby Parker's story is based on achieving a goal and doing a good deed at the same time.[19] One of its founders was in college when he lost a pair of glasses. He spent months with poor vision because cost prohibited him from affording a replacement pair. Another of Warby Parker's founders worked for a nonprofit organization that provided free glasses to people in third-world countries. He understood that the eyewear industry was controlled by a single company that kept prices artificially high. These two people, plus two others, joined forces to rectify the problem of expensive eyewear through a socially conscious company. Even the company's name suggests a journey—it's a combination of Warby Pepper and Zagg Parker, characters from Jack Kerouac literature.

The Warby Parker story is woven throughout every customer touchpoint, whether in-store or online. When buying over the internet, consumers can choose to try up to five frames. Warby Parker builds anticipation by sharing where the glasses were produced, when they shipped, and when they will arrive. The glasses don't come in a hard, black glasses case, like those of other brands; instead, they arrive in a colorful case covered in the work of artists. With every pair, the company includes a microfiber cleaning cloth, which has the company's story printed on it in one hundred words. Through this consistent connection with consumers via a story, Warby Parker has powered its Buy a Pair, Give a Pair model, which has provided over 1 million pairs of glasses to people in underdeveloped countries.[20]

Elsewhere in apparel, the roots of the North Face brand stem from a small mountaineering store in San Francisco that began in the 1960s.[21] The name refers to the side of a mountain that usually has the most unforgiving conditions, which would naturally require the best clothing and gear to tackle. Initially, the store had a reputation for its high-quality products and focus on exploration and conservation. The brand grew from a store name to a line of products when the owners began to make their own apparel and equipment, which focused on innovation and performance. To this day, North Face remains the go-to brand for high-performance apparel, equipment, and footwear, pushing the limits of innovation and design so its customers "never stop exploring."

4. VOYAGE AND RETURN

While this story type is similar to a quest in that it's about going from one place to another, this archetype is more about traversing a mental state. The traveler leaves, gains wisdom, and returns wiser for having undertaken the journey. In a voyage and return, the hero travels beyond the comfort zone into an intimidating or unfamiliar unknown. Then, the hero ultimately succeeds (or escapes) and returns safely home. *Gulliver's Travels* and *Alice in Wonderland* are perfect examples.

Experiential brands about escape or indulgence often tell stories of voyage and return, allowing their users to dive into a completely different world. Harley-Davidson is one such brand. For most people, the name Harley-Davidson evokes images of people who are free and happy. They leave the mundane behind as they ride off on a motorcycle. This perception arose because the brand has successfully created a story of escapism from the everyday routine, job responsibilities, and demographic labels.[22] However, unlike many brands, Harley-Davidson didn't settle on this story from the first day.

Rather, this was a story born of necessity after the company started to lose business to Japanese motorcycle brands in the mid-1980s. Harley-Davidson had quality issues compared to the Japanese companies, and in America, it was associated with biker gangs. Without a massive marketing budget to turn the tide, the company started Harley Owners Group—HOG, which happens to be the company's stock symbol—to connect with customers through affinity and build loyalty. It worked, and when the brand was back on its feet a few years later, it used its repositioning to form new values grounded in freedom, heritage, community, and quality.

Today, Harley-Davidson has a cultlike following of enthusiasts who not only have emotional connections to the brand but physical ones. Most consumers wouldn't get a tattoo of their favorite brand's logo, but Harley-Davidson riders aren't most consumers.

Consider the beer brand Corona. Corona's "Find Your Beach" slogan is more than a tagline.[23] It's part of an underlying story about breaking away to your own personal happy place. When this slogan was first advertised, Corona commercials focused solely on beach scenes. Every scene was relaxing, showing people with their toes in the sand, sometimes sitting in chairs with a tub of icy Corona bottles beside them. Later, commercials highlighted the social aspect of going to the beach with friends. Today, while the beach iconography remains present, the brand invites beer aficionados to discover a personal state of mind that helps them escape the mundane, whether that's a warm, sunny beach or a ski resort in the snowy mountains.

5. COMEDY

The comedic story doesn't follow the modern definition of comedy (i.e., one solely based on humor). It's more Shakespearean, where two parties must face confusion and struggles until they can finally be together. These stories, usually funny, often involve concepts like mistaken identity throughout the chaos.

What does that look like for brands, though? Ace Hardware provides the perfect answer. For Ace, the brand is about helping consumers avoid the misadventures of hardware shopping that are common in other stores. Its brand story, centered around "helpful hardware folks," focuses on providing consumers with the expertise they need to tackle their home improvement projects with confidence.[24]

Another example, Allstate, tells its customers, "You're in Good Hands with Allstate." Allstate also calls itself "The Good Hands People" and uses the visual of cupped hands to tell its story of protection in the face of misfortune. This is an example of a comedy story that focuses on the calamity that will happen if consumers do not trust the brand to protect them.

That story inspired the company's recent creative work in its "Mayhem" campaign, where mayhem personified creates a range of unfortunate scenarios covered by Allstate insurance policies. Scenarios range from being rammed by a driver at a tailgate party to watching a puppy chew up the back seat of a car. The scenarios are funny, and the comedy archetype shines through Allstate's offer to keep consumers safe when mayhem occurs.

6. TRAGEDY

While the other story archetypes we've covered are about successful heroes, this one is not. In tragedy, a character's flaw or suffering proves to be too much to overcome. This is the story without the happy ending: *Julius Caesar*, *Romeo and Juliet*, and *Hamlet* are good examples.

For most brands, tragedy makes for a bad story, but some brands can use it to their advantage. Medical companies, financial planning companies, and public safety entities often use tragedy to tell a story that encourages safer behavior from their target audiences. The tragedy archetype differs from the comedy archetype in that, while both are about using a brand to protect oneself, the stakes are higher in a tragedy. That makes tragedy effective for campaigns like public service announcements.

Sometimes, consumers are torn between whether the risk of not buying the product is greater than its cost. In specific situations, the brand needs to remind people of potentially tragic consequences. This is useful for companies such as the Kidde brand, a maker of fire safety products and related items (and part of the United Technologies family of brands).[25] The origins of the brand trace back to Walter Kidde, who was a pioneer of fire safety in the early 1900s. Today, the peace of mind offered by Kidde safety products is central to the brand.

That concept recently manifested in a Kidde TV campaign called "Technology Saving Lives." The campaign showed three real-life testimonials of people whose lives or the lives of their loved ones were saved by the use of Kidde products. "My son would not be here today," was one such verbatim reference to the potentially tragic consequences that were avoided thanks to Kidde brand products.[26]

7. REBIRTH

Rebirth is the story of change through hardship or enlightenment. In *A Christmas Carol*, Scrooge experienced a rebirth after visits from his ghosts, for example, and *Doctor Who*, one of the most popular cult TV shows, regularly depends on the rebirth of its main character every few seasons. After the rebirth occurs, the person (or brand) reborn experiences the world in a more positive way than before.

The crux of rebirth is that some fundamental component of the past must change. Many categories and brands are in the business of rebirth, including fashion and cosmetics, which communicate the transformative magic of their brands' products.

Rebirth isn't limited to beauty, though. For 120 years, The Salvation Army's brand story has been one of renewal. Its founders originally sought out people in bad situations, like sex workers and people with alcoholism, and offered them help in the name of the Christian church. Today, The Salvation Army "exists to meet human need wherever, whenever, and however we can."[27] The organization provides a wide range of services, including disaster relief assistance, human trafficking prevention, addiction treatment, unemployment assistance, and elderly care, to name a few. Its tagline, "Doing the Most Good," guides the organization to leverage donor support to better the lives of people who have been marginalized or have fallen on hard times so that they may be renewed with hope.

These seven types of stories contain the basic components of all stories told today. Some brands borrow from multiple types at once, while others subvert expectations, but the reason for their adherence to these principles is simple: these are the stories we, as humans, know and understand. To capture the attention of consumers, brands must tell their stories in a format that makes sense to their audiences.

GUIDING PRINCIPLES AND CONSIDERATIONS FOR BRAND STORYTELLING

Brand leaders should consider the following suggestions to get the most from their stories.

1. IDENTIFY YOUR PURPOSE

As detailed in chapter 4, on brand positioning, consumers are more interested than ever in the companies behind products. As such, it's not surprising that an increasing number of companies are choosing to position their brands around their unique purposes—their "why." Examples include Patagonia, PATOS, TOMS Shoes, and even B2B players like SAP. In each of these cases, the brand's purpose is arguably the most meaningful point of difference from the competition. Frequently, that purpose is one of the primary reasons customers purchase from that brand.

According to Carla Johnson, author and keynote speaker, "Brands need to identify their true, underlying story and articulate what makes them different in the world. Ideally, this difference—and the resulting story—is purposed-based. That's the most powerful foundation for a brand story."[28]

Even if a brand is not positioned around a purpose, the "why" can still be a great source for a compelling brand story. A tale about why a founder chose to launch a company is one such example, as is one about how a company lives in accordance with its values. These stories can easily fit any of the archetypes listed in this chapter. According to James Dowd in his presentation *The Science of Story*, "There's always a story behind a brand, whether it's in the product line or the company value system. It's just waiting to be told."[29] The more relevant and relatable the purpose, the more powerfully its story can affect the brand.[30]

2. CONSIDER YOUR ORIGIN

Closely related to purpose is a company's origin or roots. The manner in which it was founded can often provide great fodder for a brand story.

Jim Beam has been a family tradition since 1795. Despite several changes in ownership over multiple generations, its brand still leans heavily on the great story it has to tell about its founding and "America's native spirit." This applies to not only the Jim Beam brand but to all of the company's spirits. According to former Beam Suntory chief marketing officer, Rebecca Messina, "All of our brands have a great heritage and an incredible story to tell. When I visit our distilleries and speak with the family members of our brands' founders, I can listen to them for hours. Part of my job is to make those stories relevant and accessible to the consumers who purchase our brands."[31]

Another example of a company that draws its story from its roots is the quick-service restaurant Culver's. This brand's origin comes through brilliantly in the following carefully crafted story.

> The Culver's family is proud to call Sauk City, Wisconsin, home. This is where the Culver family opened their first restaurant, and where right up the road you'll find Culver's home office, along with a passion for great food that runs as deep as the beautiful Wisconsin River. This is a place connected to the farms that produce the dairy and grow the food that has made Culver's a family favorite nationwide. It's a small town where people use words like "Please" and "Thank you" and "It's my pleasure." Come see where your food comes from.

Importantly, Culver's vice president of marketing, Julie Fussner, points out how this story has been an inspiration for brand strategy and positioning. "This story plays heavily into our brand positioning: Welcome to Delicious. I call it our brand idea. Some people refer to it as a tagline—but it's not—it's much more than that. I think it will be around forever."[32]

3. UNDERSTAND YOUR AUDIENCE

We also covered the concept of target audiences in chapter 4, which is relevant again here. One of the key points of emphasis was that customers—although clearly a critical target audience to address—are typically not the only stakeholders of a brand. As with positioning, it is important to determine who the most important audiences are for a brand story. And, as with positioning, that usually means more than one audience.

It's easy to imagine how different audiences will gravitate to different themes, tones of voice, and other communication aspects of a story. It's another thing to account for different sets of expectations and create a brand story that pleases all of them. Regardless of which direction the story goes, it must remain consistent for audiences of any category to take it seriously.[33]

4. CREATE CONSISTENT AUTHENTICITY

An authentic story helps suspicious consumers relax, which is the first step toward earning their trust.[34] The seven story archetypes should not suggest that storytelling can be a mechanical or formulaic process. On the contrary, to approach story development in this way is a recipe for failure. Rather than identify a successful story that worked for someone else—and therefore contribute to brand monotony—allow your own voice to shine through. Overpolished, professional speech gets lost in the crowd, but a story that comes from the heart (and remains consistent across channels and audiences) piques curiosity.[35]

5. BRING OUTSIDERS INTO THE FOLD

Don't be afraid to co-create or even outsource the identity of your brand story. Inspiration for great brand stories can come from anywhere, including outside company walls. Customer testimonials and actual customer service examples are great sources for brand stories. These real-life tales also represent one of the best ways brands can avoid coming off as self-serving in their storytelling.

Here again, Carla Johnson offers great advice: "Companies are not always able to objectively identify what makes them different and special. I encourage them to turn to external sources for inspiration. It could be customers, vendor partners, industry analysts—essentially anyone who sees and experiences your brand from the outside. Very often, they bring powerful insights that would never have been surfaced internally."[36]

In other words, let audience members define the story on their own, and in the ways that are most personal and relevant to them. Singtel, a Singapore telecom company, took this concept and ran far beyond where most brands go. The company asked its Twitter followers to talk about times when fast network speeds are most useful, then turned the best suggestions into comedic skits, even bringing in Singaporean comedy icon Hossan Leong.

The merit of turning to outside sources for inspiration is based on more than just instinct. Headstream's research backs it up. According to Headstream's study, 57 percent of consumers "love" stories based on true events that happened to real people.[37]

6. IT'S NOT ABOUT THE BRAND (UNTIL IT IS)

This final guiding principle is admittedly somewhat paradoxical. However, it is important to keep in mind. Companies clearly need to avoid the temptation to make the brand story all about themselves, but they must also remember the brand story is ultimately meant to sell the brand. Balancing the conflict between entertainment and sales is a delicate balancing act that requires careful management during the creation of the brand story. Dowd's presentation reminds brands not to make themselves the heroes of their own stories. The customers are the true heroes—but they couldn't be the heroes they are without the brands by their side.[38]

WHAT TO DO ONCE THE STORY HAS BEEN CRAFTED

Crafting the brand story is only half the battle, especially in today's media-rich activation environment. Once the story is solidified, pay close attention to its dissemination to achieve maximum impact. Let's quickly review some of the most obvious methods, means, and platforms for brand story distribution.

Simply posting story-related assets on a blog is not enough. To get the message to the audience, brand marketers must follow a deliberate strategy that includes social media posts, email campaigns, traditional media placement, and other common marketing strategies. Remember, every channel has a different blend of audiences, so adjust the dissemination strategy with that in mind.[39] Don't discount paid media during this process. Although consumers distrust the direct word of brands in general, they prefer to control their own story consumption, which means brands should place their stories in convenient locations for audiences to view.

Give special attention to the role video plays in bringing a great brand story to life. Video marketing has gained popularity in recent years, as Headstream's research verifies. This is unsurprising, given the emotional nature of stories and the dramatically increased potency of audiovisual content. Apple, Dove, and Weight Watchers are just a few brands that have experienced tremendous success while communicating their stories through video.

Treat the delivery of the story with as much care as its creation. By identifying the presence of different target audiences on different channels, then executing a multiplatform approach to disseminate the message, brands can ensure their stories receive the attention they deserve.

TELL A STORY FOR THE AGES

Brand stories have gained popularity in recent years, both as a strategic asset and an activation tool. Stories have always been powerful, so the transition of the art of storytelling into the world of business has been a natural evolution. However, marketers need to understand exactly what comprises a brand story and what makes it different from other strategic and creative components of their brand.

The brand story is the narrative designed to evoke positive emotions about the brand within the target audience. These stories are woven into the fiber of the brand's being, often tracing back to the founding of the company. With such a rich history, a story can enjoy a very long shelf life in terms of relevance and appeal.

In this way, brand stories are quite different from advertisements and campaigns. Though the story might inspire a campaign, a great story will outlive nearly any campaign the company develops. Unlike an advertising campaign, which inevitably runs its course, brand stories have staying power. Brand stories can even outlast brand positioning, which can lose relevance as consumer needs, attitudes, and preferences shift over time.

Brand stories do share one common characteristic with positioning, advertising, and other aspects of branding, however: their ultimate objective is to create meaningful differentiation for the brand. As important as it is to be authentic, selfless, and entertaining (without directly selling), the brand story remains a brand strategy tool to help marketers drive a competitive advantage.

PART 3

UNIQUE NUANCES AND SPECIAL CONSIDERATIONS

Chapter 9

———

Brands in an Era of Digital Activation

With the mobile industry evolving rapidly, Vodafone needed to update its brand positioning. So in October 2017, the telecom giant announced big news: after nine years, Vodaphone would leave "Power to You" behind and focus on the capabilities of today's (and tomorrow's) new technologies. This new positioning was part of Vodafone's global rebranding exercise across thirty-six countries. It was designed to emphasize Vodafone's confidence that technological advances and digital services would have a positive effect on societal transformation and quality of life in the years ahead.

Vodafone's new brand positioning strategy and associated marketing campaigns arose from extensive research, including surveys of more than thirty thousand people in seventeen countries.[1] Market research revealed that, despite multiple global threats, respondents in all age groups believed that "their own living standards, and those of children, will have improved 20 years from now" and that "technology innovation will have the most positive influence on the future over the next 20 years."[2] Specifically, respondents believed that education and entertainment would be more immersive using virtual, augmented, and mixed reality technologies, which would in turn create demand for better, more reliable connectivity.

As a telecom brand, Vodafone believed it needed to address these evolving views in its communications. So its new brand positioning based itself in optimism about the future.[3] This new direction distinctly positioned the brand as modern and inspiring. Vodafone's new tagline became: "The future is exciting. Ready?"

Vodafone executed a brand campaign across all communication channels and touchpoints, including innovative online formats and digital screens. The company embraced digital marketing, but, more specifically, it embraced targeted, personalized content developed via internal and external sources.[4]

"As consumers evolve from the era of the internet to digital, mobile to convergence, Vodafone is evolving from being just a telecom service provider to a total communication solutions partner," said Siddharth Banerjee, executive vice president of marketing for Vodafone India. "As a part of this evolution, Vodafone's aim is to help customers and communities adapt, navigate, and prosper from the remarkable new trends reshaping the world."[5]

Vodafone's new multimedia marketing campaign utilized simple human stories of embracing technology through the eyes of its now-famous "common man" brand ambassadors, Asha and Bala. The two elderly characters represent people without much experience using mobile services. Throughout Vodafone's marketing campaigns, this couple learns to understand and use technology in simple, relatable ways, traveling the world while demonstrating to others like them how easy (and useful) technology can be.[6] The campaign also introduced Vodafone's Internet of Things technology to its Indian customer base with a simple use case scenario. In some ads, Bala demonstrates how to use the service to monitor his blood sugar to see when he can indulge his sweet tooth.

As part of its rebranding, Vodafone issued newly designed business cards in digital formats. This allowed the entire global Vodafone workforce to use the new cards on the rebrand's launch day, an undertaking that would have taken months using physical cards. "Our digital identity is today as important as our physical one, so it's imperative to be able to share and store contact information that's accessible and sendable anywhere in the world," said Joud Adada, Vodafone's head of cognitive procurement.[7]

Vodafone's successful digital rebrand empowered the company to take a leading stance in an increasingly online world. And as the line between digital and physical continues to blur, more brands should take notes on Vodafone's repositioning to think about where they fit in a tech-centric society.

DIGITAL LANDSCAPE DEFINED

Before we go further, it's important to note that this chapter is not intended to cover the latest and greatest tactics in the world of digital brand activation, nor is it meant to cover best practices of specific digital channels, vehicles, and touchpoints. Others have written entire books on these topics, and every modern-day marketing conference focuses on digital tactics. Instead, this chapter will focus on the critical role brand strategy (especially brand positioning) should play in shaping digital strategy and execution—a topic that is not covered nearly to the extent it should be elsewhere. Even savvy, disciplined marketers who tend to lead with brand strategy in the analog world sometimes abandon their brand-first mindset when they move to digital activation.

It may help to begin by defining what we mean by the "digital landscape." The application of digital technology to the world of marketing activation introduced an entirely new set of channels, touchpoints, and experiences for brands. In addition to traditional and physical touchpoints—such as radio and TV advertising, direct mail, in-store experiences, and call centers—we now have digital touchpoints, like online ads, social media, newsletters, email marketing, and much, much more. (See figure 9.1.) Today, the number, magnitude, and level of influence of these digital touchpoints are at least as great as (if not greater than) those in the physical world.

Figure 9.1
Touchpoints: Digital & Physical

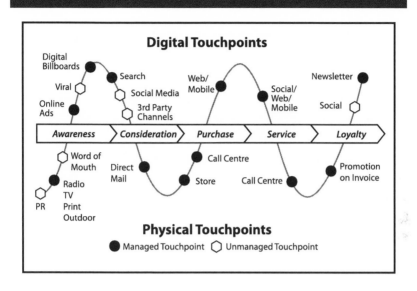

There are two important points to note about the digital landscape and its impact on brand activation. First, as illustrated in figure 9.1, it is pervasive throughout the entire purchase funnel. Digital touchpoints help establish awareness and consideration just as much as they facilitate purchases and engender loyalty. It's safe to say that today, for many businesses, the path to purchase is as much digital as it is physical.

The second point is that the lines between analog and digital activation are beginning to blur in several important ways. For starters, physical and digital touchpoints are increasingly intertwined in the customer experience. Consider customers who walk through the aisles of a brick-and-mortar store, read the retailer's point-of-sale material, and simultaneously compare prices and check reviews on their mobile phones. Additionally, as we mentioned earlier and will expand on later, customers do not delineate between physical and digital touchpoints the way marketers do. To customers, the brand experience is fluid—and the medium through which the brand delivers the experience is irrelevant.

NAVIGATING THE ROCKY TERRAIN OF THE DIGITAL LANDSCAPE

To be clear: digital activation may be the single greatest, most positive change since the dawn of brands. The challenges that follow are not meant to imply that digital has had a negative impact on brands, but rather that there are obstacles regarding its use that marketers must overcome. Properly executed, digital activation helps marketers avoid denigrating valuable brand equity and perpetuating brand monotony.

The first challenge pertains to the pervasiveness of digital activation. Given the inherent breadth and reach of digital, it's easy for a brand's message to become diluted and fragmented as it spreads across different channels on numerous occasions over long periods of time. While the same can be true in the analog world, the ubiquity, reach, and potentially viral nature of digital touchpoints exacerbates this phenomenon.

Digital activation also poses challenges of control, as much of the activity extends beyond marketers' reach. As illustrated in figure 9.1, many of the touchpoints of the digital landscape are unmanaged, meaning customers and other external influencers control the message and determine the ultimate impact of the activation. Interestingly, this is especially true for touchpoints near the top of the purchase funnel (in awareness and consideration). That means the touchpoints that are perhaps most critical in terms of forming perceptions and shaping preference (i.e., building brand equity) are the ones marketers have the least ability to dictate.

Perhaps the most serious challenge to digital activation is also the one marketers have the greatest ability to address. Digital activation—to a far greater extent than traditional brand activation—typically lacks the strategic underpinning and brand alignment that are critical for both short-term and long-term success. Not surprisingly, spending so much time and effort on selection of optimal digital channels and creative execution—without equal consideration of the underlying brand strategy—can have dire consequences.

This is neither anecdotal experience nor conjecture; market research backs up the claim.[8] According to a 2016 study from the brandgym, 91 percent of marketing directors agree that "the key to effective digital marketing is clear brand positioning." That's the good news. However, the survey also revealed that 62 percent of marketing directors feel that "with the focus on digital/social marketing, brand strategy gets overlooked." (See figure 9.2.)

Figure 9.2
Link Between Brand and Digital Strategy

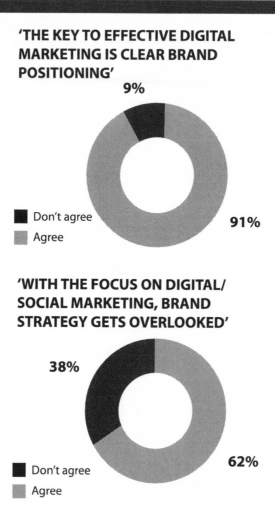

'THE KEY TO EFFECTIVE DIGITAL
MARKETING IS CLEAR BRAND
POSITIONING'

9%

■ Don't agree
▨ Agree

91%

'WITH THE FOCUS ON DIGITAL/
SOCIAL MARKETING, BRAND
STRATEGY GETS OVERLOOKED'

38%

■ Don't agree
▨ Agree

62%

Source: Brandgym

As was the case when we discussed the broader challenges of brand strategy, the solution to developing more brand-centric digital activation requires changes in both mindset and frameworks. The next two sections will detail both issues. We will cover how marketers should expand their philosophies in digital activation and modify some of the basic brand strategy frameworks behind their current approaches.

FORGING A NEW DIGITAL PATH

As with any meaningful, transformational change, forging a new digital path begins with a shift in mindset. For marketers to begin to think more strategically about the alignment of digital activation and brand strategy, they must understand the role of digital in the broader marketing mix. According to Jeff Mancini, chief strategy officer at Interbrand, "There is no visible digital strategy that isn't integrated into your larger brand and business strategy."[9]

This required shift in mindset consists of three components.

1. STRATEGY BEFORE TACTICS

Digital activation, like anything else pertaining to brand activation, begins with sound strategy. More specifically, it starts with brand positioning. Digital activation should not only be consistent with positioning but inspired by it.

"Smart marketers recognize the importance of [brand strategy], and before 140 characters are tweeted, status updates are posted, live videos are broadcast, or content is created, they begin with their brand positioning," said Darcy Schuller, chief digital marketing and brand strategist at Suvonni. "Brand positioning is at the heart of any solid brand strategy and should be the guiding element for shaping the experiences that your customers have with your brand. This is even more important in the digital space, where the opportunity for brands and audiences to engage is at the forefront."[10]

While using brand strategy to guide digital activation seems like a principle any brand marketer would embrace and follow, it is surprising how often this is not the case—even with marketers who are very strategic with other components of the marketing mix. And even when they are strategic in their approach to digital, it tends to be more from a broader business perspective, as opposed to *brand* strategy.

To be fair, this is not to suggest that driving short-term, tangible business results is not important, nor that it is less important than establishing and consistently reinforcing long-term brand equity. Rather, digital activation needs to accomplish both, not one at the expense of the other. Recent thinking in this area suggests that marketers should lean slightly more to the long-term side (about a 60:40 ratio) for peak effectiveness.[11] Marketers don't have to choose: they simply have to establish a strong base of branding upon which they can pursue their more immediate goals.

2. LEVERAGE BRAND POSITIONING AS THE PRIMARY UNIFIER

Another required mindset shift lies in the need to embrace a more holistic, unified approach to digital activation. The inherently disparate nature of digital marketing—from websites and apps to social media and video—makes it easy for brands to experience dilution and fragmentation. To rise above, marketers must think beyond the channel.

"Think of the total online consumer experience, leveraging a wide range of digital tools as is relevant to your brand and resources," said Danyl Bosomworth, cofounder of Smart Insights. "These are real touchpoints including websites, apps, social media channels, from online ads to billboards, broadcast, retail, and real estate. Your customer does not see a difference in the channel; building a seamless experience of your brand that fits the audience's new reality is now essential."[12]

Here again, brand positioning can serve as the guide that unifies strategic planning, messaging, and tone that might be otherwise disjointed (if not outright contradictory). As with any other component of the marketing mix, brand positioning should serve as a screen for digital activity. When a tactic or message is not consistent with the positioning, that component should be immediately rejected or, at a minimum, reconsidered.

3. INVEST IN BUILDING LONG-TERM EQUITY

Perhaps the most important mindset shift pertains to marketers' expectations of what digital can and should accomplish, both in near-term and long-term horizons. The immediacy and instant gratification that typically characterize the digital world, along with the ease and accuracy of online measurement, can prompt marketers to regard digital activations solely as transaction drivers. However, it's also important to think about long-term brand equity creation in digital activation. Digital isn't about next week: it's about how consumers perceive the brand's presence in the long run, both in the online world and outside it.[13]

Much of the potential of digital as a long-term equity builder lies in its inherent ability to forge deeper, more meaningful relationships with consumers. Brands can end their investments in digital activation with likes on Facebook, but by going deeper with those online relationships through the lens of brand positioning, they can take those relationships a step further.

Great digital strategies turn short-term opportunities into the building blocks of bigger relationships. Transactions are important, but when those transactions feel consistent with the brand positioning, the brand becomes more distinct in the eyes of the consumer. The greater the distinction, the more likely that consumer will choose to engage with the same brand at the next opportunity.

ADJUSTING FRAMEWORKS TO FIT THE MINDSET

With the mindset of using brand positioning to guide digital activation established, we next turn our attention to the basic brand strategy frameworks discussed earlier in this book. Following are the specific components of brand strategy that deserve reexamination in light of digital activation.

1. PROMISE

As mentioned in chapter 4, a brand promise can center on a what, how, why, or who. Regardless of the type selected, digital activation represents an opportunity to deliver on the promise in a way that would not be possible in an analog environment. Even when digital is not the primary delivery vehicle of the brand promise, whatever gets delivered must remain consistent with the essence of that promise.

According to Tim Murphy, senior vice president of digital marketing at Chubb, "Digital platforms come and go...we have Pinterest, Instagram, Snapchat, and so on. But at the end of the day, it's not about the platform. The challenge is to solidify what you know about your brand promise, and then deliver relevant content and social interactions that are consistent with it."[14]

Take Tito's Handmade Vodka, for example. Here is a brand all about authenticity. Its founder, Bert "Tito" Beveridge loves keeping the Austin, Texas-based sensation real. His philosophy—to make products both exceptional and accessible—hasn't changed since he founded the company in 1995. Highlighting the handcrafted nature of the product, Tito's message has remained consistent and rooted in authenticity.

Beveridge built his brand via word-of-mouth marketing by pounding the pavement and telling his stories. Gradually, the authenticity of those efforts transitioned into social media, but the basic promise remained the same in the digital arena. Tito's never viewed social media as another tool in the marketing repertoire. Instead, the brand uses social channels to give customers an opportunity to engage. That authentic personality stretches across all promotional platforms at every interaction, building credibility and showing customers how trustworthy the Tito's brand is.[15]

Tito's boosts its authentic feel by sharing user-generated content created by real customers on the company website. The brand's dog-centric blog, *Vodka for Dog People*, was created to rescue and protect stray animals around its rural Austin distillery. Tito's fundraises for Emancipet, a local animal clinic, and sells pet-related items to further its mission of animal welfare. The brand found a way to blend its authentic roots with a "why" that resonates with its audience and made it relevant across digital channels; customers continue to reward the company with their business.

2. PERSONA

Every brand needs a clearly defined persona, and this brand persona should be reflected consistently across all digital touchpoints—just as the persona is presented in physical environments. Persona shapes every brand component from visual identity (e.g., logo) to tone of voice (e.g., messaging), all of which are present in digital activation.

Colonel Sanders's image has been synonymous with KFC since the franchise first opened more than sixty years ago. After founder Harland Sanders died in 1980, it seemed like no one else could fill his shoes. He was a marketing genius who created an effective persona—and that persona lived on.

KFC recently embarked on a brand refresh to address a slight loss of relevance in the market. The company's brand positioning is grounded in its quirky founder and all the things he did to make the brand great, so KFC returned to those roots. Today, the Colonel's values ooze through every touchpoint, from the brand voice (including its heavy accent) to the customer experience in the restaurants. The decision to make the Colonel a foundation of the brand's marketing was based on his larger-than-life, slightly goofy personality, and it worked.

Social media is an essential part of KFC's overall strategy. The fast-food giant is always looking for new ways to engage its audience on platforms where its fans are most passionate. The Colonel's reintroduction to KFC's advertising in 2015 included a two-day round trip from the chain's hometown in Louisville, Kentucky, to its iconic Big Chicken restaurant in Marietta, Georgia, to promote new menu flavors. KFC enlisted two Instagram influencers to chronicle and compare modern-day GPS navigation technology to a cassette tape recording of the Colonel himself giving overly detailed directions, telling witty stories, and initiating amusing singalongs.[16] Cassette tapes might be decades old, but KFC drove home its commitment to do things the Colonel's way: "the hard way." When it comes to brand personas, it doesn't get much better than KFC, and it doesn't become diluted in the brand's digital activation.

3. PRODUCT OR SERVICE OFFERING

No conversation about the impact of digital on brands would be complete without addressing the product and service offering. Here, the question to ask is "How can digital technology impact a brand's core offering?"

The answer splits into at least two paths. Digital can enhance a brand's products and services by providing better options for customization of existing offerings. Even more impressively, however, digital can be used to deliver new, incremental product and service revenue streams not easily achieved in the analog world. Digital has an inherent ability to change the dynamics of space and time for brands, completely redefining the concept of location.

For more than ninety years, Ace Hardware has been known as the "place with the helpful hardware folks" in neighborhoods across the United States. Ace's brand promise is to deliver helpful, neighborly service to every customer, every time. Realizing the challenges of providing that brand promise of friendly service with a finite number of retail stores,

Ace effectively redefined the term "neighborhood" while extending the reach of its product and service offerings.

This is where The Grommet—an online marketplace and product discovery platform in Somerville, Massachusetts—came into play. Ace acquired a majority share in The Grommet in 2017, extending its virtual neighborhood to address the needs of consumers everywhere. The Grommet is more than an e-commerce site for products created by entrepreneurs: it's a discovery platform that connects inventors with customers who need new solutions to old problems.

"The Grommet has often been called a 'general store for innovation,' and Ace is a trusted destination for the goods and services homeowners need to take care of their homes," said Jules Pieri, cofounder of The Grommet. "That is a powerful combination. Both companies have a deep heritage of helping local businesses thrive, so our values are uncannily compatible. And how fitting is it that our company is named after a humble piece of hardware? There is some destiny at work here."[17] Ace doesn't just want to sell; it wants to help, and its partnership with The Grommet in the digital arena is a testament to that neighborly spirit.[18]

4. PERSONALIZED EXPERIENCE

Covered in detail in chapter 6, customer experience is the sum total of all brand touchpoints that impact key stakeholders. Today, for many brands, these touchpoints are increasingly digital.

Seattle-based cruise line Holland America recently repositioned its brand to be about the way in which travel can change the world by breaking down barriers and building a sense of community among travelers. Jarvis Bowers, vice president of digital marketing for Holland America, points out how this positioning is brought to life in the digital format. "Everything from our website visuals to our online content reinforces the captivating experience of travel. We don't just focus on the ocean, mountains, and other beautiful scenery. We demonstrate how—through exposure to immersive and enlightening experiences—travel can be truly transformative."[19]

One of the keys to great experiences—as referenced in chapter 6—is personalization. Digital technology has created an unprecedented ability to personalize brand experiences. Personalizing the experience is highly dependent on a company's ability to up its game relative to generating meaningful insights and deepening customer intimacy. As Bowers notes, "The companies who excel at delivering superior, personalized customer experiences are the ones that have the greatest sense of who they truly serve."

When it comes to personalization in the digital arena, results are somewhat mixed. As shown in figure 9.3, it appears marketers in both B2B and B2C companies are achieving at least some degree of personalization in the more easily personalized digital venues (e.g., email and, to a lesser extent, websites).[20] However, when it comes to a web applications and mobile apps, there is still much room for improvement.

Figure 9.3
Personalization in Digital Activation

**Q: In which of the following digital channels
are you using personalization?**

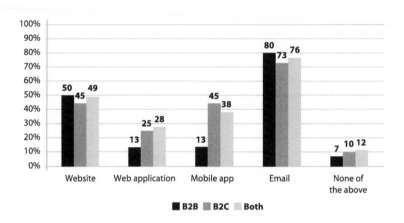

Source: Evergage & Researchscape International

Digital activation has the potential to positively and dramatically impact the customer experience more than any other aspect of a brand. Technologies and tools—such as video, virtual reality, augmented reality, live interactions, and more—have completely redefined the experience for many brands already. However, as with any other brand aspect, these touchpoints should be consistent with—and inspired by—the brand positioning.

Italian automaker Piaggio clearly understands the fashionista target audience of its Vespa scooter, and the company tailors the customer experience accordingly. A Vespa is more than a vehicle: it's a fashion accessory, a lifestyle statement, and a mode of transportation in one. These scooters have been a symbol of independence among young people of every generation. The ability of the scooters to reflect the personality of the riders, both through association with the brand and through the experience of riding one, is critical to the Vespa brand. For decades, product customization has been an essential centerpiece of Vespa's brand story, which fits nicely into the digital trend of customization happening in the broader fashion world.[21]

Piaggio has expanded its connection with young audiences through its digital activations. To renew its brand heritage, Vespa launched an augmented reality campaign in WIRED magazine that enabled users to customize, test drive, and share their personal scooter through a method that leapt off the page. The test drive feature seamlessly wove together the physical world with the AR dimension. Other wildly successful augmented reality experiments, like Snapchat and Pokémon GO, highlight the ability of AR to create immersive, engaging experiences for audiences of Millennials and members of Generation Z.

5. COMMUNICATIONS AND MESSAGING

Brand communicators regularly struggle to hit the right audience with the right message through the right medium at the right time. This is every bit as true in digital media as it is in analog. By overlaying typical purchase funnel dynamics, we can see this point more clearly.

In digital, as in all types of activation, the content of communication and the specific medium chosen should make sense with the target audience's place in the funnel. Once again, the messaging should remain consistent with the brand positioning no matter what the objectives of the activation might be.

Zendesk, which provides customer support software and cloud services, isn't in the sexiest line of work. It was, however, one of the first companies to dismiss the notion that customer service must be boring, difficult, and complicated. Part of Zendesk's brand promise says, "We do things elegantly. We do things in a sophisticated way."[22] Zendesk prides itself on its human, personable relationships with customers, as well as its charm, which shines through the brand's digital video campaigns.

When Zendesk designed its video strategy, it considered not only the purchase funnel and medium but also its opportunities to infuse its unique brand positioning into each video it created. At the top of the funnel, Zendesk uses fun, lighthearted videos to explain what it does and establish the company as a no-nonsense partner with great service. By the time prospects are in the middle stages, the videos begin to focus on people-to-people connections and the value of those relationships. Finally, Zendesk's bottom-of-the-funnel videos assure customers that Zendesk will provide better service than anyone else in the business, going into detail about their great service and convincing customers to make the purchase.

In every brand activation tactic, the positioning should shine through. Without it, even the best digital activations suffer from common issues that lead to brand monotony. When the positioning is strong and consistently reinforced, however, the brand stands out—both online and offline.

EMPOWERING EMPLOYEES TO BE DIGITAL AMBASSADORS

Chapter 12 will address employee brand engagement more broadly, but here we will focus on the topic as it relates to digital. Digital activation has narrowed the gap between employees and customers. Company blogs, employee Twitter feeds, interactions with brands on social media, and other touchpoints make it easy for employees to weigh in on brand communications. Of course, depending on how those communications transpire, they can have either positive or negative effects on a brand.

Consistent with the rest of this chapter, the lesson is obvious: those employee interactions should keep the brand's key messaging in mind. "Everything you post, share, write, tweet, reply, etc. on social media should be purposeful and in alignment with your brand positioning," said Schuller at Suvonni. "More importantly, it should always be of value to your audience."[23]

Today, it isn't just a select group of PR employees who represent the company externally. As Rose Johnstone wrote for Innovation Enterprise, "Not only does digital marketing and the digital 'experience' extend far further than the marketing team, but everyone in the company should be aware of the brand message and should interact with customers accordingly."[24]

Many companies have taken this lesson to heart. Below are a few ways in which companies have taken steps with their employees to ensure brand consistency in the digital realm.

CONTENT DEVELOPMENT

Content should always be relevant and useful to its intended audience. It should also help build relationships with customers and drive tangible business results. However, content should also consistently reinforce the brand positioning and build long-term equity. It is alarming how many marketers think little (if at all) about brand positioning as they develop their content strategy and editorial calendar. Great content connects the wants of the customers, the company's mission, and the brand's purpose together in a clean, useful way. Unfortunately, many companies neglect to consider that third component.

Red Bull, however, is an exception to the rule. According to Tessa Barrera, former global head of social media for Red Bull, "The idea was always to find a way to have the conversation about the brand, and the brand to enable it, rather than the top down approach of the brand publishing a message to reach its fans. Red Bull does not focus on what it sells; it focuses on who it is: a company that brings excitement to its advocates."[25]

In other words, Red Bull's content serves both the customer and the brand's positioning.

SOCIAL MEDIA

Kelly Services is a staffing agency that has been around for more than seventy years. Kelly markets to two different customer groups: prospects and customers, and employees and candidates. To reach both groups,

Kelly Services adopted a social media strategy that met the challenges of both modern marketing and modern recruiting.

To address this dual-audience objective, Kelly Services uses EveryoneSocial, a social selling and employee advocacy platform for marketing, sales, and HR. With EveryoneSocial in place, Kelly Services employees can log in to the application each morning and read relevant company and industry content as if it were in a magazine. Employees can also add their own streams, share interesting pieces on social media accounts, and track the engagement of each post via reporting tools.

This focus on employees helped Kelly Services keep social media activity related to its brand on-message and consistent with its positioning. Over a two-year period, Kelly saw a 1,000 percent increase in social reach and a 1,150 percent increase in daily web traffic from social media channels.[26]

CUSTOMER SERVICE

Digital activation can do more than convince people to buy a brand; it can help solidify a brand as a top provider of customer service.

Wistia, an analytics and hosting platform, provides how-to videos and personal appreciation notes to its customers online. People might glance over a long paragraph of text, even if that text holds the answers to their questions, but they will pay close attention to a video from a personable staff member. Wistia leverages its brand positioning as an easy-to-use, helpful digital provider to guide customers through their online issues. Customers who might be turned off by other providers that use traditional help systems, like FAQs, appreciate the way Wistia's videos explain difficult concepts in easy terms with visual guidance from real employees.

In the age of social media, employees can no longer hide behind the brand name. Modern consumers see every company representative as the voice of the company, even if those representatives have nothing to do with marketing or PR. Employees don't need to delete their social media profiles, but they do need to understand how their online presence can help or harm the brands of their employers. Companies, too, should understand not only how to prevent employees from inadvertently tarnishing their brands' reputation online, but how to leverage the knowledge and personalities of their employees to more effectively connect with their audiences.

DRIVING DIGITAL FOR THE LONG HAUL

Chapter 13 will address the broader role of measurement in brand strategy and effective brand management. Here, we will briefly touch on the role of measurement specifically with regard to digital activity. As with the other content in this chapter, it will represent only the tip of the iceberg relative to the vast and expansive topic of digital brand measurement.

It is encouraging to see continuing calls for proof that digital activation does more than drive short-term business results. Followers, clicks, shares, and comments are a necessary (but insufficient) outcome of digital activation. According to Peter Minnium, president of market research company Ipsos, "It's more critical than ever for all parties in the ecosystem to offer definitive proof of digital's effectiveness as a brand-building medium."[27]

At the risk of oversimplification, there are three types of metrics in digital media. (See figure 9.4.) Activity metrics, as the name implies, are metrics that measure consumers' activity online. They include things like page views, clicks, conversions, etc. This type is by far the most frequently used and easily obtained digital measurement. These also tend to be the least meaningful in terms of assessing digital's impact on long-term brand equity.

Figure 9.4
Types of Digital Metrics

Metric Type	**Activity**
Description	Pertains to the type and frequency of specific digital actions consumers take relative to a brand
Examples	• Website visits • Page views • Clicks • Shares

Metric Type	**Brand Equity**
Description	Pertains to the impact of digital activity on consumers' attitudes and perceptions of a brand
Examples	• Preference • Consideration • Purchase intent • Attribute ratings

Metric Type	**Business Outcomes**
Description	Pertains to the effectiveness digital activity has on the business performance of a brand
Examples	• Customer acquisition • Purchase • Loyalty • Share of wallet

On the other end of the spectrum are business outcome metrics. These measurements gauge the effectiveness of digital activity on actual business performance and can include things like incremental sales, changes in market share, and (when combined with spending) return on investment. Between these two types are equity metrics, which assess the impact of digital activity on things like brand perceptions, associations, and favorability. This category of metrics is the least prevalent today, but it is perhaps the most important when it comes to ensuring digital activity leads to building long-term equity, differentiation, and sustainable competitive advantage.

Fortunately, marketers are taking steps in the right direction. The Association of National Advertisers, the Interactive Advertising Bureau, and the American Association of Advertising Agencies are collaborating on the Making Measurement Make Sense initiative. The charter of this initiative is to identify clear, standards-based metrics for interactive advertising comparable to those in legacy media. This will empower brands to measure the effects of their digital activations on their long-term branding. It's a real first step toward validating the effectiveness of digital activation as an approach to brand-building (as opposed to only driving transactions), but much work still lies ahead.

One of the most important areas to measure is brand lift. Brand lift refers to the increase in interaction with a brand as a result of an ad campaign. Although these interactions vary by brand and campaign, they typically cover the perception-related metrics that comprise the AIDA funnel: awareness, interest, and desire. (See figure 9.5.)

Figure 9.5
Brand Lift Metrics

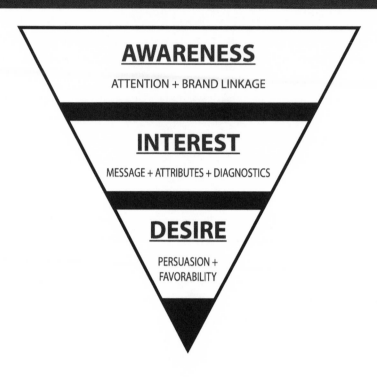

Source: "The Definitive Guide to Digital Brand Lift,"
Marketing Land

Here, it is important to understand and distinguish between metrics that measure the effectiveness of a specific digital campaign (e.g., behaviors and transactions) and those that measure the impact of the campaign on key *brand attributes*. While both are important, the latter merits more attention, as it represents the enduring impact (or lack thereof) of digital activity on the long-term viability of the brand. These metrics also help marketers understand the extent to which digital activation establishes meaningful differentiation for their brands. As Peter Drucker noted, "Long-term results cannot be achieved by piling short-term results on top of short-term results."

One example of measured brand lift comes from Kantar Millward Brown's Brand Lift Insights solution. This tool evaluates all digital advertising formats, including online, mobile, tablet, and social media platforms. Importantly, the tool goes beyond merely assessing campaign performance through metrics like exposures and format effectiveness. It also measures changes in attitudes and perceptions, as well as associations important to the brand positioning that result from the campaign. These kinds of measurements enable brand managers to assess the impact of their digital activities on long-term brand equity—not just short-term market results.

As Minnium from Ipsos noted, "Bringing the same metrics used to measure and optimize advertising effectiveness in the analog world to the digital one is a valuable starting point to strengthen brand marketer trust in digital advertising." The better the measurements become, the more equipped brands will be to gauge the effectiveness of their long-term strategies.

DIGITAL WITH A PURPOSE

Lack of brand-centric strategic intent and purposeful direction have allowed digital activation to contribute to the increasing problem of brand monotony. The good news is that, with the right mindset and tools, digital activation has the potential to play a key role in solving the problem it partially contributed to.

To do so, marketers must shift their mindset to put strategy before tactics and consider how brand positioning should inform every digital campaign across both short-term and long-term horizons. By making this mindset change and adjusting brand frameworks as outlined in this chapter, marketers can prevent digital activation from perpetuating brand monotony and use digital tools for their intended purpose: to make brands indispensable.

Chapter 10

———

Brand-Building in the World of B2B

Maersk is a 114-year-old, $35 billion business conglomerate based in Copenhagen, Denmark. It conducts business in 150 countries around the world, and it has over eighty-eight thousand employees. It is the largest container ship and supply vessel operator in the world.

The container shipping industry is about as traditional and quintessentially B2B as it gets. But when you look at the way Maersk has gone about building its brand, you would think it more closely resembles a consumer packaged goods powerhouse like Unilever or Nestle. Following a decade of consumer, competitive, economic, and regulatory turbulence that plagued both Maersk and the industry overall, the company realized that establishing and maintaining an impeccable reputation among key stakeholders was imperative. But even more importantly, it recognized that reputation is an outcome, not a means. And it realized that building a stellar corporate brand—grounded in a solid strategic foundation—was the key to achieving this desired outcome.

So how did the company do this? Nick Blythe, from BLUE Communications, sums it up well. "Maersk delved to the depths of what its brand stood for to build an organization founded on 'care,' one that was working to create an industry that is truly sustainable and that could evolve successfully with the current and future demands of the global economy, trade, and society. What they achieved in a comparatively short span of time was significant: transforming their communications, exploiting all channels—online and offline—with the singular aim of building a company that people could trust."[1]

According to the company's website, "At Maersk Line, we move more than cargo. We propel ambitions. This means that, whether you run a corner shop or a conglomerate, we have the expertise, global network, and stability you need to drive your business forward." It underscores this brand promise with the payoff "Let us propel your ambitions."

There are several things that make this promise powerful and a solid example of effective brand positioning. First, it rings true to the company's strategic intent of demonstrating care and establishing trust. Additionally, the promise is a very compelling end benefit—it clearly articulates what Maersk will do for its customers. But what's perhaps most interesting is the way it taps into a higher-order, more emotional payoff: "Let us propel your ambitions." While this tagline may not seem all that edgy, it is clearly a departure from the functional, stodgy, and more conservative communication that typically characterizes this industry—and, quite frankly, many other B2B sectors as well.

Where the Maersk brand-building story becomes even more interesting, however, is the way it went about activating its new brand strategy. Here again, if you didn't know who we're talking about, you would assume it was a classical consumer packaged goods company or a technology startup. Specifically, Maersk took its story to the digital arena in a big way. In a relatively short period of time, it gained 1.1 million Facebook fans, seventy-three thousand followers on Twitter, and thousands more on LinkedIn, Google Plus, Instagram, Flickr, YouTube, and Pinterest. Let's look more closely at what Maersk is doing across these channels.

MAERSK'S CONTENT STRATEGY

Content represents the foundation of any successful digital strategy. Maersk's content strategy focuses on telling brand stories to engage customers and provide shareable, innovative, differentiated content, like time-lapse videos and thought-provoking branded journalism. It takes an objectives-based approach to every piece of content and marketing channel. It has already transitioned from using social media to engage with the community to using it as a bottom-line driver of customer insights, collaborative thought leadership, and enhanced lead generation.

Maersk depends largely on digital content for engagement. Maersk's first head of social media communications (and, originally, only department member), Jonathan Wichmann, discovered a treasure trove of digital images of ships and ports when he first joined the company. "I wasn't sure exactly how we'd be able to engage with people when I started, but in my first week, I found our digital archive, which no one was using," said Wichmann. "It had 14,000 photos on file—mainly ships, seascapes, ports, etc. I knew I could share them and add stories to them. That rich history was something I could share that was unique to Maersk, and people really responded to it. Now, people who don't even know who we are take and post photos of Maersk ships."[2]

FACEBOOK

Maersk views Facebook as both a B2C and B2B tool and uses it to reach current and potential employees, competitors, suppliers, regulators, and shipping enthusiasts with regular visual posts. One recent post was of a whale tragically killed by a Maersk ship. It had a one-to-one like-to-share ratio, which far exceeds normal results. While this was a sad event, Maersk was transparent and spoke in the authentic voice the company uses in all of its communications. One commenter remarked, "After reading this post, I am amazed at Maersk Line's honesty and wish more companies would follow such practices."

TWITTER

Maersk features more serious content on Twitter than it does on Facebook. Thanks to the immediate nature of tweets, the company uses this platform primarily as a news source and vehicle for distributing press releases. For example, the largest container ship in the world, the *Emma Mærsk*, routinely travels through the Suez Canal. Several years ago, during riots in the area, an online rumor claimed the ship was sinking. In truth, the ship was damaged but safely in port. By tweeting the status of the ship, the company nipped the rumors, stemmed rising panic, and avoided the necessity of a communication plan to make customers aware of the situation.

LINKEDIN

LinkedIn speaks to a different audience. According to Maersk's social media management, LinkedIn subscribers prefer to communicate with the company via this channel. So the company uses LinkedIn to provide shipping industry news, inviting select users to participate in discussions with experts on industry challenges and opportunities. On its company page, Maersk describes core products and ideas for peers to recommend in a way reminiscent of sites like TripAdvisor. Of course, the company also uses LinkedIn to recruit talent.

IS IT PAYING OFF?

Despite its initial and continued success with social media, Maersk's management eventually (and understandably) pushed for a greater understanding of how its 1.1 million followers on Facebook affected its bottom line. In his earliest calculations, Wichmann estimated a 1,500 percent return on investment on a $100,000 Facebook investment. He also said that Maersk's Twitter users were fifteen times more influential than average users, so when the brand shared on Twitter, the content tended to ripple out into networks where the company sought relevance.

The social media team now integrates with the sales and customer service teams to track photos to post. Internally, the team asks new employees how much of an impact social media had on their decision to join the company. Maersk is an impressive example of how even a B2B brand that operates in a traditional, staid environment can make the most of the social media tools at its disposal—even if it begins with only one person working the department.

Once again, however, digital activation is only a small part of this story. The bigger takeaway here is how this traditional, old-world B2B company has gone about building a world-class brand. Are brands important in maritime, and in B2B more broadly? Once again, BLUE Communication's Blythe states it well: "As the majority of people would acknowledge, the marine industry is naturally traditional and perhaps reticent to change, but up to 25 percent of the purchasing decision-making process within transport and logistics sectors is derived from brand. Brand as an intangible also represents a significant part of overall enterprise value; it's worth investing in."[3]

THE ROLE OF BRANDING IN B2B

As discussed in earlier chapters, the origin of brand management traces back to the world of consumer packaged goods. However, since its inception, many of the concepts of brand management (and the foundation of brand strategy) have applied effectively to other B2C and B2B businesses. Despite this, many B2B marketers still question whether brands are as important in the world of B2B as they are in B2C. Those who do recognize the importance of brands in B2B wonder whether the same basic principles, practices, frameworks, and guidelines still apply.

Increasing evidence shows that brands are just as important in the world of B2B. Interbrand's Best Global Brands 2017 Rankings—which evaluates brands across financial performance, consumer choice influence, and ability to command a premium price—included multiple B2B brands in the top twenty-five, like IBM.[4] Numerous other studies and research have confirmed the importance of branding in B2B. One 2017 study from B2B International showed that, among marketing executives, branding is the single most important marketing strategy on their plates.[5] That places branding ahead of strategies like product development, market segmentation, and pricing. (See figure 10.1.) Additionally, CEB, now part of Gartner, found that B2B marketers increasingly turn to branding to win preference, drive purchases, and achieve premium pricing. (See figure 10.2.) The CEB study, which was conducted with fifty-five CMOs, found branding to be the second-highest priority among marketing executives.[6]

Figure 10.1
Branding vs. Other Marketing

Q: Which of these marketing strategies are you focusing on at present?

	WAVE 2017	WAVE 2016	WAVE 2015
Branding — 60%	60%	50%	64%
Product development — 55%	55%	52%	51%
Customer Satisfaction — 55%	55%	51%	54%
Value Marketing — 51%	51%	51%	50%
Market Segmentation — 41%	41%	48%	52%
Competitor Analysis — 38%	38%	31%	32%
New Industry Sector Opportunities — 38%	38%	29%	37%
Route-to-Market — 32%	32%	24%	30%
New Country Opportunities — 23%	23%	20%	23%
Environmental Positioning — 16%	16%	3%	12%
Raising Prices — 13%	13%	9%	9%
Low Cost Leadership — 9%	9%	6%	6%
Volume Sales at Low Prices — 3%	3%	3%	3%

Significantly Higher
Significantly Lower

Source: B2B International

Figure 10.2
Rising Importance of Branding

Impact of B2B Brand Connections

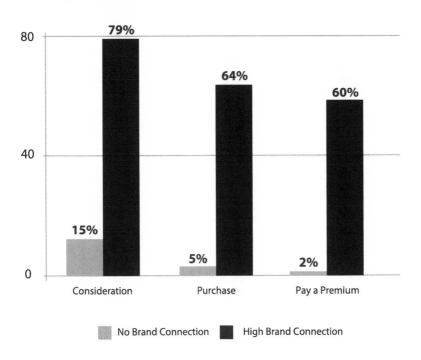

Source: "From Promotion to Emotion, Connecting B2B
Customers to Brands," CEB

Despite this recognized importance, the same B2B marketing executives do not believe they are successful in building strong brands. In the B2B International study, only 38 percent of marketing executives in the United States believed their corporate brand had a strong unique selling proposition. The number is only slightly higher in Europe, at 43 percent.[7] (See figure 10.3.)

Figure 10.3
Perceived Strength of USP

Q: To what extent do you believe your organization has a USP (unique selling proposition) that sufficiently drives differentiation of your corporate brand?

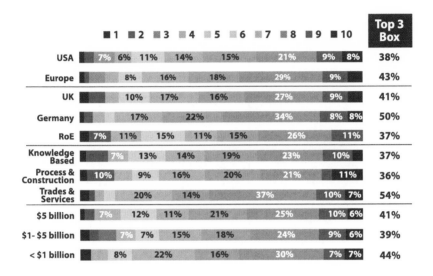

	1	2	3	4	5	6	7	8	9	10	Top 3 Box
USA	7%	6%	11%	14%	15%		21%		9%	8%	38%
Europe		8%	16%	18%		29%			9%		43%
UK		10%	17%	16%		27%			9%		41%
Germany		17%	22%		34%			8%	8%		50%
RoE	7%	11%	15%	11%	15%		26%		11%		37%
Knowledge Based	7%	13%	14%	19%		23%			10%		37%
Process & Construction	10%	9%	16%	20%		21%			11%		36%
Trades & Services		20%	14%		37%			10%	7%		54%
$5 billion	7%	12%	11%	21%		25%			10%	6%	41%
$1- $5 billion	7%	7%	15%	18%		24%			9%	6%	39%
< $1 billion	8%	22%	16%		30%			7%	7%		44%

Source: B2B International

Additionally, our brand strategy consulting firm, FullSurge, conducted market research in 2015 to understand exactly how successful high-growth companies achieve their impressive results.[8] The sample included more than 550 business executives from large-cap and mid-cap market companies in both B2C and B2B businesses across virtually all industries. Our goal was to understand what high-performance growth companies (those with greater than 15 percent three-year compound annual growth rate) do differently in branding, marketing, and innovation.

While we expected to find differences, the magnitude of difference in responses between high-growth companies and the rest was shocking. (See figure 10.4.) These higher-growth companies—which we dubbed "Growth Gurus"—accounted for 19 percent of the total sample. They view and approach the vital business functions of branding, marketing, and innovation in fundamentally different ways than their lower-growth peers. Specifically, B2B Growth Gurus were 33 percent more likely to say their companies had value propositions that were well-defined and clearly understood by their employees. They were also 31 percent more likely to state that their company's brand portfolio was logically organized and well understood by customers. Growth Gurus were an astonishing 79 percent more likely to rate their company's brand-building capabilities as a great deal stronger than the capabilities of their competitors.

Figure 10.4
Brand Performance in B2B

Strength of Agreement
"Our company's brand-building capabilities are a great deal stronger than those of our competitors.'"

Growth Gurus | 24%
Non-Growth Gurus | 13%

Strength of Agreement
"Our corporate brand is a great deal stronger than our competitors.'"

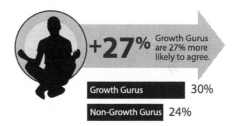

Growth Gurus | 30%
Non-Growth Gurus | 24%

Strength of Agreement
"We have brand value propositions that are formally documented and well-understood by customers."

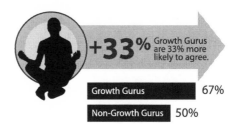

Growth Gurus | 67%
Non-Growth Gurus | 50%

Source: "The Anatomy of a Growth Guru," FullSurge

So the current state of brand-building in B2B seems to be a mixed bag. While most marketers recognize the importance of building and maintaining strong brand assets to establish competitive advantage and achieve superior business results, most do not currently believe they do a good job of it. Those who succeed, like our Growth Gurus, reap the benefits of their efforts.

B2C VERSUS B2B: ARTICULATING THE DIFFERENCES IN BRAND STRATEGY

Before we delve into the similarities and differences in brand-building in B2B and B2C, it is important to distinguish between brand strategy and the marketing activation that supports it. Clearly, approaches to marketing activation (e.g., advertising, communication, and social media) differ dramatically for B2B organizations. Conversely, when it comes to brand strategy, there are far more similarities than differences. Most of the principles and best practices are equally relevant in both environments. Additionally, the frameworks for brand strategy are essentially the same regardless of industry or product category.

Even though the basic principles and frameworks for brand strategy are equally relevant, though, there are a few characteristics common to many B2B businesses that should be considered when discussing brand strategy. Below, we will cover five general "truths" about the nature of B2B businesses and how these "truths" may affect the way B2B marketers need to approach brand strategy. To be clear, these "truths" are vast generalizations. There is a tremendous amount of variability among different types of B2B businesses. However, by and large, the following tenets hold true for many B2B organizations.

1. BUSINESS COMPLEXITY

In general, B2C products tend to be simpler and more straightforward, especially those in consumer packaged goods. Even more sophisticated B2C products, like automobiles and televisions, require only a very manageable level of knowledge and research to master.

Conversely, B2B products tend to be more technical in nature. Many, if not most, require at least a base level of expertise to use effectively. Even when B2B products are simple and straightforward, they are often components of more complex solutions. Additionally, while consumer products are typically uniform, B2B ones frequently require customization to meet the unique needs of customers.

Beyond the product offering, the decision-making process also differs between B2C and B2B businesses. B2C purchase decisions, like for groceries and clothing, are generally made by individuals (or at most, a family). However, B2B purchase decisions are often made by groups, committees, or procurement departments. They may include formal processes, such as lengthy proposals and pitch presentations. In some cases, convoluted qualification processes require vendors to be approved before they are allowed to do business with a company. All this means that while B2C brands must be relevant to individuals, B2B brands must be compelling to a broader group of people.

According to Steve Wnuk, vice president of marketing for Milwaukee-based Quad/Graphics, "Big businesses, in particular, can be very complex. Purchases tend to be highly considered and not very straightforward. It's harder to explain your product. Getting your message across typically takes a lot more thoughtfulness than for your typical consumer packaged goods item that shows up in a grocery store."[9]

2. SALES CYCLE

Closely related to the above factor, sales cycles also tend to differ between B2C and B2B. Many B2C categories have very short cycles—sometimes measured in only minutes or seconds. Meanwhile, B2B companies tend to have longer cycles, in part because of the number of stakeholders involved and the formal processes referenced above.

The role branding plays in the B2B purchase decision may be slightly different given this dynamic. In the case of B2C, especially consumer packaged goods, purchases are often less involved and more impulsive. In B2B, however, where the sales cycle is typically much longer, the objective of the brand is to help build confidence and trust with customers over multiple phases of longer, more complex sales cycles. Even when the sale is over, it can take months or years for a B2B customer to form a solid impression of the purchased product or service.

Ed Keller, chief marketing officer at Navigant, a global professional services firm based in Chicago, spoke about this dynamic. He said, "Sales cycles are long, and product use cycles are even longer. Clients may purchase a technology product from us, or they may purchase a consulting service, such as an audit. They may not know for a year whether they like our product or whether they're having a good brand experience. It can take a long time—even several long purchase or sales cycles—for us to establish credibility as a vendor and build trust in our brand."[10]

3. PURCHASE PRICE AND COMMITMENT TERMS

While B2C purchase prices vary widely depending on category, they tend to be less expensive than B2B purchases and require far less of a commitment. Consumers are often motivated by low price points, discounts, and deals, but cost is rarely the sole driver of purchase outside a few highly price-sensitive consumer segments.

Conversely, B2B purchases are more expensive, often totaling six- or seven-figure amounts, or more. Many of these purchases represent long-term investments. Depending on the nature of the business, binding contracts between supplier and customer may be necessary. Some of those contracts may involve exclusivity, and even if they don't, the hard and soft costs associated with switching are often prohibitive. All of these factors combine to raise the stakes on getting it right the first time and place increased pressure on the brand to instill confidence and trust among customers.

4. FEWER CUSTOMERS, FEWER SEGMENTS

Unlike B2C companies, B2B companies generally compete for business among a smaller set of prospective buyers. It's not uncommon for B2B companies to have fewer than one hundred customers. In some cases, a small handful of customers account for the vast majority of a B2B company's revenue and an even higher proportion of profits.

One natural outcome of fewer customers and prospects is that B2B markets generally have fewer needs-based segments than B2C ones. It stands to reason that a smaller group of customers can only be segmented so finely before the distinctions between segments become meaningless. The other reason B2B markets tend to have fewer needs-based segments is that their customers' needs tend to differ to a lesser degree than the needs of those in consumer markets. Common B2B market segments include price-sensitives, quality seekers, best-in-class performance drivers, and collaboration seekers.

All other things equal, fewer distinct segments typically means fewer brands are required to go to market. As Navigant's Keller said, "In almost any consumer segmentation, you're going to have six, seven, or even eight segments. We have far fewer segments. I don't need a big portfolio of brands when I'm not trying to appeal to six different client segments."[11]

5. IMPORTANCE OF RELATIONSHIPS

At the risk of overgeneralizing, B2C branding tends to be more transactional than relational. Even with digital marketing, social media, and other advances in activation that have deepened customer relationships, the depth of those relationships still pales in comparison to the highly personal face-to-face relationships that characterize many B2B businesses.

Unsurprisingly, B2B branding is all about building customer relationships. Products and services are often sold and delivered through salespeople or broader account teams. The brand must stand for something greater than the products it sells: it must house an entire solution, or offering, and provide an experience that is both desirable to customers and in line with the promise of its brand positioning. Executed effectively, the benefits can be significant, as many B2B customer-supplier relationships carry high degrees of loyalty and multiyear engagements.

Consider the strong, enduring relationships that Serta Simmons Bedding enjoys with its retail customers. This is a quintessential B2B2C business, where the customer is the retail partner that is essentially an intermediary between the manufacturer and the end consumer.

Andrew Gross, executive vice president of marketing for Serta, said that Serta aims to create a strong relationship with its customers by being retailers' partners in growth: "For some retailers, that means helping them to better advertise our national product line. So we do a lot of work on strengthening co-op programs where we provide them tools to give them access, for instance, to media that they would never be able to access on their own. And then for other retailers, it's really making big plays with differentiated products that are logical extensions of our national lines… We're always working on our ability to consistently serve retailers on time and to strengthen our relationships with them."[12]

Two additional issues that cause ongoing debate about B2B branding, both of which merit further discussion, are targeting and brand promise.

Should target audiences be defined at the individual level or at the company level, and what (if anything) is the role of emotion in B2B brand positioning? The following two sections address these questions in greater detail.

TARGETING IN B2B MARKETS

As noted earlier, B2B companies often market and sell to groups and committees. When thinking about the target audience in brand positioning, does it make sense to do so at the company level? The individual buyer level? Or something in between? Let's explore this common debate further.

Many B2B organizations, whether attempting to formally segment the market or merely define a target customer, talk in terms of organizations. They may define their targets as large hospital systems or Fortune 500 companies. This is sometimes referred to as firmographic segmentation. The obvious drawback to this approach is that companies don't make purchase decisions; people do, even if that means a *group* of people. With that in mind, establishing a brand target of large hospital systems, Fortune 500 companies, or financial services providers is dangerous. This assumes that the individual or group decision-makers in those institutions have similar needs and purchase drivers based solely on the makeup of their companies or the nature of their sectors. So while "large hospital systems" may in part describe the target—either implicitly or explicitly—defining the target also needs to include more individual, buyer-specific characteristics.

To be fair, some B2B companies already segment their markets and define target audiences in a more sophisticated manner. These companies have taken a page out of B2C companies' segmentation playbook and established attitudinal-based or needs-based segments and brand positioning targets at the buyer level. Once again, even if B2B buyers are groups—not individuals—this approach remains valid. This idea is perhaps best expressed through the words of Ann Rubin, vice president of corporate marketing for IBM. "It's not about B2B or B2C," she said. "It's about B2I. Business to individual. We don't talk to companies because companies don't buy our products and services—people do. We have to understand buyers at the individual level—and in their personal lives—in order to be relevant in their business lives."[13]

Perhaps an even more effective way to define a brand's target audience is through *combining* buyer functions (or roles) with more attitudinal-based or needs-based factors. According to Steve Wnuk, "We look at buying groups. We start with job function, and then we overlay personas. So we essentially have four different personas across two different buying groups and titles within those groups (including both purchasing and marketing)."[14]

GE Healthcare, the $18 billion division of General Electric that sells medical imaging products and related services, recently changed from a traditional B2B segmentation based on firmographics at the institutional level (e.g., total revenue, number of beds) to one based on buyer-centric needs. GE now focuses on four key buyer segments: decision-makers, who can be administrators or medical practitioners; clinical differentiation, which covers entities that want to distinguish themselves by using GE Healthcare equipment; equipment productivity, addressing how many daily exams the buyer needs the equipment to perform; and value-added services, for buyers who want additional services like data management in addition to equipment. This segmentation approach has resulted in higher growth and greater cost savings for the division.

B2B BRAND PROMISE: RATIONAL VERSUS EMOTIONAL

Another ongoing debate in B2B brand strategy is the extent to which emotion-based promises make sense as compared to rational-based ones. Conventional wisdom dictates that business decision-making is more rational than consumer decision-making. As such, it makes sense for the promise component of B2B brand positioning to be rational as well. However, B2B marketers are increasingly recognizing the flaws and shortsightedness of this mindset.

Let's revisit the market research of CEB. Researchers distinguished between business value and personal value. Business value was defined as appealing "to logic/reason in areas such as functional benefits (e.g., high performance, structure/order) and business outcomes (e.g., achieving business goals)."[15] Put simply, these are rational factors that pertain more to the business than the individual.

Personal value, meanwhile, was defined as "emotional appeals in areas such as professional benefits (e.g., being a better leader, simplifying my life), social benefits (e.g., fitting in with colleagues, admiration from others), emotional benefits (e.g., confidence, excitement, happiness), and self-image benefits (e.g., doing good for society, feeling of accomplishment)." In other words, these are personal factors that tend to skew more emotional.

CEB tested the relative importance of the factors against fourteen business outcomes, including consideration, purchase, premium payment, and advocacy. The research found that, across this set of commercial outcomes, personal value had twice as much impact as business value.[16] CEB went on to conclude that with B2B buyers, emotion matters more than logic and reason. (See figure 10.5.)

Figure 10.5
Personal Value vs. Business Value

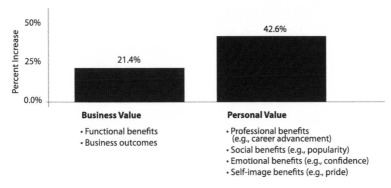

Impact of Perceived Brand Benefits on Commercial Outcome

- Percent Increase axis: 50%, 25%, 0.0%

Business Value — 21.4%
- Functional benefits
- Business outcomes

Personal Value — 42.6%
- Professional benefits (e.g., career advancement)
- Social benefits (e.g., popularity)
- Emotional benefits (e.g., confidence)
- Self-image benefits (e.g., pride)

Source: "From Promotion to Emotion, Connecting
B2B Customers to Brands," CEB

Even more interestingly—given a key premise of this book is that we are in the midst of a brand monotony crisis—is that business value (arguably the most common form of brand promise in B2B) is not seen by B2B buyers as a differentiator. According to the research, only 14 percent of B2B buyers perceive enough meaningful difference between brands' business values to be willing to pay extra for that difference. (See figure 10.6.) This appropriately led CEB to conclude "Business value (rational factors) is just table stakes. It gets suppliers into a buyer's consideration set but doesn't make them stand out within the consideration."[17]

Figure 10.6
Business Value is not Differentiating

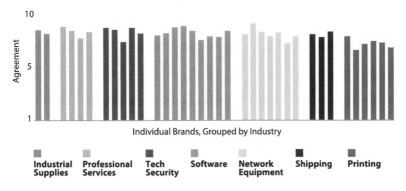

**Average Agreement with Statement:
"This brand will help us achieve business goals."**

Individual Brands, Grouped by Industry

Industrial Supplies · Professional Services · Tech Security · Software · Network Equipment · Shipping · Printing

Source: "From Promotion to Emotion, Connecting
B2B Customers to Brands," CEB

One final note from the research is that, contrary to popular belief, B2B buying is highly personal. In fact, the CEB study found that B2B buying is even more personal than B2C buying. The researchers believe this is because buyers feel a great deal of *personal risk* in their business-related purchase decision-making. (See figure 10.7.) Specifically, the report states B2B buyers feel three primary personal risks: losing time and effort if a purchase goes poorly, losing credibility if they recommend an unsuccessful purchase, and losing their jobs if they are found responsible for a bad purchase.

Figure 10.7
B2B Buying is Very Personal

**Relationship Between Number of Perceived
Personal Risks and Emotional Connection**

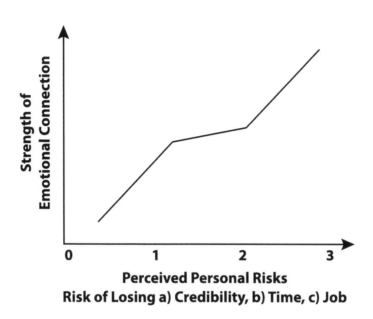

**Perceived Personal Risks
Risk of Losing a) Credibility, b) Time, c) Job**

Source: "From Promotion to Emotion, Connecting
B2B Customers to Brands," CEB

Consider the case of Snap-on Inc., based in Kenosha, Wisconsin. Snap-on makes high-end tools and equipment for home projects and industrial work alike. The company doesn't sell to consumers through retailers, but rather through independent dealers and franchises. These franchises represent Snap-on's business customers.

Snap-on's vice president of marketing, Yvette Morrison, talked about how it feels to operate in that environment. "The stakes for success are so much higher," she said. "There are more significant implications if I don't get it right. It's not that Snap-on could go under: it's an independent franchisee that could go under. This is someone whose family may need to go without if we don't get it right for him. So the personal risk to me is great, and I don't take it lightly in terms of what we're tasked with doing."[18]

After spinning off its mobile phone business from its main company, newly minted Motorola Solutions (which focuses on government and enterprise customers) decided to focus both internally and externally on the impact its products and solutions make. Its new brand proposition, "To help people be their best in the moments that matter," is a holistic proposition that applies to Motorola's myriad product offerings. From an emotional perspective, the positioning focuses on both mission-critical situations of first responders and life-enhancing scenarios of people like retail sales associates.[19]

Squarespace provides another example. The website building and hosting company's brand positioning states, "Squarespace makes beautiful products to help people with creative ideas succeed."[20] Its website looks nothing like a traditional function-oriented website, but instead has beautiful imagery and speaks about empowering people who are "shaping the world's most iconic businesses." Both its language and its visual style convey success.

Importantly, none of this is to say that logic-based promises are irrelevant in B2B environments. Rationality always has been, is, and will continue to be an important component of B2B branding. However, as we learned from the CEB market research study, rational benefits (or business value) are little more than table stakes for B2B companies today. Those benefits are necessary, of course, but not sufficiently differentiating. B2B companies that can leverage their rational benefits into an emotion-based brand payoff can achieve meaningful differentiation—and that differentiation drives the competitive advantage brands need to deliver superior business results.

MOVING FORWARD IN B2B BRANDING

Branding is every bit as relevant and important in B2B as it is in B2C. Encouragingly, the skill gap in brand-building between B2B and B2C marketers is narrowing, especially as many B2B companies seek to hire marketers who have been classically trained in the consumer packaged goods world. Both the importance of brand and the enhanced skillsets of B2B marketers are evident across rankings like Interbrand's Best Global Brands Ranking, Kantar Millward Brown's BrandZ Top 100 Global Brands, and CoreBrand's 100 Most Powerful Brands.

For the most part, when it comes to brand strategy in B2B versus B2C, there are more similarities than differences. Most principles and best practices are equally relevant in both arenas, and they share similar frameworks. However, as detailed in this chapter, B2B branding does have a couple of nuances worth keeping in mind.

First, it is important to remember that people, not companies, make purchasing decisions. As such, marketers must avoid the temptation to define target audiences at the organizational level. Second, contrary to popular belief, research proves that emotions play a critical role in B2B decision-making. Therefore, it is important to ensure that B2B brand positioning features a compelling emotional element.

Chapter 11

————

Long Live the Corporate Brand

By virtually any measure, IBM is an example of a stellar corporate brand. The company is more than one hundred years old and conducts business in more than 170 countries. It has remained relevant, even revered, through several dynamic business transitions, including one from hardware manufacturer to software and services solutions provider. The decades-old financial saying "No one ever got fired for buying IBM" is a testament not only to the strength of the company and its services but to the enduring equity of its corporate brand. A quick glance at the Interbrand and BrandZ rankings referenced throughout this book shows that IBM is consistently in or near the top ten brands in terms of value, power, and prestige.

CASE STUDY OF A STELLAR CORPORATE BRAND: IBM

IBM is a shining example in the way it has developed and consistently maintained its corporate brand strategy.[1] It follows many of the principles and best practices outlined in the earlier chapters of this book, including some of the updated strategic frameworks and other tools we have discussed. Although it would be impossible to do the company and its corporate brand justice in the space of a few paragraphs, this chapter begins with an overview of the critical components of the IBM corporate brand strategy and how those components combine to position the company for competitive advantage and continued business success.

DEFINING AND UNDERSTANDING THE TARGET

In terms of target audience, IBM got it right in several respects. As referenced in chapter 10, the company resists the temptation to rely on a company-level, firmographic market segmentation. IBM acknowledges the importance of individual buyers within companies and understands that not all customers in the same sector have the same business needs. Instead, the company embraces the notion of B2I (business to individual) and recognizes that people, not companies, make purchase decisions.

IBM didn't stop after it identified its target buyers, of course. The company has gone to great lengths to understand the underlying motivations of individuals within certain buyer roles. At the corporate level, IBM identified a mindset and persona that defines its target customers: forward-thinking. To IBM, forward-thinkers embrace the role of science and technology in business and society. They seek to make a difference and to change the world for the better. This target mindset will make perfect sense when we review the brand's positioning. Additionally, beneath the corporate level, IBM has identified specific highly nuanced buyer roles and personas at the individual business-unit level.

One final note about target audience: although IBM clearly places current and prospective customers at the top of the list in terms of priority, the company also recognizes the importance of the other stakeholders the corporate brand must serve effectively. Specifically, the IBM brand caters to employees, industry analysts, and investors, as well as other internal and external constituencies.

IDENTIFYING AN ENDURING IDEA

With a solid understanding of both target audience and its internal competencies, IBM set out to identify and articulate something it dubbed an "enduring idea." As the name suggests, this concept captures the essence of what the company, people, product, and brand do for target audiences and for society overall. In the case of IBM, "world-changing progress" is the brand's enduring idea. This is not the corporate brand positioning, which we will cover next; rather, it is more like what we discussed in earlier chapters about brand purpose.

ARTICULATING THE CORPORATE BRAND POSITIONING

For years, the IBM brand had been positioned around the idea of a "Smarter Planet." The premise was to make the world's systems smarter through the application of technology to better serve our needs as individuals and societies. Recently, however, the company has evolved its corporate brand positioning to a new angle: "Let's Put Smart to Work."

According to Ann Rubin, IBM's vice president of corporate marketing, "This positioning is about taking all of the great technology we have and helping companies apply it at scale across their organizations to do things they could have never done before. With Smarter Planet, it was let's change large systems that interact with other systems. With our new positioning, it's let's change things across the board—large and small—for individuals, companies, and societies. Let's Put Smart to Work is also an invitation...come work with us to change the world. *Let's* do this together."[2]

She goes on to provide a tangible example of this. "With Smarter Planet, we might have thought about improving the healthcare system—for example, putting electronic medical records in place. But now, we have so much more technology available and so many more companies and professionals embracing it. We can use technology to help patients, to help doctors make diagnoses, to help researchers find cures. Now, it's not improving the healthcare system. It's about applying smart technology to help hospitals, doctors, patients, and researchers—making it better across the board."

Clearly, this concept represents a powerful and inspiring promise for the IBM corporate brand. It meets all the criteria discussed earlier. The positioning is both relevant and compelling—who isn't in favor of worldwide progress? It is differentiating, as IBM is uniquely qualified to deliver on this goal. IBM's positioning is also highly credible: in its most recent annual report, IBM cited fifty examples of companies that are applying new technologies at scale to change their businesses and their industries.

ESTABLISHING AND DEPLOYING 'HERO BRANDS'

In addition to its corporate brand, IBM has five hero brands: Cloud,

Watson, Services, Security, and Research. These are essentially massive business platforms that cut across IBM's myriad businesses and product lines. (Chapter 5 went into significant detail on brand portfolio strategy and architecture, so there's no reason to repeat the discussion here.) The company carefully and deliberately defined a positioning and identity for each hero brand, along with each brand's relationship with the corporate master brand—including standards and guidelines for usage. As Rubin noted, "Each hero brand has its distinct differentiators, and regardless of the application, the hero brand must be used in a way that is consistent with its positioning. We have one IBM Cloud and one Cloud narrative. And it doesn't matter what Cloud is being applied to; we need to be really consistent in how we talk about it."

LIVING BRAND VALUES

Finally, IBM identified a set of core values for its corporate brand and company overall. Those values are dedication to every client success, innovation that matters for the company and for the world, and trust and responsibility in all relationships. Importantly, these are more than mere platitudes or statements in a brand book. They are practices and behaviors reinforced in day-to-day interactions.

For each brand value, the company provides a list of behaviors and practices that help IBM employees understand how to live the value and, equally importantly, how not to. For example, IBM offers specific direction on what "trust and responsibility in all relationships" looks like. Employees are encouraged to unite with team members, recap when needed, determine what is needed to do the job well, and collaborate on solutions.

Above all, Rubin recognizes the potential benefits that accrue within organizations with a strong corporate brand strategy. She said, "It gives your company purpose and meaning and represents your core values. It also helps your employees answer questions and make important decisions. Those decisions impact everything we do across the company, so we need to make sure we get it right."

IBM is one of the largest companies in the world and clearly has one of the most respected corporate brands. However, companies do not need to become as large as IBM to emulate its success in branding: they simply need to understand what makes a corporate brand effective and learn to leverage that brand to achieve business goals.

THE SIGNIFICANCE OF THE CORPORATE BRAND

To be fair, sometimes the distinction between corporate brand and product brand becomes blurred. Even some of the world's most powerful corporate brands also serve a product branding role. Hershey's, Coca-Cola, and Hyatt are just a few examples.

As is the case with brand strategy in B2B versus B2C, when it comes to corporate brand versus product brand, there are far more similarities than differences. For the most part, the basic principles and best practices that have been covered in this book apply regardless of whether the brand in question is corporate or product. The strategic frameworks we have discussed, such as those for brand positioning and brand experience, are equally relevant for each brand type. That being said, there is undeniably a special role for the corporate entity in the world of branding. As stated earlier, for many companies, corporate brand represents the single most important brand asset within the overall portfolio.

THE RISING IMPORTANCE OF THE CORPORATE BRAND

Companies can no longer rely solely on product and service differentiation strategies as their mainstay for meaningful differentiation and competitive advantage. This is due, in part, to the increasing sophistication of consumers who now consider the social, environmental, and ethical makeup of the companies from which they purchase.

After a decades-long lapse, the importance of the corporate brand has become increasingly evident in the world of advertising. According to Kantar Media, corporate brand advertising rose 17 percent in 2012 compared to the previous year, even though total ad spending rose just 3 percent.[3] This resurgence has occurred in several meaningful ways. First, branded house companies like General Electric, Google, and ExxonMobil have begun messaging around topics broader than their individual product and service offerings. Their campaigns have recently touted the broader benefits they provide to the marketplace and society overall. These companies understand the importance of enhancing their corporate reputation (i.e., building and maintaining a stronger corporate brand) as opposed to only providing calls to action that are designed to drive near-term transactions.

Branded house companies aren't the only ones experiencing the resurgence, however. Several traditional house of brands consumer packaged goods companies, which trade on the equity of their strong consumer-facing product brands, are also embracing the trend. For example, SC Johnson, manufacturer of world-class product brands like Pledge, Raid, and Ziploc, began talking about its status as "A Family Company" back in 1998. That simple message was intended both to reinforce the company's heritage and to instill trust in its products among consumers. In early 2018, the company evolved that tagline to say, "A Family Company at Work for a Better World."

"SC Johnson has a long legacy as a family company committed to doing what's right for our consumers, communities, and the environment," said SC Johnson Chairman and CEO Fisk Johnson. "This is something we have been doing for generations, and we want people to know more about the many ways we are at work for a better world."[4]

Other more recent examples include The Hershey Company, which embraced its corporate brand in 2016 with a new tagline: "Hello Happy. Hello Hershey's." Even though different executions feature a specific Hershey's brand, such as the chocolate bars or Hershey's syrup, the focus remains primarily on the emotional connection between Hershey and consumer memories. The Hershey Company also merged multiple social media channels for each brand into master Hershey accounts on Facebook and Twitter.[5]

Another recent example of a company embracing its corporate brand comes from The Coca-Cola Company. In 2017, Coca-Cola began to position itself through advertising as a total beverage company, as opposed to merely the flagship brand at the heart of its corporate name. With language like "more than our name suggests," the creative content behind this branding shift includes less well-known brands like Honest Tea, Odwalla juice, and Smartwater. To be fair, part of this strategic shift is likely in response to the increasing health concerns that surround sugary carbonated drinks.[6]

THE CASE FOR CORPORATE BRAND-BUILDING

Companies that invest in building a strong corporate brand enjoy numerous benefits. A strong corporate brand can:

- Provide significant returns on investment and other financial benefits
- Reflect and communicate a company's purpose and mission
- Mitigate business risk and help organizations navigate challenging times
- Penetrate new markets more easily and cost-effectively
- Provide efficiencies in marketing spend and investment
- Become a source of pride and esprit de corps for employees
- Endure for the long haul, while individual product brands may come and go

As is hopefully evident from this list, the sky is the limit when it comes to monetizing the benefits of a strong corporate brand. We will cover each benefit individually in more detail throughout the remainder of this chapter, including examples, statistics, and anecdotal evidence that support the notion that a corporate brand is a worthwhile investment.

1. FINANCIAL SECURITY AND INFLUENCE

Former Coca-Cola CEO Roberto Goizueta once famously declared, "All our factories and facilities could burn down tomorrow, but you'd hardly touch the value of the company; all that actually lies in the goodwill of our brand franchise and the collective knowledge in the company."[7]

No discussion on the financial benefits of a corporate brand (or any brand, for that matter) would be complete without first addressing the concept of brand valuation. One of the most common ways of determining the economic value (i.e., worth) of a brand is based on the future income potential associated with it. This approach estimates future financial benefits, then discounts them to assign a present value.[8]

Thanks in part to advances in the sophistication of brand valuation, the Internal Financial Reporting Standards (IFRS) Foundation recently stated that brands and other acquired intangible assets could be reported on balance sheets. According to Interbrand's Best Global Brands 2017 Ranking, Apple is the most valuable brand in the world at a staggering $185 billion.[9]

However, mere economic valuation of brands is not always an important (or even relevant) data point for companies. Other indicators can also substantiate the financial benefits of building and maintaining a strong corporate brand. Take, for example, the impact corporate brands can have on market capitalization. According to CoreBrand's Corporate Branding Index, a company's corporate brand can account for up to 7 percent of the organization's market capitalization.[10]

Yet another example, which is related to the above point of market capitalization, pertains to mergers and acquisitions activities. Rick Wise, CEO of brand consultancy Lippincott, discussed the topic in *Wharton Magazine*. "We have seen advantages in the financial markets, both for buyers and sellers," he wrote. "Research shows that a strong corporate brand can enhance value, as the brand can help signal the quality and reliability of earnings and the future growth potential of the company. For buying companies, the enhanced economics of being able to quickly fold an acquired company under the parent name can yield significant synergies."[11]

Wise is not the only one in this camp. According to Interbrand, "In an M&A context, brand continues to be a key driver of acquisition premiums. Often, it is the latent potential of the brand that is driving this premium through its ability to enter new markets and extend into adjacent categories. A broad skill set, combining market research, brand, and business strategy, together with business case modeling, is required to quantify the latent financial potential of the target brand."[12]

Clearly, financial benefits come to companies that consistently invest in, nurture, and protect their corporate brands. Whether it's in pursuit of an enhanced balance sheet, improved income statement, higher stock price, or a more lucrative capital event, corporate brands make for solid financial investments.

2. PURPOSE THROUGH CORPORATE BRANDING

A recurring theme of this book is that we live in an age of transparency. Along with the internet, this transparency is behind much of the shift in power dynamics relative to branding from manufacturer to consumer. We now know that to many consumers, especially Millennials, the people behind the brand matter. Rebecca Messina, former chief marketing officer of Chicago-based spirits maker Beam Suntory, shared her thoughts on this topic. "I do not believe any company is exempt from consumers' desire to know that the company they're buying products from has integrity," she said. "I think [corporate transparency] is an area where consumers will always want to know more. We're getting to the point where they want to know as much about the companies making the products as the products themselves."[13]

Savvy marketers are proactively embracing this movement. In addition to advertising and other forms of creative activation, we are increasingly seeing this trend reflected in brand strategy, especially in positioning. As referenced in chapter 4, perhaps the most extreme manifestation of this shift occurs in for-profit companies whose primary reason for being (i.e., purpose) is reflected in their brand positioning. So-called purpose branding is not a fad; purposes will likely be reflected in brand positioning for many years to come.

Although many credit Simon Sinek's famous TED Talk about "start with why" as the impetus of purpose-based branding, the truth is that this concept has existed for much longer and covers much more than what was addressed in Sinek's presentation.[14] Purpose-based branding means the company looks to its brand to declare not only the promise it makes to customers through its products and services, but to communicate the broader purpose it serves to all its stakeholders.

As such, it should be no surprise that one of the many benefits of a strong corporate brand—regardless of whether it's formally reflected in its positioning—is the ability to signal to customers and other external stakeholders what the company believes in. We will cover *internal* stakeholders later in this chapter.

According to John Marshall and Lippincott's Rick Wise, "People matter as much as products. In today's radically transparent business environment, understanding a company's integrity, values, and, most importantly, intentions, matters more than ever. For customers, the purpose of the company can often be as important as the performance of its products. For employees, there is a heightened need for a corporate brand that connects."[15]

In chapter 4, we showcased several purpose brands positioned around their "why." Patagonia essentially sells outdoor clothing, but those unfamiliar with its corporate brand might not know that it defines itself through conservation, sustainability, and environmental protection. It reflects that definition in its mission statement: "Build the best product, cause no unnecessary harm, use business to inspire and implement solutions to the environmental crisis."[16]

Two additional examples of purpose brands not showcased in chapter 4 include TOMS Shoes and REI. TOMS Shoes is perhaps one of the most famous examples of a corporate purpose brand. When TOMS sells a pair of shoes, a new pair goes to a child in need. When the company sells eyewear, a part of the profits goes to save or restore eyesight for people in developing countries. The company also champions other causes, including safe drinking water, improved maternal health, and safer childbirth. Importantly, this goes beyond mere corporate philanthropy, which most companies of any notable size embrace. This is the very purpose behind TOMS, the driving force of its corporate brand.

REI is another example of a corporate purpose brand. It began as a small company run by twenty-three mountain-climbing buddies. Today, it is the country's largest consumer cooperative. From the beginning, the brand has focused on the outdoors and preservation of natural resources: "At REI, we inspire, educate, and outfit for a lifetime of outdoor adventure and stewardship."[17] In 2015, REI gave all its employees a paid day off on Black Friday, the busiest retail day of the year, so they could spend time with their families instead of crazed shoppers. The company extended the campaign beyond its walls and beyond Black Friday, encouraging everyone to join in the mindset: "#OptOutside isn't just about Black Friday. It's become a movement much larger than us. It's a mindset. It's about choosing to spend more time outside all year long and of recognizing the importance the outdoors has on our health and well-being."[18] REI encouraged outdoor enthusiasts to share pictures on Instagram via #OptOutside and featured select photos from customers on the REI website.

These corporate brands stand for more than profits. They stand for causes that resonate with their target audiences, and because of that, they are powerful assets for the companies behind them.

3. RISK MITIGATION DURING CHALLENGING TIMES

Examples abound of companies that have masterfully navigated through tragedy and crisis with world-class public relations. Johnson & Johnson's 1982 handling of consumer deaths related to cyanide-laced Tylenol, for instance, immediately became a textbook case study on how to respond proactively and responsibly manage through crisis and adversity.[19]

While it would be foolish to downplay the importance of skillful public relations in times of crisis, it's also important to note that these are inherently reactive tactics in response to negative events. Arguably, the most carefully conceived and thoughtfully executed PR response during a time of tragedy can only be so successful if the corporate brand behind the outreach is weak. Conversely, when a well-intentioned company mishandles a bad situation, the strength and goodwill of its corporate brand—developed over many years—can be invaluable to help it weather the storm.

Think about a corporate brand like a bank account. Efforts to infuse the brand with positive equity increase the account's balance. When something negative happens, the abuse draws down previously deposited funds. Continual investment in the corporate brand (i.e., consistently infusing it with positive goodwill) eventually pays back the investing company many times over during moments of need.

The 2010 BP Deepwater Horizon oil spill in the Gulf of Mexico will likely go down in history as one of the biggest hits to a corporate brand.[20] This disaster, which killed eleven people and leaked 4 million barrels of oil into the sea, caused widespread adverse effects to wildlife habitats in the area, not to mention the fishing and tourism industries.[21] People around the world will forever remember the underwater shots of oil continuing to leak from the rig after BP claimed the spill had been contained. BP CEO Tony Hayward was skewered by the public for saying he would "like his life back" after the disaster affected so many people.[22] Fines and other payments cost the company more than $60 billion.[23]

BP provides an example of how the goodwill of a strong corporate brand can enable a company to survive a devastating catastrophe that carried with it both financial and reputational consequences. Without BP's previously established brand equity, the company might not have survived this incident. Instead, BP is still in business, did not undergo massive layoffs or defections, and is expected to turn a profit in 2018.

Another major company, Wells Fargo, is in the middle of its own recovery process. Amid the admission that the company created potentially 2 million fake customer accounts in 2016 (and engaged in other questionable practices), the Wells Fargo brand suffered severely.[24] In 2018, the company began running mea culpa ads to acknowledge trust issues with consumers and promise that things were going to change. It remains to be seen whether this new strategy and accompanying tagline—"Established 1852. Re-established 2018."—can overcome the beating the brand has taken.

The larger the company, the more disastrous a PR crisis can be. When negative press starts to pour in, the time for investment in the corporate brand has passed. Companies must invest in their corporate brands even in the best of times, so that if and when they do face a crisis, they have enough equity and trust established in their corporate brands to withstand the consequences.

4. BRAND-POWERED MARKET PENETRATION

Chapter 5, which covered brand portfolio strategy, detailed how brands within a corporate portfolio can align strategically to become more than the sum of their parts. To do so, companies often link their brands in ways that benefit at least one, if not more, of their portfolio brands. This is essentially the concept of brand architecture.

Among other points, the chapter covered how by providing an explicit endorsement to a lesser-known branded entity within a portfolio, a strong master brand can essentially transfer equity to the lesser-known brand and help it gain traction in the market. While these master brands do not necessarily have to be corporate brands, they are more often than not. In these cases, investments in the corporate brand pay dividends by allowing the corporate brand to transfer equity and goodwill to the lesser-known brand, thus helping it gain quicker adoption when entering new categories and markets.

"Companies continue to look to new products and brands to produce growth, but the continued decline in consumer trust in brands means new brands must clear an increasingly high hurdle," noted Denise Lee Yohn in *Harvard Business Review*. "When new brands are able to draw upon a master brand's existing equity, they have a greater likelihood of success than those that start from scratch. By conveying credibility, quality perceptions, and sometimes simply familiarity, master brands make the introduction of new sub-brands easier and usually more successful."[25]

5. CORPORATE BRANDING AND COST-EFFECTIVE OPERATIONS

As noted throughout this book, both the one-time and ongoing costs of launching and supporting a world-class brand can be astronomical. That said, one single campaign that unifies all of a company's products generates economies of scale.

While not always a primary motivation, many companies realize economic efficiencies when they lead with a master brand strategy. Often, the master brand behind that strategy is a corporate brand. "Promoting a single brand with a single campaign naturally makes for a more efficient marketing spend, but in today's fragmented media landscape, the advantage is even more pronounced," Yohn said. "Despite the lower levels of reach that broadcast media outlets deliver today, as well as the proliferating niche social media channels, an advertiser can still maximize the exposure it generates in a single media channel by spreading it across multiple brands and products."[26]

Yohn's argument also points out how efficiencies manifest in increased flexibility. "Because many companies are operating with lower margins today than in the past, they need increased flexibility to better manage costs and inventory," she said. "Emphasizing its master brand gives a company flexibility in brand portfolio management and in advertising and promotion. When costs, demand, or other factors change the strategic importance of the products and brands in its portfolio, a company can delete, modify, or combine them with less risk of confusing customers or losing market salience."

The Coca-Cola Company's recent focus on its corporate brand is one such example. With this strategy and the campaigns behind it, the company has strengthened its corporate brand. However, other brands in the portfolio, such as Honest Tea and Smartwater, also receive benefits through association. They have lower levels of awareness and equity, but they benefit from operating under The Coca-Cola Company's banner.

In the B2B arena, SAP offers a similar example of consolidation and efficiencies. This move is more about portfolio strategy and architecture than it is about advertising and promotion, but it yields efficiency benefits all the same. In 2016, the company announced that it would move to a corporate endorsement strategy for its sub-brands, which include SAP Ariba, SAP Fieldglass, and SAP Hybris. In this case, SAP gains significant branding efficiencies by leaning more heavily into its master brand, which also happens to be the corporate brand, through architecture and messaging.

Of course, there are downsides to leaning too heavily on a corporate brand at the expense of individual product brands. By definition, this approach allows for less segmentation and targeting from individual (i.e., product) brands. Dependence on the corporate brand assumes more of a mass audience and universal message. This can also increase business risk. If the corporate brand encounters turbulent times, it can become difficult for product brands to shield themselves from negative backlash.

These are serious concerns, to be sure, but for companies that are confident in their corporate brands and looking for a more cost-effective approach to marketing, bringing portfolio brands closer to the corporate brand—through both strategy and activation—can yield significant savings.

6. INTERNAL ESPRIT DE CORPS

As we will cover in chapter 12, there is a difference between employer branding and employee brand engagement. Employer branding refers to the efforts of companies to attract top-notch talent, which is inherently an externally focused effort. Conversely, employee brand engagement is the process by which a company shapes its current employees' everyday work behavior to make it consistent with the brand identity of the organization. This is clearly more internally focused. However, for both concepts, the corporate brand plays a vital role.

When carefully developed and executed, the corporate brand represents the external manifestation of a company's business strategy. Internally, the same brand can serve as an organizational guide for employees. The Apple brand, for instance, has a strong position as a design-driven, innovative company that offers many types of products and services. Its corporate brand encapsulates the body and soul of the company to employees, as well as inspiring consumers to buy Apple products.[27]

For employees across all levels of an organization, the name on the building and on their business cards is one of the fundamental components of their professional identities. The corporate brand can be a tremendous source of pride. It is not uncommon after mergers and acquisitions for longtime employees—especially those at acquired companies whose legacy brands are being phased out—to struggle with a change in identity. In some cases, employees will refer to their legacy company's brand name years after the name was retired. This is strong evidence of the power of a corporate brand and the deep level of attachment employees develop with it.

The same concept applies to candidates in the recruitment process. As any hiring manager or HR executive will attest to, it would be a vast understatement to say that a company's reputation in the market weighs heavily on a potential recruit's choice of employer. That reputation reflects the perceptions job candidates have of the corporate brand. So whether the brand acts as a recruitment tool or a source of pride for existing employees, the corporate brand clearly matters to employees as much as it does to customers and other stakeholders.

As Rick Wise observed, "Today's employees are less loyal than they were a decade ago, but at the same time workers and managers are 'badged' with their employer's brand like never before. Having a clear corporate story that resonates with employees and recruits is just as important as a resonant story for product brands."[28]

Amazon recently purchased Zappos, an online retailer of shoes, clothing, and other personal items. When the news became official, Zappos sent an announcement to its employees that said, "Zappos and Amazon sitting in a tree..."[29] That distinctive spirit remains with Zappos today as the company functions like a standalone entity with Amazon in the distant background. Although Zappos is a $1 billion company by revenue, its core values don't sound like those of traditional businesses. Those values, which include directions like "create fun and a little weirdness," are clearly intended to generate esprit de corps and help employees feel like they're part of something special.[30]

7. STAYING POWER: LONG LIVE THE CORPORATE BRAND

In an ever-changing, increasingly fickle consumer environment, success in individual product and service lines is never a guarantee. Though many successful product brands have come and gone, great corporate brands continue to thrive. Markets today suffer disruption easily, and rapid innovation has shortened product lifespans. When products and services are fleeting, the brand must be enduring. Once again, more often than not, that brand is corporate.

With a few exceptions, companies tend to outlive specific product and service offerings. So it stands to reason that corporate brands outlive their product brand counterparts. Therefore, it makes sense to invest in the asset with a longer shelf life and greater reach.

Examples of corporate brands outliving product brands are common in many industries, including the automobile industry. Model brands such as the Ford Probe and the Chevy El Camino no longer exist. Even big names like Oldsmobile and Saturn have been retired. In the world of consumer packaged goods, the Pepsi corporate brand has outlived many of its child brands, including WOW Chips, Pepsi A.M., Slice, and Teem. Lifebuoy, the world's first deodorant soap, was Unilever's oldest product. The soap first hit shelves in 1894. It is no longer in existence, but Unilever is still going strong. Young consumers today may have never heard of the Walkman, but they likely know Sony.

Even the most established product brands don't last forever. But history has proven over and over again that corporate brands—with the exception of a possible phase-out following M&A activity—are the brands most likely to withstand the test of time.

THE CORPORATE BRAND OF TOMORROW

The importance of the corporate brand has grown steadily in recent years, and all indications are this trend will continue. Consumers consider the social, environmental, and ethical makeup of the goods and services they select, both as individuals and as corporations. Many consumers today care as much about the company making the products as they do the products themselves.

The trend in corporate brand investment applies not only to B2B and other branded house companies, but even to traditional consumer packaged goods companies that typically go to market based on the strength of their individual product brands. Companies like SC Johnson, The Coca-Cola Company, and The Hershey Company are all examples of this.

Building and maintaining a corporate brand provides numerous benefits, including financial return, risk mitigation during challenging times, leverage to enter new categories and markets, and employees' overall sense of pride. With such power, it's no surprise that the majority of the world's most valuable brands are corporate brands.

PART 4

MANAGING THE INDISPENSABLE BRAND

Chapter 12

Employee Brand Engagement

A number of high-level executives file into a large room in a building located in the middle of Ross Perot Jr.'s Circle T Ranch outside of Dallas, Texas. The facility is part of Deloitte University's seven-year-old, 110-acre campus. The purpose is to participate in a Deloitte Greenhouse engagement, a highly immersive and interactive session that helps leaders address complex business challenges.[1]

Participants in this Greenhouse session include approximately twenty-five executives from a large automotive company that wants to reconstitute its ERP leadership team, which has been struggling lately. The cause of the problem (though the team might not recognize it at the time) is an inability to communicate effectively. Also attending this session are six Deloitte professionals, including Jeff Suttle, Deloitte University's client experience leader and the facilitator of the session. Interestingly, while Suttle tells the Deloitte client team members that they are allowed to be in the room and participate, they are only allowed to speak in questions, never statements.[2]

The setup of the room is equally interesting. For one thing, there is a giant forty-foot mural of an owl on the wall. It doesn't look like an owl at first glance, though—more like a brown tree with eyes peering around.

There is no standard office furniture in the room, but there are comfortable couches and chairs, as if participants had been invited into an unusually large living room. Shockingly, given the profile of the attendees, no one is allowed to carry a laptop or mobile phone.

Once everyone has arrived, the session begins. Suttle tells each participant to pick up one of the black cards lying on the floor and to keep the picture on the back of the card secret. He then instructs them to line up on a spectrum from "zoomed in" to "zoomed out," using only their words to describe their pictures. Participants mill about and consult with one another. Music plays in the background. The executives struggle... and struggle...and struggle a bit more. Finally, after several minutes, they form a line—only to discover they are all holding different parts of the same picture.

One card shows a desert scene. Another shows a cruise ship. Others show spaceships, airplanes, and roosters. One picture shows an island, where people interact with a postman carrying a letter. On that letter is a stamp, and on the stamp is a desert. In the desert is a cowboy watching television. The television shows a city scene, and in that scene, there is a bus. On that bus, there is an ad for a cruise ship. Within that cruise ship ad is a boy on the deck, holding a magazine with a picture of a village, where another child is pictured with a rooster. Each individual picture holds a truth of the whole, but discovering that truth requires effective communication and teamwork.

This exercise allows Deloitte's clients to see the communication problems that plague them in a new light. During the debrief, Suttle asks, "What made it so hard to line up correctly?" Participants reply, "Well, it's the language we used." When Suttle asks what problems the language created, they say it wasn't specific enough, that they looked only at their own cards and used only their own perspectives. Suttle jokes, "Oh, so you mean nobody else has another perspective?"

In less than thirty minutes, Suttle and Deloitte effectively demonstrated the problem: the way this team communicated and shared (or didn't share) the perspectives of their colleagues was holding the group back. Through this exercise and those that followed, Suttle and Deloitte accomplished something that the group had been struggling to do for months. The clients walked out impressed by Deloitte's threefold solution.

First, Deloitte showed participants the obvious truth of their communication problems. Second, Suttle gave participants real actions they could implement when they left. Third, the exercise showed participants that Deloitte is a company willing to throw a bunch of important people in the middle of a room and teach them to "look again."

This is where the story reveals how brand positioning, customer experience, and employee brand engagement can come together to produce magic. Those two words, "look again," are essential to Deloitte's brand positioning. It's a play on words—you think Deloitte is just an accounting firm? Better look again. (In fact, this group represents the firm's business consulting—not accounting—function.) More importantly, though, it's about what Deloitte does for its clients. This is a Big Four professional services firm that can look at problems through multiple lenses and bring innovative, strategic thinking to the table. Deloitte consultants help their clients "look again" at business problems from new perspectives, turning them upside down to see what they didn't before. In that process, Deloitte helps its clients discover all kinds of possible solutions and home in on the best one.

So why does this represent a strong example of employee brand engagement? It shows the way Deloitte demonstrates (rather than lectures) to its employees how to successfully deliver the brand promise to its clients. Critically, Suttle never pulled his Deloitte partners aside and told them they need to attend a training session to learn about the company's brand positioning, "look again," or how to deliver it to clients.

"The last thing partners at Deloitte want is to be told they need to go somewhere for a few days so they can be taught how to live the brand," he said. "So instead, we show them organically." In the process, Suttle demonstrated what the Deloitte brand is all about and how to bring it to life through the client experience. "To be fair, they would never tell me, 'Hey, I just lived the brand.' But they know what the essence of the brand is, and when we debrief a Greenhouse experience, they say things like, 'This is "look again," isn't it?' And I say, 'You think?'"

Deloitte, through its "show, don't tell" approach, provides a textbook example of employee brand engagement on steroids. Let's talk more about what we mean by employee brand engagement and why it's so important to building indispensable brands.

EMPLOYEE ENGAGEMENT: BUILDING A RELATIONSHIP

Before we delve into employee brand engagement, though, let's take a step back and talk more broadly about employee engagement on its own (i.e., beyond how it relates to brand). Employee engagement is the emotional connection employees feel toward their employment organization, which influences their behaviors and level of effort in work-related activities, according to BusinessDictionary.[3]

Companies use several popular models for thinking about employee engagement, many of which are helpful in developing connections between employees and the organizations that employ them. The "Hands, Heads, Hearts" framework is one such model. As the name implies, companies must first get concepts into the hands of employees so they can learn about them. The next step in the progression, heads, is about comprehension. Employees must understand the concepts communicated and know how they pertain to them personally and the company's expectations of their performance. Finally, the hearts component covers the all-important emotional connection these new concepts must establish with employees. In this stage, employees buy into what the learning concepts stand for. They believe in, care about, and become committed to the company's message.

EMPLOYEE ENGAGEMENT AS IT RELATES TO BRAND

Employee *brand* engagement is the process by which a company shapes its employees' everyday work behavior to ensure that it is consistent with the brand identity of the organization. Importantly, this should not be confused with employer branding, which describes how companies influence the *external* perceptions of their brands from a workplace perspective. Employer branding is most often used in recruiting efforts as a means to attract top-notch talent. Conversely, employee brand engagement focuses less on prospective employees and more on the ones already in the building.

Recall that in chapter 6, we covered the importance of brand experience. That chapter focused primarily on external constituencies—customers, in most cases. However, as illustrated in figure 12.1, internal audiences (namely employees) are equally important to successful brand-building. This figure clearly demonstrates a strong link between internal perceptions and business outcomes (in particular, the way external stake-holders experience the brand).

Figure 12.1
Employee Brand Engagement & Customer Experience

Aligning the brand

Experience brand through
Product use
Service relationship
Advertising
Reputation

Experience brand through
Recruitment
Training & Development
Internal communication
Culture/environment
Reward & Incentive

THE BRAND

External stakeholders

Internal stakeholders

Customers' experience of employee
Employees' experience of customers

William J. McEwen, PhD, is the author of *Married to the Brand*. He eloquently describes the inextricable linkage between brand experience and employee brand engagement: "Our research shows a strong positive correlation between a company's level of employee engagement and its level of customer engagement. Each builds upon the other. Energized, passionate employees help create passionate customers. And, in return, customer enthusiasm clearly contributes to the morale and enthusiasm of any employee who comes in contact with those customers. It works hand in glove."[4]

As opposed to customer-focused brand experience, employee brand engagement focuses internally to address how companies should recruit, train, communicate with, and incentivize employees in a manner consistent with the brand strategy. The corporate brand resides at the intersection of these two concepts, informing both as they pursue disparate (yet related) strategies for different audiences.

While employer branding (building the company's brand reputation externally) has gained popularity in recent years, unfortunately, this is not the case with employee brand engagement. This disparity defies logic. As with anything else in branding, how can a company establish positive perceptions externally before it does so internally?

According to BrandingBusiness, a brand strategy agency dedicated to building B2B brands, "A successful brand launch is not possible if the brand is not first successfully launched internally. Gaining employee buy-in and ensuring every individual in the organization understands how they can live the brand is key to building a powerful brand. Companies need to pay as much attention to their internal audiences as they do to their external constituents."[5]

The benefits of employee brand engagement are well documented, both directly and indirectly. One Gallup study found that companies with highly engaged employees have earnings per share that outperform those of companies in the same industry with less engaged employees by 147 percent.[6]

A CASE STUDY: MGM RESORTS

In 2014, MGM Resorts repositioned its brand from a casino company to a worldwide resort and entertainment company. MGM wanted to be known not only for excellent gaming venues but also for world-class restaurants, clubs, hotels, theater facilities, and more. Think of the Bellagio or the MGM Grand in Las Vegas.

Lilian Tomovich, the first chief experience officer (and chief marketing officer) of MGM, had the challenge of ensuring the new brand strategy would succeed. In an effort to drive marketplace impact as quickly as possible, many companies make the mistake of launching their brands externally first and following with internal efforts later (if they do any internal brand engagement at all). Tomovich and her team took a different approach.[7] They socialized the brand's positioning from the inside out, engaging all employees in an effort titled "We Are the SHOW," the cornerstone of which was the following acronym:

- S for smile and greet the guest

- H for hear the story

- O for own the experience

- W for wow the guest

MGM clearly understands that employee brand engagement is a vital component of effective branding and, ultimately, company success. Additionally, as this case demonstrates, employee brand engagement consists of two related components: The people component represents the "who" of employee brand engagement and includes audiences and facilitators. The content and process component represents the "what" and the "how" and includes the materials and activities that comprise the overall initiative. The following two sections cover these components in turn.

COMPONENT 1: PEOPLE (THE "WHO")

The first component of employee brand engagement pertains to people. By people, we mean both the people within the organization who need to be engaged (i.e., audiences) and the people best suited to lead that effort (i.e., facilitators).

Once again, McEwen sheds important light on the topic of employee engagement. "In their attempts to build stronger customer relationships, many companies emphasize managing the traditional 4 Ps of marketing—Product, Price, Place, and Promotion—while appearing to overlook an essential fifth P: People." He goes on to say, "Our research has shown that, when it comes to building customer loyalty, the 'people' factors are often the most important element, outweighing the combined impact of product features, convenient locations, and even low prices."

Let's further break down and explore the "people" component.

Audiences

Who are the people organizations need to engage in brand education? Some companies mistakenly believe that only their frontline employees (e.g., sales representatives and customer service teams) need onboarding and training in brand strategy delivery. However, as pointed out in chapter 9, digital activation and social media have turned employees from every business function into customer-facing roles. Employees across all functions must understand and embrace brand strategy if the effort is to succeed.

At MGM Resorts, the company's top seven thousand leaders participated in a kickoff conference during the reveal of the new branding initiative. Top management highlighted the shift in positioning and discussed its implementation in detail. Other managers learned why the brand needed to transform, how that transformation would take shape in the organization, and how the assembled group would further that strategy. Attendees then trained in their new roles as cultural ambassadors, practicing with their peers to roll out the changes to their seventy-seven thousand employees.

Other companies have used similar tactics. General Electric, for example, invited its 350,000 employees to participate in a brand ambassador program to train its workforce on how to represent the brand both at work and off the clock.[8]

Facilitators

The second factor in the people component, facilitators, refers to the people responsible for communicating brand strategy within the company. Should these be representatives from HR? Perhaps the CMO, or even the CEO? To be sure, leaders within both marketing and HR play vital roles in this effort. However, without visible and broad-based C-suite support, the message may ring hollow.

However, senior-level management is only part of the answer when it comes to spreading the word. Leaders must not only communicate the message themselves but also learn to identify, nurture, and leverage brand champions within their organizations. As the name implies, brand champions are employees who understand, embrace, and behave in accordance with the brand. Their collective influence is second only to the C-suite in its ability to help others buy into the brand strategy.

So how do you find these individuals? You can start by looking at employees' social media activity. According to research from Weber

Shandwick and KRC Research, 39 percent of employees have shared praise or positive comments online about their employers.[9] Additionally, the research shows that 21 percent of employees fall into an "activist" category. These workers voluntarily take positive actions (and no negative actions) regarding their employers, including but not limited to defending and advocating for the brand online.

Social media offers leaders an avenue to find and recruit brand champions, but other creative options exist as well. Leaders should seek to find these brand advocates wherever they can and give them the recognition and resources they need to spread the word.

Human Resources

HR plays an important, unique role in employee brand engagement. Brands have values, and employees should embody those values. As such, companies need formal mechanisms in place to assess brand fit among both existing and potential new employees. HR must determine to what extent a prospective new employee seems to represent the values of the corporate (or business unit) brand and, therefore, the organization.

According to Paul Barton, author of *Maximizing Internal Communication*, "Authentic brands are built from the inside out, and effective internal communication is crucial to branding success. I believe the best way to build an authentic brand starts with hiring people who already embody some of the brand's characteristics and then reinforcing the brand through training, appropriate policies, and ongoing internal communication."[10]

In practice, the role of HR in employee engagement can take many forms. When Dell decided to infuse more branding into its hiring process, the company turned to its internal agency, Dell Blue, to develop a campaign that hit job listings, social platforms, and events. Dell ensured that every employee, future and present, received proper training on how to embody the company brand.[11] QuikTrip, a convenience store company based in Tulsa, Oklahoma, provides another example of employee engagement.[12] This company positions itself on its unwavering commitment to customers (what it calls its "special sauce"). Every job applicant must complete a personality assessment process, which is designed to identify traits and skills that support QuikTrip's brand positioning.[13]

In-person interviews follow the tests to ensure applicants can provide specific stories to back up their answers.

These factors combine to form a comprehensive view of the people factor—but, as mentioned earlier, people make up only half of the whole.

COMPONENT 2: CONTENT AND PROCESS (THE "WHAT" AND "HOW")

The second component of employee brand engagement pertains to the activities used to facilitate the engagement: content and processes. Unfortunately, these activities are often superficial at best. The marketing department issues a memo outlining the brand strategy, distributes some posters and mousepads containing key brand messages, and calls it a day. Slightly more ambitious companies may go a step further to include a limited round of employee training. While these are worthy tactics, an employee brand engagement initiative needs to be a formal, strategic, and ongoing effort if it is to succeed in the long run. Let's break down content and process in greater detail.

Content

One content tool to consider is brand stories. As discussed in chapter 8, brand stories are an important part of any brand strategy. Done well, they endear customers and other external stakeholders to the brand, but they also have the potential to be persuasive internally by educating and engaging employees on brand strategy.

"In order to make the story we tell externally, we have to make sure that our employees understand it and can make it come alive," said Carla Johnson, author of *Experiences: The 7th Era of Marketing.* "As marketers, we spend so much time creating the promise of what a customer or prospect can expect in doing business with us...We have to create promise keepers: the people who make all of those external promises come true, and they can't do it without understanding the story we're trying to tell and the promises we're making."[14]

In a post for *Content Marketing Institute*, Johnson discussed how Motorola Solutions leveraged the power of brand story in employee engagement.[15] When Motorola split into two separate companies, employees eventually found themselves working for new employers when the realignment finished. Rather than assume employees would get the gist, Motorola rebranded more than thirty locations over the weekend, celebrating the new brand promise and helping employees understand what that promise entailed.

Numerous companies have used brand story in this manner. Nike's cofounder and University of Oregon track coach Bill Bowerman once put melted rubber into his family's waffle iron to make a better sole for his runners.[16] That sole later became the iconic Nike waffle sole. While this brand story appeals to consumers, Nike also uses it to reinforce the "Just Do It" attitude of its brand positioning to its employees.

Another tool, employee value proposition, has been gaining favor in recent years. As the name implies, employee value proposition is like a brand positioning or value proposition, except this proposition focuses exclusively on an internal audience. Importantly, however, brands must tightly link this value proposition and the external one or risk creating a disjointed brand.

Chapter 4 provided an excellent prescription to guard against this. In that chapter, we discussed how to create stakeholder translations for brand positioning by audience type. If a company considers its employees to be a relevant stakeholder group—and it absolutely should—an employee value proposition could be as simple as developing a stakeholder translation of the brand promise for that important stakeholder group.

Social media management platform Hootsuite provides an excellent example of an employee brand value proposition. The company's blog proclaims, "At Hootsuite, we're revolutionizing communications via social and transforming messages into meaningful relationships. Our team is comprised of passionate, egoless peeps having fun building something bigger than themselves. Each day, you will bring our core values to life through your actions and collaboration with our team, our customers, and our community."[17] Hootsuite's employee value proposition effectively conveys the essence of the brand to employees, helping them understand their high-level role in delivering that brand to outside audiences.

The last employee branding tool we will cover is the brand playbook. More than a mere style guide—which outlines how the brand should be presented visually and in text—the brand playbook establishes guidelines for how employees should present the brand holistically. This includes details on procedures, processes, and rules that cover what it means to live the brand. Among other things, an effective brand playbook clearly delineates which types of activities and behaviors are consistent with the intent of the brand strategy and which are not. Hootsuite built an entire library of branding for this purpose, which resulted in a 50 percent increase in qualified job applicants.

The brand playbook includes the employee value proposition, as discussed earlier in this section, but that's not all. It also provides instructions for how employees should act in accordance with brand guidelines in every situation, from face-to-face interactions to social media communications.

Process

In terms of the processes and activities brands can use to deliver content to employees, options are virtually limitless. Town hall meetings, offsite company functions, and formal training sessions are traditional avenues. However, today's digital landscape provides companies with a variety of other options for activation channels, including company intranet, YouTube videos, and social media sites (both internal and public).

It's helpful to think about process as an ongoing effort rather than a solo event or moment in time. As is the case with external audiences, employees need repetition and continuity to absorb complex concepts and messages. Workers should be exposed to consistent messages over time, ideally in new and creative manners, to get those messages to stick. New employees will always need onboarding, so companies should use that time as a starting point.

Both during and after the eight-month rollout at MGM Resorts, brand leaders used an internal communications plan to keep the brand positioning top of mind.[18] Daily leadership and team member updates kept employees engaged through digital channels. Back-of-house posters showed team members living the brand values under the headline "This is my stage." Employee surveys completed after the rollout yielded positive feedback about the company; combined with increases in revenue, net income, and revenue per available room, MGM's strategy was a resounding success.

Miller Brewing Company provides another example of effective processes.[19] Miller positions itself on a heritage of craftsmanship dating back to the mid-1800s. The company's founder, Frederick Miller, is at the heart of that positioning. To help employees live the brand values of pride in their work, tradition, and passion for great beer, the company implemented an internal branding effort that included multiple engaging components. Larger-than-life posters of workers as heroes throughout breweries, "I Make Miller Time" T-shirts, and booklets that celebrated the tradition of beer all contributed to the effort. The company even featured employees talking about their passion for brewing Miller beer in TV commercials, turning an internal campaign into an external asset as well.

The content and processes of employee brand engagement take good ideas and turn them into reality. By understanding the roles these tools play, companies can get their employees on board and excited about their brands.

EMPLOYEE BRAND ENGAGEMENT DESERVES THE SPOTLIGHT

Employee brand engagement is a critical, yet often overlooked, aspect of brand strategy. As marketers, we are trained to take an outside-in approach. Market research and other efforts help us gain a deep understanding of the wants, needs, attitudes, and perceptions of customers and other external stakeholders. We use that information to develop outward-looking brand strategies. This is certainly a best practice that we should maintain, but just because it's necessary does not make it sufficient.

No brand strategy—no matter how compelling or unique—can succeed in the long run if it is not understood, embraced, and lived by the employees who are responsible for its delivery. This includes all employees, not just marketing or customer service departments. When companies develop entire workforces of people who are committed to their brands, they can achieve things far beyond the reach of companies that fail to turn that branding focus on themselves.

Chapter 13

Brand Measurement and Marketing Accountability

Xerox is an information technology company headquartered in Norwalk, Connecticut. With annual revenue exceeding $10 billion, Xerox sells print and digital document solutions, plus document technology products, in more than 160 countries around the world.[1] This company has a venerable corporate brand by any measure, including its position on Interbrand's Best Global Brands 2016 Ranking.[2]

Although several factors contribute to Xerox's stature as a respected corporate brand, one of the most important is the attention the company dedicates to measuring and managing its brand's reputation. Among other partnerships, the company actively uses Young & Rubicam's Brand Asset Valuator (BAV) tool. As referenced earlier in this book, BAV measures brand qualities and metrics that drive marketplace success. The BAV model breaks a brand down into two core components: brand strength, which refers to future growth potential, and brand stature, which refers to a brand's current operating value. Brand strength is a function of two pillars: differentiation and relevance. Brand stature is a function of two other pillars: esteem and knowledge. Brands that score highly on both strength and stature are considered leaders in their respective categories.

Xerox provides a great example of how brand measurement (in this case with the BAV tool) can drive effective decision-making and nurture a strong corporate brand. The company evaluated more than forty-eight attributes across the four BAV pillars referenced above, then assessed these measurements for its own brand, key competitive brands, and other brands across the broader technology landscape. From there, Xerox conducted a factor analysis that resulted in seven territories that it believes drive brand strength.

Next, Xerox further evaluated the seven territories across the components of brand strength—differentiation and relevance. The company sought to determine which territories most effectively drove differentiation, which drove relevance, and which drove both effectively. This analysis led to the identification of four factors that formed the basis for evaluating and managing the brand going forward.

Xerox then prioritized those four factors to align with its goals. The company's leaders determined that they were satisfied with the current performance of one factor and sought to maintain it. For two others, they determined that the factors were important and had room for improvement, so they sought to strengthen them. The last factor, which Xerox called "bold," consisted of seven attributes: daring, dynamic, energetic, independent, fun, social, and carefree. More than all the rest, Xerox determined that this factor was critically important and had the most potential for meaningful differentiation for the brand. As such, Xerox decided to focus on significant performance improvement for this factor.

"When we initially looked at 48 attributes, it was a bit unwieldy, but once we conducted the factor analysis with Y&R, it became much more obvious what we should be doing, and much more manageable," said Barbara Basney, vice president of global brand, advertising, and media for Xerox. "Differentiation is a big problem in our category. There really isn't anyone who is successfully standing out in the competitive set. But we know that 'bold' is the one thing that if we focus on and implement right, it is going to help us break through the clutter with relevance."[3]

To be sure, many companies use tracking and measurement tools like Y&R's BAV. This story is more interesting, though, because of the way Xerox chose to consistently incorporate the tool into its decision-making and campaign development. As Basney noted, "When we determined that 'bold' was one of the factors we wanted to emphasize and own, we began to develop initiatives that were much less expected and much more breakthrough. It also provided the marketing communications team with 'marching orders'—things to be mindful of when activating and messaging."

Importantly, Xerox strives to correlate its marketing activity and marketplace outcomes to better establish a cause-and-effect relationship. "Something we do for every brand initiative is we identify certain needles we're trying to move regarding the perception of the brand with our target audiences," said Basney. "We want to make sure our initiatives are resulting in a lift on these brand perceptions. And we also want to increase other performance metrics like business interest, likelihood of doing business with us, willingness to learn more, willingness to accept a proposal, etc. So we always do a pretest on attributes before anything goes live, and when we see a double-digit or more increase on these measures, we know we've been successful."

Xerox provides a great demonstration of how brand measurement must consist of more than simple attribute tracking and basic diagnostics. Beyond both of those functions, effective brand measurement needs to be prescriptive so that it can actively help marketers manage their brands more effectively.

MARKETING ACCOUNTABILITY AND MEASURING OUTCOMES

Before we dive into the topic of brand measurement, we should first consider the broader definition of marketing accountability. Marketing accountability covers the use of data to connect marketing campaigns and strategies to bottom-line outcomes. As is the case with many of the topics we've covered, others have written entire books on marketing accountability, and their expertise and perspectives need not be rehashed here. For our purposes, though, it will help to gain a high-level understanding of why marketing accountability is important and how brand measurement can help achieve it.

Traditionally, marketers have struggled to establish tight correlations between their activities and business outcomes. This is largely because many factors affect the latter, which makes it challenging to isolate the impact of marketing activities and investments. While this is true for most business functions, it's arguably most true for marketing. It should not be surprising, therefore, that chief marketing officers last an average of four years in their position, about half as long as the tenure of the average CEO.[4]

So CMOs clearly need to strive for greater levels of marketing accountability. One recent *Forbes* study noted that, "Without broad understanding and consensus measures of the contribution of marketing to enterprise value, marketers, organizations, and the economy will suffer."[5] The study found that low accountability was tied to low returns on investment and damage to CMOs' reputations.

Increasing marketing accountability is easier said than done, though. In a post for Marketo, Jon Miller broke down the journey to greater marketing accountability into five sequential stages: denial, fear, confusion, self-promotion, and, finally, accountability.[6]

The denial stage, as the name implies, describes the initial refusal of the CMO to believe an accountability issue exists. This stems from the belief that because marketing is an inherently inexact science, it is not possible to hold marketers as accountable for business results as other functions. Miller argues that this stage can cause other members of the C-suite to withdraw from the CMO, leaving the lone executive isolated and vulnerable.

In the fear stage comes the recognition of the need to prove the return on investment of marketing activities. Here, Miller says many CMOs choose to avoid the spotlight for fear of exposure. Once again, this does not bode well for the CMO's relationships with fellow cross-functional leaders.

The confusion stage comes next. Here, the CMO is prepared to act but is unsure what to do. Perhaps the CMO puts in place simple tracking plans, but those basics do little to demonstrate how marketing activities and investments directly (or even indirectly) contribute to bottom-line performance.

According to Miller, the self-promotion stage is fraught with desperation. Myriad marketing metrics, data points, facts, figures, charts, and graphs appear in this stage under the guise of marketing accountability but with none of the gravity of the real thing. Typically, these include only "softer" measurements, like basic brand health and customer perceptions, and are difficult to tie to real business results, like revenue and profit.

Accountability, the final stage and the desired destination, eventually arises from the rubble of the other phases. Here, the CMO finally determines the right measurements to track—not just traditional marketing metrics, but also financial and other business performance metrics. The CMO understands how to link marketing activities and investments to business outcomes in a credible, effective manner. This builds credibility within the C-suite, especially with the CEO and CFO. At this point, Miller notes, marketing ceases to be a cost center and becomes a generator of profitable revenue and growth.

FURTHER EVIDENCE OF C-SUITE DISHARMONY

Importantly, Miller's perspectives regarding marketing accountability are supported by empirical data, especially the part about the isolation CMOs often experience within the C-suite.

According to a report issued by the CMO Council and Deloitte—*CMOs and the Spark to Drive Growth*—there is a significant gap between how CMOs and the C-suite view the role of marketing. Specifically, the study found that 95 percent of business leaders believe their CMO's top priorities should include revenue growth (versus 70 percent agreement among CMOs). Additionally, 49 percent of business leaders believe their CMO's top priorities should include increasing market share (versus 32 percent agreement among CMOs).[7]

Clearly, this represents an important lack of alignment between CMOs and their C-suite counterparts. In a recent article from Marketing Insider Group discussing this report, Michael Brenner wrote, "Marketing leaders need to go way deeper into the data and analytical side of marketing in order to ensure marketing decisions and cross-department engagement are achieving end-game results. Not just engagement, lead generation, and brand trust signals but increases in sales across different channels and a more aggressive approach to gaining market share."[8]

The report is a sobering call to action for marketers to move beyond the domain of brand and to think more holistically about customers and business results. Increasingly, CMOs are being charged with mastering a deeper sophistication of the businesses their brands serve, which is a precursor to marketing accountability. According to Diana O'Brien, global chief marketing officer at Deloitte, "CMOs today are very challenged to pick their head up and take an enterprise view. It's critical that they see themselves not as just the manager of the brand and the marketing plan, but as a growth driver for the organization. It's in that role that they have a voice in the strategy and can help influence how the organization moves forward."

To be clear, marketing accountability is about far more than brand measurement. However, it should be evident from the above context that measurement plays an important role in achieving that final stage of accountability—and in ensuring the continued success of the CMO.

CLEARING THE CONFUSION AROUND BRAND MEASUREMENT

Ask most brand managers how they feel about brand measurement, and you will likely conjure up memories of lengthy, mind-numbing presentations from market research agencies. These presentations tend to focus on brand health metrics, like awareness and consideration. If the brand managers are lucky, they might see a few brand-specific measures in these presentations, such as attributes that pertain specifically to their brand positioning.

Traditional brand tracking, as described above, is certainly important. However, that is just the tip of the iceberg when it comes to implementing a comprehensive brand measurement system. More important than brand tracking is what marketers do with the data they capture. How do they analyze and manipulate their data to improve decisions and create a competitive advantage?

Marketers benefit by thinking about measurement along three distinct time horizons, each with a different capacity to drive decision-making capabilities and affect business performance.

DIAGNOSTIC: THE PAST

At a minimum, brand tracking should help brand managers diagnose the impact of their past activities and the overall health of their brands. This is mostly a historical, backward-looking approach, but it does have its uses. Digital brand measurement, as discussed in chapter 9, has taken diagnostic capabilities to an entirely new level. Digital attribution models can diagnose results and explain whether (and to what extent) specific activities contribute to business performance metrics, such as new customer acquisition. While this is still a once-removed measurement from establishing a correlation between marketing activity and its ultimate impact on long-term brand equity, it's certainly a step in the right direction.

PRESCRIPTIVE: THE PRESENT

More powerful than simple diagnosis of past performance and current brand health is the use of that same data in a prescriptive way. Marketers can set objectives and targets for select brand metrics that trigger certain tactics or changes in strategic direction. For example, a company in the midst of repositioning to a more aspirational brand promise may establish market-driven milestones on certain brand attributes that, when achieved, trigger a shift in focus to bolder, more ambitious aspects of positioning. In this sense, brand metrics help marketers make more objective, data-driven decisions as they manage their brands.

PREDICTIVE: THE FUTURE

If diagnostic measurement is steeped in the past and prescriptive in the present, then predictive capabilities are all about the future. These analytics help marketers determine the likelihood of events to come and use that knowledge to prepare accordingly. This measurement science is in its infancy, but it could have powerful implications for how marketers manage brand equity.[9] Sophisticated modeling could help executives make both tactical and strategic decisions that consider short-term effects on business performance, as well as projected long-term effects on brand equity.

These three time-based lenses and respective capabilities showcase the powerful effect that brand measurement can (and to an extent already does) have on a CMO's ability to achieve true marketing accountability. With these in mind, let's take a closer look at the current state of brand measurement.

THE CURRENT STATE OF BRAND MEASUREMENT

With our understanding of the broader context of marketing accountability, the importance of brand measurement should be apparent. However, as with several other aspects of brand strategy covered in this book, marketers do not believe they are doing a good job of brand measurement, despite the widespread agreement on its importance. Once again, market research backs this up.

Nielsen subsidiary Visual IQ is a leading marketing intelligence provider. The company recently published a study that examines the extent to which marketing executives are confident in their tracking of the overall performance of their brands.[10] The study also covers executives' confidence in their measurement of the effects created by individual campaigns on different channels. The report is aptly titled *Branding Measurement in Today's Accountable World: A Tale of Two Marketers.* In it, Visual IQ points out that marketers have made significant strides in brand measurement (especially due to the increasing use of digital channels and their inherent measurability). However, the study maintains that marketers still have a long way to go. CMOs' capabilities have increased, but so have CEOs' expectations.

The good news is that the study shows an increased recognition of the importance of brand measurement. According to the research, 75 percent of marketers surveyed in the United States view the metrics they use to measure and optimize branding campaigns as "very" or "extremely" important. However, when it comes to organizations' demonstrated ability to measure the impact of marketing activity on brand equity (especially beyond digital channels), marketers are not very confident. Eighty percent of marketers surveyed indicated that measuring the impact of branding efforts is more challenging than measuring the impact of direct response efforts. This perspective on the challenge of measurement carried through to the marketers' perceptions of their own capabilities. While 85 percent of the respondents said they were "very" or "extremely" confident in their organization's ability to quantify the impact of direct response efforts, only 64 percent said the same about branding efforts.

Visual IQ's study attempted to diagnose the underlying issues of this measurement challenge. Unsurprisingly, the key problem appeared to be a lack of sufficient tools with which to measure and optimize branding efforts. When asked which challenges or obstacles stand in the way of effective measurement and optimized branding, the top responses were:

1. Lack of advanced measurement tools or methodologies (46 percent)
2. Inability to tie multiple brand engagement activities into a single brand metric or overall score (42 percent)

3. Lack of analytical expertise and resources to measure or optimize branding efforts (39 percent)
4. Inability to tie brand engagement to business outcomes (33 percent)

This last set of findings is consistent with takeaways from the *Forbes* study referenced earlier in this chapter. That study had this to say about the primary obstacles in front of effective marketing accountability: "There are five primary obstacles holding marketing organizations back from achieving higher levels of marketing accountability and performance. Most involve establishing common standards, measures, organizational competencies, and codified approaches to communicating, measuring, and managing the contribution of marketing investment to enterprise value."[11]

With so many challenges in front of them, the question for marketers becomes: What can we do about it?

UNDERSTANDING TYPES OF METRICS

Types (or categories) of brand metrics that companies can potentially track differ by industry. For example, B2B companies prioritize different metrics than B2C organizations, and companies in product-based industries don't look at the same things as those in service-based sectors. Metric types also differ based on the goals and intended uses of the metrics by organizations. Companies interested in linking brand activity to business performance must track more and different types of metrics than those interested only in tracking basic brand health.

In general, though, three types of metrics comprise a comprehensive and effective brand measurement system. (See figure 13.1.) The first two categories are entirely about the customer and the brand, while the third considers the impact of the first two types on the organization itself.

Figure 13.1
Types of Brand Metrics

 Perception Metrics *How they VIEW you*

Funnel
General brand health metrics

Awareness
Consideration
Purchase Intent

Image
Brand-specific attributes

Convenient
Irreverent
Humorous

 Behavior Metrics *What they DO*

Passive
Lower Levels of Commitment

Browsing a website
Writing a review
Downloading an article

Active
Higher Levels of Commitment

Submitting a contact form
Requesting a proposal
Making a purchase

 Performance Metrics *What you ACHIEVE*

Non-financial
Business and market impact

Market Share
HH Penetration
Share of Wallet

Financial
Economic impact

Unit Sales/Revenue
Earnings/Profitability
Gross/Net Margin

PERCEPTION METRICS

Brand perception metrics are all about how customers view the brand. These can be further broken down into two subcategories: brand funnel and brand image.

Brand funnel metrics are perhaps the most common metrics in use today. Most companies that engage in brand measurement include this metric type in their tracking systems. Funnel metrics tend to be fairly consistent across companies and help marketers understand the underlying health of their brands. Although the traditional model of a linear purchase funnel (e.g., awareness, consideration, purchase) is a bit murkier in a digitally activated brand environment, it still provides a suitable framework for these purposes.

Brand image metrics also pertain to brand health. Unlike the brand funnel metrics, though, they tend to be more specific to an individual brand, especially that brand's positioning. As referenced in the Xerox example that opened this chapter, most every company is interested in tracking specific attributes that contribute to the brand's levels of differentiation and relevance. These metrics help companies understand how audiences perceive their brands in the marketplace, what target audiences believe about those brands, and what feelings the brand evokes.

Brand equity refers to enduring perceptions, and perceptions refer to the ways in which customers think and act in relation to the brand.[12] Stronger positive perceptions are more likely to influence purchase decisions and add value to a business. If marketers don't understand consumers' perceptions of their brands, they cannot effectively grow their businesses. However, by tracking and quantifying customer perceptions, marketers can see where their brands stand in the market relative to the competition. This includes, among other things, where the brand has high-potential white space opportunities for positioning within the category.

BEHAVIOR METRICS

If perception metrics are all about how consumers think and feel, behavior metrics explain what consumers actually do. These are sometimes called engagement or interaction metrics. Behavior metrics have become increasingly popular with the emergence of digital marketing and social media.

Behavior metrics break down into two subcategories: passive and active. Passive behavior metrics typically occur earlier in the purchase funnel and include low-involvement and low-commitment forms of interaction. Browsing a website, reading a review, and downloading an article all fall under this subcategory. According to Pew Research Center, more than 80 percent of internet users seek online product reviews, discussion forum recommendations, or feedback from social media before making a purchase decision for the first time, which makes these metrics critically important to marketers.[13]

Active behavior metrics move a little further down the purchase funnel. Here, the levels of interest, involvement, and effort are higher than they are with passive metrics. Examples of active behaviors include reaching out to a company for information, filling out a contact form, sending a request for proposal, and, of course, actual purchase. These examples all demonstrate a high level of engagement and interest, even though a commercial transaction may not have yet occurred.

PERFORMANCE METRICS

Performance metrics are essential for organizations to connect the dots between the investments, initiatives, and activities of their brands and the financial results of the business. Marketers can and should consider these metrics from both a nonfinancial and financial perspective.

Nonfinancial performance metrics are business results that, although not inherently quantifiable from an economic standpoint, tend to be strong indicators of financial performance. Often, they represent a link between brand activity and direct financial measurement. Examples of nonfinancial performance metrics include market share; household penetration; customer acquisition, retention, and loyalty; and share of wallet. It's easy to see how increases in each of these metrics can ultimately lead to improvement in one or more financial performance metrics.

Conversely, financial performance metrics are the ones typically found on a company's income statement or other financial documents. Driving performance on these metrics, of course, is the ultimate goal of any for-profit business, so it is natural that marketers should want to understand the extent to which brand efforts affect the business's bottom line. Examples of financial performance metrics include revenue, profitability, and margin.

As we previously established, business performance metrics (financial and nonfinancial) are a central component of any marketing accountability effort. Unless marketers can move beyond the first two categories of metrics (which are all about the brand and customers) and demonstrate tangible proof of impact on business results, they have little hope of achieving accountability. The challenge is to establish a credible link (or at least a strong correlation) between the first two categories of metrics and the third.

HOW TO IMPLEMENT EFFECTIVE BRAND MEASUREMENT

The optimal way to approach brand measurement varies by company and industry. There is no single, universally accepted best way to measure. Still, some measurement—even just basic brand health tracking—is better than no measurement at all. The approach for any given company will differ based on its goals, but all companies can follow these guiding principles that tend to hold true regardless of industry or measurement objectives.

GUIDING PRINCIPLE 1: USE A MIX OF METRIC TYPES

Marketers should include a mix of the different types of metrics described earlier. Each type of metric (perception, behavior, performance) has merit. However, the real power in measurement comes when a marketer can look at the brand—and, by extension, the business—and gain a holistic perspective using a variety of data points. This is the aspect of a metric system that enables a company to move along the continuum from diagnostic to prescriptive and potentially even predictive.

GE Healthcare measures the success of its brand across all three metric types. Through a combination of continuous tracking and an annual brand health study, GE Healthcare tracks measurements such as awareness, familiarity, consideration, purchase interest, likelihood to recommend, and Net Promoter Score. The company correlates these metrics with commercial and financial performance metrics, like revenue and customer acquisition, to create an accurate assessment of the brand's impact on business objectives.

GUIDING PRINCIPLE 2: BENCHMARK AGAINST THE COMPETITION

Brand metrics, no matter how robust or comprehensive, are of little use without a relevant frame of reference. Marketers must choose other brands against which to track and compare performance. The obvious brands to include in a dashboard are those of close category competitors, but best-in-class companies with aspirations of building world-class brands tend to include brands outside their competitive sets—sometimes even those in different industries.

IBM obviously tracks its corporate brand along with those of its key category competitors. But, as mentioned in an earlier chapter, it also tracks and benchmarks its brand against technology companies outside its own category. On several select metrics, IBM compares itself to world-class brands in completely unrelated industries, providing a unique perspective on opportunities to improve.

GUIDING PRINCIPLE 3: ESTABLISH BASELINES AND TARGETS

Companies should establish baselines and targets for brand measurement. As is the case with the above principle of competitive benchmarking, any given metric at any point in time lacks meaning without context, including how that metric is trending and how it compares to an upcoming milestone target. In large part, it is this aspect of a measurement system that can help elevate it from diagnostic to prescriptive.

Visa Europe is diligent about establishing goals and targets for key brand metrics within its measurement system. The company sets clear objectives both annually and in relation to specific programs and activities. For the latter, Visa Europe determines the success of brand-related activities relative to a set of predetermined objectives, which makes it easy to gauge which branding initiatives are most successful.

GUIDING PRINCIPLE 4: CORRELATE BRAND PERFORMANCE WITH BUSINESS RESULTS

This principle has been a consistent theme throughout this chapter. Ultimately, brand measurement operates in service of improved business performance and enhanced marketing accountability. To accomplish these objectives, a measurement system must include both brand and business performance metrics, as well as tools, processes, and approaches to help establish relationships between the two, preferably with a distinct cause-effect connection. At minimum, business performance metrics should include key performance indicators like sales leads, unit volume, and market share. Ideally, they also include financial metrics such as revenue, profit, and margin.

Hewlett-Packard is an example of a company that does an outstanding job correlating its brand programs with broader business measurements. One metric of interest to the company is customer loyalty—the extent to which business customers continue to purchase from HP and spend disproportionately on the brand. Through premeasurements and post-measurements, HP establishes a link between its branding activities and one of its most important business metrics.

GUIDING PRINCIPLE 5: KEEP IT SIMPLE

One of the most common pitfalls of brand measurement systems is allowing them to become overly ambitious or too complex to manage. When this happens, marketers may lose confidence in the credibility of their systems and sometimes even abandon them altogether.

However, as mentioned earlier, some measurement is almost always better than none. While it is important to establish meaningful and aspirational objectives, it is equally important that the system be realistic in both its scope and pace. This might mean initially limiting the dashboard to include only the most important metrics or capping the extent to which correlations are drawn between metrics. Marketers would be wise to increase their measurement efforts gradually over time, adding new capabilities as their proficiency increases.

Teradata embraces the notion of simplicity with regard to brand measurement. The company believes that if the system is too complicated, it won't be leveraged. As such, Teradata uses multiple forms of research and tracking to inform its measurement system, but it does not obsess over trying to coordinate them or reconcile apparent discrepancies. Teradata also recognizes the value of softer qualitative input to support its otherwise quantitative dashboard.

No two companies are alike, and as such, no two approaches to brand measurement will be identical, either. These guiding principles can apply to a wide variety of situations, though, and provide an excellent blueprint for marketers to begin measuring their brand-building efforts more effectively.

A FINAL WORD ON ACCOUNTABILITY

Most marketing executives recognize the importance of marketing accountability in the digital age and understand the role a good measurement system plays in achieving that accountability. The rapid emergence of digital activation channels and advances in data analytics have greatly increased marketers' ability to measure brand performance and its impact on business outcomes. Despite this, research indicates that most marketing executives remain uncomfortable with their organizations' capabilities in this vital aspect of brand management.

To make meaningful contributions to business performance, increase marketing accountability, and secure their tenure in the C-suite, CMOs need to become more adept in brand measurement. They must move beyond mere tracking and diagnosing in brand-related measurement and begin to understand how their most valuable assets—their brands—and the initiatives and programs behind them impact business results.

Chapter 14

The Challenges and Opportunities Ahead

In the previous chapters, we have covered topics ranging from brand positioning and architecture to brand experience and employee engagement. The objective behind these chapters was to help marketers overcome the current state of brand monotony that characterizes so many product and service categories today. Additionally, the goal was to help put forward a blueprint for making brands indispensable to the customers they're intended to serve. Let's put everything together and see just how powerful an indispensable brand can be.

The Hershey Company's "Shared Goodness" promise embraces many of the concepts we've discussed.[1] This promise is simple but powerful, spanning more than one hundred years of a brand that does much more than provide a name for a label. The "Shared Goodness" promise continues the legacy of Milton Hershey, guiding the Hershey brand to champion the shared futures of today's children, the shared business of sustainable practices, the shared planet upon which we all live, and the shared communities in which The Hershey Company operates.

Hershey's promise includes, among other aspects, its corporate brand, positioning, promise, experience, story, and employee engagement. That promise succeeds because it represents more than a platitude or eye-popping piece in a corporate social responsibility report—it's compelling, genuine, and authentic. As The Hershey Company president Todd Tillemans said, "These represent the intentions of (our founder) Milton Hershey. We're 125 years old, and we represent one of the original purpose-driven brands."[2]

In the process of living its purpose, Hershey has clearly become an indispensable brand. Each of its products (and associated brands) carries a distinct taste profile, an iconic form, and the same promise that Hershey infuses in all its brands. As Tillemans noted, "Others have tried to emulate us by launching their answer to Kisses or their version of peanut butter cups, but they're shown as imposters. We have been able to own these entities and forge special relationships with consumers through our brands. Because more important than all of these tangible (product) features, there is the Hershey brand promise that makes our products and brands special."

Other brands may attempt to copy Hershey, but even if they were able to replicate ingredients and recipes, they will never dethrone the king. The brands of The Hershey Company are indispensable, and in that distinction lies tremendous power and value.

THE JOURNEY FROM INDISTINGUISHABLE TO INDISPENSABLE

Business leaders, authors, professors, marketers, and consultants have consistently posed a rhetorical, yet important, question: If your product, brand, or company were no longer available tomorrow, would anyone care? And if so, why? In other words: Are you indispensable?

In his article for the *Harvard Business Review* "The Ten Questions Every Change Agent Must Answer," Bill Taylor identified the critical questions effective leaders must ask themselves and their organizations.[3] Two of those critical questions are essentially proxies for indispensability. One is "If your company went out of business tomorrow, who would miss you, and why?" while the other is even more direct: "Can your customers live without you?"

This book began by declaring war on brand monotony. Whether we call it sameness, homogeneity, commoditization, or monotony, it doesn't matter. Brand monotony leads to myriad negative consequences, as referenced in the opening chapter, including lower price points, reduced margins, declining market share, and lower profitability. Brands that linger in monotony (as defined by customers) for extended periods of time risk commoditization and, eventually, extinction.

Conversely, the antithesis of monotony—and the ultimate goal of world-class brands—is indispensability. Here again, experts ask a variety of questions to measure the end state. Is your brand preferred? Is it relevant? Is it engaging? Would you recommend it? Each question leads to an important discussion, and we will address each in the next section. However, the truth of indispensable brands remains simple: to be indispensable is to be absolutely necessary in the lives of your customers. It means your brand is one customers cannot live without. If you were no longer available tomorrow, they would care deeply. Your absence would represent a significant void in their lives.

PROXIES FOR INDISPENSABILITY

Once again, indispensable brands take many forms and can be defined in a variety of ways. This section covers how several world-class market research agencies and management consulting firms think about, address, define, and quantify this highly ambitious—yet incredibly worthy—objective.

PROPHET: RELEVANCE

Every year, brand and marketing consultancy Prophet surveys approximately 13,500 customers on 275 brands across 27 industries to discover which companies are relevant in its *Brand Relevance Index*. According to Prophet, "Relentlessly relevant brands engage, surprise, and connect. They delight, disrupt, and deliver. They are restless. They push themselves to earn and re-earn customers' loyalty—and they define and redefine what's possible in their categories and in our world."[4] Prophet breaks down what it means by "relentlessly relevant" into multiple factors: customer-obsessed, ruthlessly pragmatic, distinctively inspired, and pervasively innovative.[5] Each factor contributes to a brand's indispensability, whether through the needs its products fulfill or through the allure of its positioning to audiences.

In 2017, Prophet's five most relevant brands were Apple, Google, Amazon, Netflix, and Pinterest.[6] These brands undeniably own vast amounts of real estate in consumers' minds, and to their target audiences, they are as indispensable as it gets.

HARRIS INTERACTIVE: REPUTATION

While Prophet measures relevance, market research firm Harris Interactive measures reputation. The Harris Poll *Reputation Quotient* studies audience perceptions of brands across twenty attributes and six dimensions, which allows Harris to track specific drivers of reputation changes over time.[7] The dimensions and their associated attributes are:

1. Social responsibility: supports good causes, environmental responsibility, community responsibility
2. Products and services: high quality, innovation, value, brand support
3. Vision and leadership: market opportunities, leadership quality, vision for the future
4. Emotional appeal: positive sentiment, admiration, respect, trust
5. Financial performance: competitive standing, a record of profitability, investment risk, growth prospects
6. Workplace environment: employee reward structures, workplace morale, quality of talent

With the goal of measuring reputation, Harris Interactive came up with the following top five list of brands: Kraft Heinz, Amazon, UPS, Microsoft, and Wegmans.[8] Amazon makes both this list and Prophet's, which should surprise no one, given both Amazon's relevance to consumers' daily lives and its impressive market footprint and performance track record.

GALLUP: ENGAGEMENT

Research-based management consultancy Gallup measures brands through a different lens: engagement. Gallup's research says that consumers are more likely to make purchase decisions based on emotional factors, not logical factors, and that brands must elicit strong emotions from their audiences if they seek to stand out. The survey Gallup uses, called *The Gallup CE*[3], distinguishes between customers who are fully engaged, indifferent, or actively disengaged. Companies that hope to command a premium price point for their brands should pay close attention to this measurement, as Gallup found that fully engaged customers lead to a 23 percent boost in revenue, profitability, and share of wallet.[9]

BAIN & COMPANY: NET PROMOTER SCORE

Let's cover one final metric and its relationship to brand indispensability: Net Promoter Score (NPS) from Bain & Company. Fred Reichheld and a Bain team, working with data from Satmetrix, tested a variety of questions to see how well they correlated with customer behavior.[10] As it turned out, one question reigned supreme for mature, competitive industries: "What is the likelihood you would recommend Company (or Brand) X to a friend or colleague?"

By asking enough customers, companies can find their own Net Promoter Score, which ranges from –100 to 100.[11] If every customer rates the likelihood of recommendation at 6 or lower, the company would score a –100. However, if every customer rates the brand a 9 or 10, the brand would score a perfect 100. Not only is this single-number metric easy to comprehend, but research proves that companies with a higher Net Promoter Score grow faster and succeed more than their competitors.[12] (See figure 14.1 for results of the 2018 NPS study by industry.) It's safe to say that the closer the NPS is to 100, the more likely the brand is indispensable to the customers it serves.

Figure 14.1
2018 Net Promotor Score (NPS) Leaders, by Industry

Industry	Leader	Leader's NPS
Airlines	Jet Blue	74
Auto Insurance	USAA	73
Banking	USAA	79
Brokerage & Investments	Vanguard	70
Cable & Satellite TV	Verizon Fios	32
Cell Phone Service	Cricket	58
Credit Cards	American Express	60
Department & Specialty Stores	Costco	79
Drug Stores & Pharmacies	Walmart Pharmacies	32
Grocery & Supermarkets	H-E-B	72
Health Insurance	Kaiser Permanente	40
Home & Contents Insurance	USAA	78
Hotels	Ritz Carlton	75
Internet Service	Fios (a Verizon brand)	28
Laptop Computers	Apple	63
Life Insurance	Allstate	44
Online Entertainment	Netflix	62
Online Shopping	Nordstrom.com	64
Shipping Services	DHL	45
Smartphones	Apple	60
Software and Apps	Turbo Tax	55
Tablet Computers	Amazon	68
Travel Websites	Airbnb	43

Source: NICE Satmetrix

Relevance, reputation, engagement, and willingness to recommend are all worthwhile goals to pursue and metrics to track. Each in its own way represents a proxy for determining the extent to which a brand is truly indispensable.

THE PATH TO BECOME AN INDISPENSABLE BRAND

Becoming an indispensable brand is a challenging but worthwhile goal. Few brands are so integral in their customers' lives that they would be missed if they disappeared, but those that do become indispensable enjoy an unmatched level of marketplace dominance and financial returns. This book holds all the information marketers need to make their brands indispensable, which is recapped in the form of ten imperatives here.

IMPERATIVE 1: REASSERT INFLUENCE; LEAD, DON'T FOLLOW

The internet, digital activation, and social media have leveled the playing field of marketing and brand management. In many ways, these factors have tilted the balance toward the consumer. While it's true that brand managers no longer have the same degree of control over their brands they enjoyed in the early days of brand management, the pendulum has swung too far in the opposite direction. Marketers must reassume their leadership role relative to customers and resist the temptation to follow so-called best practices blindly. They must stop copying what they like about their competitors' strategies and tactics and develop their own, inspired by strategic brand positioning. Marketers still have the ability to exert influence in the commercial equation, and they should resume doing so to a much greater extent.

IMPERATIVE 2: POSITION FOR MULTIPLE STAKEHOLDER GROUPS

The early days of brand management were a simpler time. Many of the traditional frameworks for brand strategy certainly reflect that. This is perhaps nowhere truer than it is in the advertising-centric model of brand positioning, where the notion that each brand has only one target audience to please is shortsighted and naively limiting. In today's complex and highly competitive marketplace, brands need to serve multiple audience segments—and not just customers but other important stakeholders, too. As such, the traditional model for brand positioning must evolve to reflect modern-day reality. Marketers need to define brand positioning more holistically to better serve a broader, more diverse stakeholder ecosystem.

IMPERATIVE 3: CONSIDER MULTIPLE FORMS OF DIFFERENTIATION

Yet another aspect of brand positioning needs to evolve. Conventional wisdom says the promise component of a positioning statement, which typically represents a brand's primary point of difference, must be a customer end benefit. Since any given category has only a handful of meaningful end benefits (and some contain only a single, universal benefit), this perspective is one of the greatest contributors to brand monotony. As an ever-increasing number of competitors strive to differentiate through a limited set of distinct customer benefits, it's easy to understand how brands across so many categories have become indistinguishable from one another. Rather than limit promises to end benefits, marketers should consider the "how," or proof points; "who," or target; and "why," or purpose, as potential sources for brand promise—and, therefore, their primary point of difference.

IMPERATIVE 4: IDENTIFY AND ARTICULATE THE BRAND'S PURPOSE

This essentially covers the "why" component of the previous imperative. Regardless of whether a brand's formal positioning is purpose-based, defining that purpose is more important than ever before. Customers in this era of increased transparency care as much about the companies behind the offers as they do the products and services themselves. As with all aspects of brand strategy, however, purpose must be genuine and authentic. Today's savvy customers see right through (and resent) insincere brands.

IMPERATIVE 5: KEEP CUSTOMER EXPERIENCE TRUE TO BRAND POSITIONING, NOT "BEST PRACTICES"

There is no such thing as the ideal customer experience. Customers are inherently different from one another, seeking different solutions from different products and different brands. The same is true relative to the experiences brands provide. Customer experiences should be brand experiences in the truest sense, inspired more by the brand's positioning than a hypothetical (and uniform) ideal experience that could come from any brand within the same category.

IMPERATIVE 6: USE BRAND POSITIONING TO INSPIRE, NOT ONLY RESTRICT, BRAND EXTENSION

Incremental line extensions do not lead to transformative business growth. They also do not create indispensable brands. Reducing brands to a mere set of features and attributes and defining them narrowly through the categories in which they compete is unnecessary and stifling. Marketers should instead use the intrinsic, emotional aspects of their brand positioning to inspire brand extensions. However, they should always do so in a responsible manner, recognizing that careless brand extension (especially on a continued basis) can lead to brand dilution and degradation.

IMPERATIVE 7: EMBRACE THE POWER OF STORY

Stories have transformative power, and brand stories are no exception. Companies with interesting brand stories to tell should leverage them toward competitive advantage. When carefully crafted, brand stories have long shelf lives and incredible staying power. An authentic brand story can easily outlive creative campaigns and even compelling brand positionings. In crafting and communicating the story, marketers should remember to make the customer, not the brand, the hero of the tale.

IMPERATIVE 8: INVEST IN A STRONG CORPORATE BRAND

Corporate brand advertising has seen a resurgence in recent years, as has the overall investment level in corporate brands. The current era of transparency partly explains this trend, now that customers care more than ever about the companies behind the products and services they buy. Regardless of whether an organization operates as a branded house or house of brands, marketing leaders within those companies should invest in their corporate brands to realize myriad benefits. Strong corporate brands lead to marketing spend efficiencies, greater financial clout (e.g., stock price, advantageous merger and acquisitions activity), risk mitigation during a crisis, and employee esprit de corps.

IMPERATIVE 9: IDENTIFY AND EMPOWER INTERNAL BRAND EVANGELISTS

Employees must fully buy into and support the brands for which they work. If they do not, companies have little hope that external stakeholders (especially customers) will become loyal to their brands. Marketers should identify and nurture internal brand champions to inspire employee brand engagement, which leads to increased external engagement as well. Importantly, this employee focus applies to all departments, not just the marketing and branding teams.

IMPERATIVE 10: USE DIAGNOSTIC, PRESCRIPTIVE, AND PREDICTIVE MEASUREMENT

Marketers today operate in a business environment of increasing accountability. Marketing executives—and chief marketing officers in particular—must be equipped to justify the investments they make in their brands and marketing initiatives. Quantitative measurement is a key component in the establishment of marketing accountability. Marketing leaders must ensure their measurement systems are not only diagnostic but also prescriptive and hopefully even predictive. In the spirit of accountability, marketers should establish inextricable links between brand investments and their corresponding impact on business and financial key performance indicators.

There you have it: everything a marketer needs to transform an ordinary, indistinguishable brand into an indispensable one. In an environment that facilitates brand monotony and with frameworks that encourage the status quo, marketers have their work cut out for them. These imperatives (and the preceding chapters they summarize) hold the keys to change. It won't be easy, but building indispensable brands is an ambitious and attainable goal that is well worth the effort required.

Notes

CHAPTER 1

1   Patrick Barwise and Seán Meehan, "Making Differentiation Make a Difference," *strategy+business*, November 30, 2004, https://www.strategy-business.com/article/04412?gko=aa86e.

2   David Taylor, *Brand Stretch: Why 1 in 2 Extensions Fail, and How to Beat the Odds* (Chichester, UK: Wiley, 2004), 25.

3   Kevin J. Clancy and Jack Trout, "Brand Confusion," *Harvard Business Review*, March 2002, https://hbr.org/2002/03/brand-confusion.

4   Kevin Clancy and Peter Krieg, *Your Gut Is Still Not Smarter Than Your Head: How Disciplined, Fact-Based Marketing Can Drive Extraordinary Growth and Profits* (Hoboken, NJ: Wiley, 2007), 8.

5   Pat Conroy, Anupam Narula, and Siddharth Ramalingam, "A Crisis of the Similar," Deloitte Insights, January 1, 2012, https://www2.deloitte.com/insights/us/en/industry/consumer-products/a-crisis-of-the-similar-innovation-in-the-consumer-products-industry.html.

6   Nigel Hollis, "It Is Not a Choice: Brands Should Seek Differentiation and Distinctiveness," Millward Brown: Point of View, 2011, http://www.millwardbrown.com/docs/default-source/insight-documents/points-of-view/MillwardBrown_POV_Brand_Differentiation.pdf.

7   "Commoditization in Wireless Telecoms," Strategy&, last modified 2017, https://www.strategyand.pwc.com/wirelesscommoditization.

8   Andrew Smith, "Evaluating AT&T's Postpaid Phone Churn Rate Trend after 3Q17," *Market Realist*, November 10, 2017, https://marketrealist.com/2017/11/evaluating-atts-postpaid-phone-churn-rate-trend-3q17.

9   Kantar Millward Brown, *2015 BrandZ Top 100 Global Brands*, 2015.

10 "The Story of the BrandAsset Valuator Investigation," Brand Science, Young & Rubicam, n.d., http://ruby.fgcu.edu/courses/tdugas/ids3332/acrobat/bav.pdf.

CHAPTER 2

1   Greg Sterling, "It's Official: Google Says More Searches Now on Mobile Than on Desktop," *Search Engine Land*, May 5, 2015, https://searchengineland.com/its-official-google-says-more-searches-now-on-mobile-than-on-desktop-220369.

2   Alina Tugend, "Too Many Choices: A Problem That Can Paralyze," *New York Times*, February 26, 2010, http://www.nytimes.com/2010/02/27/your-money/27shortcuts.html.

3   Alexander Chernev, *The Psychology of Choice Overload: Implications for Retail Financial Services* (Filene Research Institute, 2011), https://pdfs.semanticscholar.org/5e47/70e194927ef20b4d389702a0d24429c894cd.pdf.

4   John Hagel III, John Seely Brown, Tamara Samoylova, Kasey M. Lobaugh, and Neha Goel, *The Retail Transformation: Cultivating Choice, Experience, and Trust* (Deloitte University Press, 2015), https://www2.deloitte.com/content/dam/Deloitte/za/Documents/consumer-business/ZA_RetailTrans_ConsumerBusiness_101515.pdf.

5   Aaron Smith and Monica Anderson, *Online Shopping and E-Commerce* (Pew Research Center, December 19, 2016), 5, http://assets.pewresearch.org/wp-content/uploads/sites/14/2016/12/16113209/PI_2016.12.19_Online-Shopping_FINAL.pdf.

6   Greg Sterling, "Survey: Amazon Beats Google as Starting Point for Product Search," *Search Engine Land*, June 28, 2016, https://searchengineland.com/survey-amazon-beats-google-starting-point-product-search-252980.

7   Myles Anderson, "88 Percent of Consumers Trust Online Reviews as Much as Personal Recommendations," *Search Engine Land*, July 7, 2014, https://searchengineland.com/88-consumers-trust-online-reviews-much-personal-recommendations-195803.

8   Yuyu Chen, "84 Percent of Millennials Don't Trust Traditional Advertising," *ClickZ*, March 4, 2015, https://www.clickz.com/84-percent-of-millennials-dont-trust-traditional-advertising/27030/.

9   Lauryn Chamberlain, "53 Percent of Millennial Shoppers Are 'Better Connected' Than Store Associates," *GeoMarketing*, November 15, 2017, https://geomarketing.com/53-percent-of-millennial-shoppers-are-better-connected-than-store-associates.

10   David Taylor and Jon Goldstone, "How to Reboot Brand Strategy for the Digital Age," *Campaign*, October 31, 2016, https://www.campaignlive.co.uk/article/reboot-brand-strategy-digital-age/1413429.

CHAPTER 3

1   Tom Fishburne, "Why Don Draper Types Can't Control Brand Content Anymore," Content Marketing Institute, September 15, 2013, http://contentmarketinginstitute.com/2013/09/draper-types-cant-control-brand-content/.

2   Adobe and Econsultancy, *Digital Intelligence Briefing: Taking Advantage of the Mobile Opportunity*, July 2016, https://files.acrobat.com/a/preview/3aa69674-f9e9-4603-8dff-d0b0bb80749c.

3   Yi Zhu and Anthony Dukes, "When It's Smart to Copy Your Competitor's Brand Promise," *Harvard Business Review*, March 23, 2017, https://hbr.org/2017/03/when-its-smart-to-copy-your-competitors-brand-promise.

4   Brian Barrett, "Hey Spotify: Not Every Tech Company Needs to Be Everything," *Wired*, May 21, 2015, https://www.wired.com/2015/05/hey-spotify-not-every-tech-company-needs-everything/.

5   Zach Epstein, "132-page Internal Document Shows How Samsung Set Out to Copy the iPhone Pixel by Pixel," BGR, August 8, 2012, http://bgr.com/2012/08/08/apple-samsung-patent-lawsuit-internal-report-copy-iphone/.

6   Nielsen, *Nurturing Innovation: How to Succeed in Years Two and Three*, June 2015, http://markedsforing.dk/sites/default/files/nielsen__sustaining_growth_report_0.pdf.

CHAPTER 4

1   Philip Kotler and Kevin Lane Keller, *Marketing Management* (Boston: Prentice Hall, 2006).

2   Jack Trout, "'Positioning' Is a Game People Play in Today's Me-Too Market Place," *Industrial Marketing* 54, no. 6 (June 1969): 51–55.

3   Al Ries and Jack Trout, *Positioning: The Battle for Your Mind* (New York: McGraw-Hill, 1981).

4   Michelle Greenwald, "The Evolution of Brand Marketing Strategy from One to Infinity," *Forbes*, January 21, 2018, https://www.forbes.com/sites/michellegreenwald/2018/01/21/the-evolution-of-brand-marketing-strategy-from-one-to-infinity/#2d24e0ae4afa.

5   Nate Dvorak and Robert Gabsa, "Failed Brand Ambassadors," *Gallup Business Journal*, January 10, 2017, http://news.gallup.com/businessjournal/201692/companies-dont-have-effective-brand-ambassadors.aspx.

6   Larry Light and Joan Kiddon, *Six Rules for Brand Revitalization: Learn How Companies Like McDonald's Can Re-Energize Their Brands* (Upper Saddle River, NJ: Prentice Hall, 2009).

7   Deloitte, *Oil and Gas Reality Check 2015: A Look at the Top Issues Facing the Oil and Gas Sector*, 2015, https://www2.deloitte.com/content/dam/Deloitte/global/Documents/Energy-and-Resources/gx-er-oil-and-gas-reality-check-2015.pdf.

8   Suzanne McCarron (vice president of public and government affairs, ExxonMobil), in phone interview with the author, June 2018.

9   "IBM Builds a Smarter Planet," IBM, accessed September 10, 2018, https://www.ibm.com/smarterplanet/us/en/.

10 "Popular Destinations," Airbnb, accessed September 10, 2018, https://www.airbnb.com/belong-anywhere.

11 Leigh Gallagher, "How Airbnb Found a Mission—and a Brand," *Fortune*, December 22, 2016, http://fortune.com/airbnb-travel-mission-brand/.

12 "Belong Anywhere," Airbnb, accessed September 10, 2018, https://blog.atairbnb.com/belong-anywhere/.

13 "Accenture Launches New Brand Campaign Designed to Take Company's 'High performance. Delivered.' Positioning to Next Level," Accenture, November 17, 2011, https://newsroom.accenture.com/news/accenture-launches-new-brand-campaign-designed-to-take-companys-high-performance-delivered-positioning-to-next-level.htm.

14 "Accenture's (ACN) CEO Pierre Nanterme on Q3 2016 Results—Earnings Call Transcript," Seeking Alpha, June 23, 2016, https://seekingalpha.com/article/3983958-accentures-acn-ceo-pierre-nanterme-q3-2016-results-earnings-call-transcript?referrer=.

15 Philip Kotler, "Brand Positioning Statement Example: Zipcar," *Branding Strategy Insider*, April 17, 2012, https://www.brandingstrategyinsider.com/2012/04/brand-positioning-statement-example-zipcar.html.

16 CA Technologies, "Reasons to Celebrate Customer Experience Day," *Medium*, October 3, 2017, https://medium.com/@@CATechnologies/reasons-to-celebrate-customer-experience-day-233a0e0ff398.

17 "About Tesla," Tesla, accessed September 10, 2018, https://www.tesla.com/about.

18 Simon Sinek, "How Great Leaders Inspire Action," TED, September 2009, https://www.ted.com/talks/simon_sinek_how_great_leaders_inspire_action?language=en.

19 Michelle Keaney, "Consumers Are Willing to Pay More for Purposeful Brands," *Marketing Week*, September 19, 2016, https://www.marketingweek.com/2016/09/19/consumers-are-willing-to-pay-58-more-for-purposeful-brands/.

20 Nielsen, *The Sustainability Imperative*, October 2015, https://www.nielsen.com/us/en/insights/reports/2015/the-sustainability-imperative.html.

21 "Patagonia's Mission Statement," Patagonia, accessed September 10, 2018, http://www.patagonia.com/company-info.html.

22 Julie Barrier, "A Brand Is Just a Brand—Unless It Has a Purpose," *Forbes*, September 22, 2015, https://www.forbes.com/sites/sap/2015/09/22/a-brand-is-just-a-brand-unless-it-has-a-purpose/#31e83ab8672b.

23 Radley Yeldar, "2016 Fit for Purpose Index," 2016, http://ry.com/services/brand/fit-for-purpose-2016/.

24 Steve Olenski, "How This 21-Year-Old Built a Brand with a Cult Following, and What a CMO Can Learn from It," *Forbes*, January 4, 2018, https://www.forbes.com/sites/steveolenski/2018/01/04/how-this-21-year-old-built-a-brand-with-a-cult-following-and-what-a-cmo-can-learn-from-it/#7ceef3002582.

25 Jillian Berman, "Here's Why Mountain Dew Will Survive the Death of Soda," *HuffPost*, December 6, 2017, https://www.huffingtonpost.com/2015/01/26/mountain-dew-regions_n_6524382.html.

26 "Karisma and Margaritaville Announce Partnership," Margaritaville, February 9, 2017, https://blog.margaritaville.com/2017/02/karisma-hotels-resorts-margaritaville-holdings/.

27 Peter Migut, "Margaritaville: A Brand Anything but Wasting Away," *Beneath the Brand* (blog), TalentZoo, accessed September 10, 2018, http://www.talentzoo.com/beneath-the-brand/blog_news.php?articleID=15368.

28 Chris Willman, "Jimmy Buffett Cashes In on 'Margaritaville' Brand with Restaurants, Spirits, More," *Variety*, July 10, 2018, https://variety.com/2018/music/news/jimmy-buffett-margaritaville-brand-restaurants-retirement-communities-1202868859/.

29 Jenny Rooney, "In Advance of PTTOW!, Target, Coca-Cola, Warby Parker Execs Get Candid about Courting Next-Generation Consumers," *Forbes*, May 1, 2013, https://www.forbes.com/sites/jenniferrooney/2013/05/01/in-advance-of-pttow-summit-targets-jeff-jones-coca-colas-joe-tripodi-warby-parkers-neil-blumenthal-get-candid-about-courting-next-generation-consumers/#322539a4ee4f.

30 Richard Sandomir, "Jack Trout, Who Fought for Consumers' Minds and Money, Dies at 82," *New York Times*, June 7, 2017, https://www.nytimes.com/2017/06/07/business/jack-trout-dead-marketing-strategist-product-positioning.html.

CHAPTER 5

1 Nirmalya Kumar, "Kill a Brand, Keep a Customer," *Harvard Business Review*, December 2003, https://hbr.org/2003/12/kill-a-brand-keep-a-customer.

2 Serena Ng, "P&G to Shed More Than Half Its Brands," *Wall Street Journal*, August 1, 2014, https://www.wsj.com/articles/procter-gamble-posts-higher-profit-on-cost-cutting-1406892304.

3 David A. Aaker and Erich Joachimsthaler, *Brand Leadership* (New York: The Free Press, 2009).

4 David A. Aaker, *Brand Portfolio Strategy* (New York: The Free Press, 2004).

5 "3M Consumer," 3M, accessed September 10, 2018, https://www.3m.com/3M/en_US/consumer-us/.

6 Deanna Ting and Greg Oates, "Every One of Marriott's 30 Hotel Brands, Explained," *Skift*, September 21, 2016, https://skift.com/2016/09/21/every-one-of-marriotts-30-hotel-brands-explained/.

7 "Moxy Hotels," Marriott International, accessed September 10, 2018, https://hotel-development.marriott.com/brands/moxy-hotels/.

8 "Performance PE polymers," ExxonMobil, accessed September 10, 2018, https://www.exxonmobilchemical.com/en/products-and-services/polyethylene/performance-pe-polymers.

9 Yinka Adegoke, "Comcast Seeks Reputation Change with Xfinity Brand," Reuters, February 9, 2010, https://www.reuters.com/article/comcast-xfinity-idUSN0515328620100209.

10 "Company History," COTG, accessed October 19, 2018, https://www.cotg.com/company-history.

11 Magda Adamska, "Brand Architecture Part 2: The Difference between Sub-Brands and Endorsed Brands," *BrandStruck* (blog), September 12, 2016, https://brandstruck.co/blog-post/brand-architecture-part-2-difference-sub-brands-endorsed-brands/.

12 Tim Donnelly, "How to Maintain Brand Consistency across Product Lines," *Inc.*, November 18, 2010, https://www.inc.com/guides/2010/11/how-to-maintain-brand-consistency-across-product-lines.html.

13 Leonor Ciarlone, *Building a House of Brands: Whirlpool Corporation's Blueprint for Success* (The Gilbane Report, August 2005), https://gilbane.com/case_studies_pdf/CTW_Whirlpool_Final.pdf.

14 David Aaker, "Ries and Trout Were Wrong: Brand Extensions Work," *Harvard Business Review*, April 5, 2012, https://hbr.org/2012/04/ries-trout-were-wrong-brand-ex.

15 "4 Brand Extensions and Why They Were Successful," Washington State University, accessed September 10, 2018, https://onlinemba.wsu.edu/resources/all/articles/4-brand-extensions-and-why-they-were-successful/.

CHAPTER 6

1 Robert Mandelbaum, "Select-Service Hotels: Efficient and Profitable," *Lodging*, March 2017, http://www.cbrehotels.com/EN/Research/Pages/Select-Service-Hotels--Efficient-and-Profitable.aspx.

2 Steven Dominguez (vice president of global brands, Hyatt Hotels Corporation), in phone interview with the author, March 2018.

3 B. Joseph Pine II and James H. Gilmore, *The Experience Economy: Work Is Theatre and Every Business a Stage* (Boston: Harvard Business School Press, 1999).

4 Ed Keller and Brad Fay, "Word-of-Mouth Advocacy: A New Key to Advertising Effectiveness," *Journal of Advertising Research* 52, no. 4 (December 2012): 459–64, https://doi.org/10.2501/JAR-52-4-459-464.

5 Jacques Bughin, Jonathan Doogan, and Ole Jørgen Vetvik, "A New Way to Measure Word-of-Mouth Marketing," *McKinsey Quarterly*, April 2010, https://www.mckinsey.com/business-functions/marketing-and-sales/our-insights/a-new-way-to-measure-word-of-mouth-marketing.

6 Mounica Vennamaneni, "Whole Foods Market, Marketing Strategies, and Programs Analysis," *Medium*, July 15, 2017, https://medium.com/@@mounicav/whole-foods-market-marketing-strategies-and-programs-analysis-53d6f12b6055.

7 "Whole Foods Market to Sack Disposable Plastic Grocery Bags by Earth Day," Whole Foods Market, January 22, 2008, https://media.wholefoodsmarket.com/news/whole-foods-market-to-sack-disposable-plastic-grocery-bags-by-earth-day.

8 Elliot Maras, "Amazon's Whole Foods Market Acquisition Points to a Changing Role for Physical Stores; Millennials Hold the Key," Retail Customer Experience, June 20, 2017, https://www.retailcustomerexperience.com/blogs/amazons-whole-foods-bid-points-to-a-changing-role-for-physical-stores-millennials-hold-the-key/.

9 Carolyn Tisch Blodgett (senior vice president of brand marketing, Peloton), in phone interview with the author, June 2018.

10 Christine Dahm (vice president of marketing, Noosa Yoghurt), in phone interview with the author, June 2018.

11 Javier Chavez Ruiz, "Branded Wallets Cinépolis: Connecting Real Solutions, to Real Problems, with Real Benefits," LinkedIn, July 23, 2015, https://www.linkedin.com/pulse/merchants-successful-apps-real-solutions-problems-javier-chavez-ruiz/.

12 Dani Levy, "Cinema Chain Builds Jungle Gyms in Theaters," *Variety*, March 7, 2017, https://variety.com/2017/biz/news/cinepolis-junior-jungle-gym-theater-kids-1202003872/.

13 Jeff Chu, "Can Apple's Angela Ahrendts Spark a Retail Revolution?" *Fast Company*, January 6, 2014, https://www.fastcompany.com/3023591/angela-ahrendts-a-new-season-at-apple.

14 Interbrand, "Best Global Brands 2017 Rankings," 2017, https://www.interbrand.com/best-brands/best-global-brands/2017/ranking/.

15 CustomerExperience.io, "3 Top Lessons on How LUSH Employees Improve Customer Experience," *Medium*, December 3, 2015, https://medium.com/@@_cxio/3-top-lessons-on-how-lush-employees-improve-customer-experience-6f2ab6db07bd.

16 Michael Million, "Perspectives on Orchestrating Customer Experience," http://cdn2.hubspot.net/hubfs/858343/Articles/Perspectives-on-Orchestrating-Customer-Experience.pdf?t=1462290037021.

17 Million, "Orchestrating Customer Experience."

18 Fiona Swerdlow, "The Walgreens Path to Omnichannel Success," National Retail Federation, February 5, 2013, https://nrf.com/blog/mobile/the-walgreens-path-omnichannel-success.

19 Dominguez, interview.

CHAPTER 7

1 Brittany Shoot, "Moleskine Turns the Page with Expanded Brick-and-Mortar Stores," *Fortune*, November 18, 2014, http://fortune.com/2014/11/18/moleskine-stores/.

2 Davey Alba, "Review: Moleskine Smart Writing Set," *Wired*, April 6, 2014, https://www.wired.com/2016/04/review-moleskine-smart-writing-set/.

3 Gavin Brown, "Moleskine Builds Brand Experience to Engage Creative Minds," *Persuasive Products* (blog), March 13, 2016, http://persuasiveproducts.net/brand-innovators/moleskine-brand-experience/.

4 Amanda Wright, "Moleskine's Brand Extension: A Café for the Creative," *The Branding Journal*, September 2016, https://www.thebrandingjournal.com/2016/09/cafe-creative-moleskine-brand-extension/.

5 Vanessa de Nardi, "Moleskine Limbers Up as a Lifestyle Brand," *Luxury Society*, October 13, 2017, https://www.luxurysociety.com/en/articles/2017/10/and-stretch-moleskine-limbers-lifestyle-brand/.

6 Shoot, "Moleskine Turns the Page."

7 Volker Staack and Branton Cole, *Reinventing Innovation: Five Findings to Guide Strategy through Execution* (PwC, 2017), https://www.pwc.com/us/en/advisory-services/business-innovation/assets/2017-innovation-benchmark-findings.pdf.

8 Julia Cupman, "How B2B Marketers Are Embracing Brand as the Top Driver of Growth," *MarketingProfs*, March 16, 2018, http://www.marketingprofs.com/articles/print/2018/33760/how-b2b-marketers-are-embracing-brand-as-the-top-driver-of-growth.

9 Carolin Wobben, "Success Factors of Brand Extension in International Marketing," (master's thesis, University of Hamburg, 2006), 6, https://www.grin.com/document/58639.

10 Jake Swearingen, "How the Camera Doomed Google Glass," *The Atlantic*, January 15, 2015, https://www.theatlantic.com/technology/archive/2015/01/how-the-camera-doomed-google-glass/384570/.

11 "Wingscapes WSCA04 Timelapse Outdoor PlantCam (Discontinued by Manufacturer)," Amazon, accessed September 10, 2018, https://www.amazon.com/exec/obidos/ASIN/B002M2TLLI/ref=nosim/womensgolfsho-20.

12 "The 10 Biggest Market Research Fails of All Time," TrendSource, June 2, 2017, http://trustedinsight.trendsource.com/trusted-insight-trends/the-10-biggest-market-research-fails-of-all-time.

13 Eustacia Huen, "The Museum of Failure Dishes on the Worst Products of All Time," *Forbes*, April 30, 2017, https://www.forbes.com/sites/eustaciahuen/2017/04/30/the-museum-of-failure-dishes-on-the-worst-products-of-all-time/#31e5f2b8609c.

14 Wikipedia, s.v. "Premier (cigarette)," last modified August 1, 2018, 17:33, https://en.wikipedia.org/wiki/Premier_(cigarette).

15 David Taylor, *Brand Stretch: Why 1 in 2 Extensions Fail, and How to Beat the Odds* (Chichester, UK: Wiley, 2004), 25.

16 Dave Ansett, "Brand Extension and the Cannibal Effect," *Truly Deep* (blog), accessed September 10, 2018, http://www.trulydeeply.com.au/2015/01/brand-extension-and-the-canibal-effect-brand-strategy-melbourne/.

17   "Avoiding Brand Extension Failures," Pierpont, August 12, 2011, https://www.piercom.com/insight/
     avoiding-brand-extension-failures/.

18   "The Business of Excellence," Tata, accessed September 10, 2018, http://www.tata.com/aboutus/articlesinside/
     Business-excellence.

19   "Brand Extension Success—New Profit Growth," *China Business Philippines*, January 2010, http://
     chinabusinessphilippines.com/index.php?option=com_content&view=article&id=1453:br
     and-extension-success-new-profit-growth&catid=31:asian-brand-strategy&Itemid=73.

20   "Case Illustration 1: The Armani Brand Extension Success Story," Martel Fashion, November 10, 2016, http://
     www.martelnyc.com/luxury-fashion/case-illustration-1-the-armani-brand-extension-success-story.html.

21   "Giorgio Armani—The Iconic Global Fashion Brand," MartinRoll, November 2016, https://martinroll.com/
     resources/articles/branding/giorgio-armani-the-iconic-fashion-brand/.

22   Rasa Stankeviciute and Jonas Hoffmann, "The Slippery Slope of Brand Expansion," *Marketing Management*
     20, no. 4, (Winter 2011), 26–31, https://archive.ama.org/archive/ResourceLibrary/MarketingManagement/
     documents/Slippery Slope.pdf.

23   "The Origin of Mr. Clean," Mr. Clean, accessed September 10, 2018, https://www.mrclean.com/en-us/
     about-mr-clean.

24   Pete Canalichio, "Brand Licensing and Brand Equity," *Branding Strategy Insider*, November 29, 2013, https://
     www.brandingstrategyinsider.com/2013/11/brand-licensing-and-brand-equity.html#.WuzLG9PwajQ.

25   Elise Shapiro, "West Elm Workspace's Retail Advantage," *Work Design Magazine*, March 2, 2018, https://
     workdesign.com/2018/03/west-elm-workspace/.

26   Diana Budds, "West Elm Reinvents Its Office—and Itself," *Fast Company*, October 19, 2016, https://www.
     fastcodesign.com/3064749/west-elm-reinvents-its-office-and-itself.

27   Diana Budds, "West Elm Breaks into the Boutique Hotel Business," *Fast Company*, September 26, 2016, https://
     www.fastcodesign.com/3064081/west-elm-breaks-into-the-boutique-hotel-business.

28   "The Locations," west elm Hotels, accessed November 5, 2018, https://westelmhotels.com/locations/.

29   Jena Tesse Fox, "West Elm Wants You to Recline on Their Sofa, in Their Hotel," *Hotel Management*, January 30,
     2018, https://www.hotelmanagement.net/development/west-elm-wants-to-recline-their-sofa-their-hotel.

CHAPTER 8

1   "History," Gatorade, accessed September 10, 2018, https://www.gatorade.co.nz/history/.

2   "Football Fever: Inventions That Shaped the Modern Game," InventHelp, accessed September
     10, 2018, https://inventhelp.com/archives/08-05/inventhelp-newsletter-august-2005/
     football-fever-inventions-that-shaped-the-modern-game.

3   Manouk Akopyan, "Gatorade Is Fueling Athletic Performance, and Marketing, with Innovation," AList, April 25,
     2017, http://www.alistdaily.com/strategy/gatorade-fueling-athletic-performance-marketing-innovation/.

4   *Encyclopaedia Britannica Online*, Academic ed., s.v. "Paleolithic Period," updated July 19, 2018, https://www.
     britannica.com/event/Paleolithic-Period.

5   David Damrosch, "Epic Hero," *Smithsonian Magazine*, May 2007, https://www.smithsonianmag.com/history/
     epic-hero-153362976/.

6   James Dowd and Digital Surgeons, *The Science of Story: How Brands Can Use Storytelling to
     Get More Customers*, SlideShare, April 13, 2017, https://www.slideshare.net/digitalsurgeons/
     the-science-of-story-understanding-how-stories-work-for-brands.

7 Wikipedia, s.v. "TED (conference)," last modified September 6, 2018, 00:12, https://en.wikipedia.org/wiki/TED_(conference).

8 Forbes Agency Council, "Six Critical Elements That Make TED Talks Compelling," *Forbes*, July 25, 2016, https://www.forbes.com/sites/forbesagencycouncil/2016/07/25/six-critical-elements-that-make-ted-talks-compelling/#71709571768d.

9 Headstream, *The Power of Brand Storytelling: How Brand Storytelling Can Meet Marketing Objectives*, SlideShare, June 22, 2015, https://www.slideshare.net/Headstream/the-power-of-brand-storytelling.

10 Christopher Booker, *The Seven Basic Plots: Why We Tell Stories*, (London: Continuum, 2004).

11 Bryan Rhoads, "7 Ancient Archetypes Your Brand Storytelling Should Use," Content Marketing Institute, September 11, 2014, https://contentmarketinginstitute.com/2014/09/ancient-archetypes-brand-storytelling-should-use/.

12 ReferralCandy, "Nike's Brilliant Marketing Strategy—Why You Should Be (Just) Doing It, Too," *Medium*, September 11, 2017, https://medium.com/the-mission/nikes-brilliant-marketing-strategy-why-you-should-be-just-doing-it-too-d3680d9254ba.

13 Scott Davis, "When Geico Accelerated Past Allstate," *Forbes*, March 10, 2014, https://www.forbes.com/sites/scottdavis/2014/03/10/when-geico-accelerated-past-allstate/#1b3f4c42d2ab.

14 "The Johnnie Walker Story," Johnnie Walker, accessed September 10, 2018, https://www.johnniewalker.com/en-us/whisky-knowledge/the-johnnie-walker-story/.

15 "Our History," Walmart, accessed September 10, 2018, https://corporate.walmart.com/our-story/our-history.

16 Colin Dodds, "Sam Walton: Early Life and Education," Investopedia, accessed September 10, 2018, https://www.investopedia.com/university/sam-walton-biography/sam-walton-early-life-and-education.asp.

17 "About Us," Walmart, accessed October 31, 2018, https://corporate.walmart.com/our-story.

18 Barbara Farfan, "Best Sam Walton Quotes: Walmart Business, Retail Competition, Leaders," *The Balance Small Business*, April 29, 2017, https://www.thebalancesmb.com/best-sam-walton-quotes-2892160.

19 "History," Warby Parker, accessed September 10, 2018, https://www.warbyparker.com/history.

20 Lisa Lacy, "10 Amazing Brand Story Examples," Linkdex, February 3, 2016, https://www.linkdex.com/en-us/inked/brand-story-examples/.

21 "Our Story: Behind the Brand," The North Face, accessed September 10, 2018, https://www.thenorthface.com/about-us/our-story.html.

22 Stewart Hodgson, "Born in the USA: Get Your Motor Running...The Harley-Davidson Brand Story," Fabrik, January 8, 2018, http://fabrikbrands.com/born-in-the-usa-harley-davidson-brand-story/.

23 Andrew Davis, "Your Brand Narrative," *Beneath the Brand* (blog), TalentZoo, accessed September 10, 2018, http://www.talentzoo.com/beneath-the-brand/blog_news.php?articleID=11076.

24 "About Us," ACE, accessed September 10, 2018, https://myace.com/about-us/.

25 "Kidde History," Kidde, accessed September 10, 2018, https://www.kidde.com/home-safety/en/us/about/history/.

26 Kidde United Technologies, "Kidde United Technologies TV Commercial, 'Technology Saving Lives,'" iSpot TV, 2017, https://www.ispot.tv/ad/wkv5/kidde-united-technologies-technology-saving-lives.

27 "What We Do," The Salvation Army, accessed September 10, 2018, https://www.salvationarmyusa.org/usn/home/#whatwedo.

28 Carla Johnson in phone interview with the author, July 2018.

29 Dowd and Digital Surgeons, *The Science of Story*.

30 Christel Quek, "Make Your Brand Story Meaningful," *Harvard Business Review*, June 14, 2013, https://hbr.org/2013/06/make-your-brand-story-meaningf.

31 Rebecca Messina (former chief marketing officer, Beam Suntory), in phone interview with the author, May 2018.

32 Julie Fussner (vice president of marketing, Culver's), in phone interview with the author, June 2018.

33 Christoph Trappe, "7 Brand Storytelling Best Practices to Grow Your Audience," *Content Science Review*, April 26, 2017, https://review.content-science.com/2017/04/7-brand-storytelling-best-practices-to-grow-your-audience/.

34 Ilya Pozin, "4 Ways to Use the Power of Story to Build Your Business," *Inc.*, August 11, 2017, https://www.inc.com/ilya-pozin/bwhy-authentic-storytelling-should-be-your-marke.html.

35 Enakshi Sharma, "7 Things That Make Brand Storytelling Authentic," Brandanew, June 1, 2015, http://www.brandanew.co/7-things-that-make-brand-storytelling-authentic/.

36 Johnson, interview.

37 Headstream, *The Power of Brand Storytelling*.

38 Dowd and Digital Surgeons, *The Science of Story*.

39 Trappe, "7 Brand Storytelling Best Practices."

CHAPTER 9

1   Vodafone Group, "Vodafone Announces New Brand Positioning Strategy," London Stock Exchange, October 5, 2017, http://www.londonstockexchange.com/exchange/news/market-news/market-news-detail/VOD/13386612.html.

2   Ann-Marie Corvin, "Vodafone/ 'The Future Is Exciting. Ready?'/ Team Red, WPP," *Alf Insight* (blog), October 11, 2017, https://www.alfinsight.com/content-library/campaign-spotlight/2017/vodafone-the-future-is-exciting-ready-team-red-wpp/.

3   "A Creative Campaign around Vodafone's New Positioning," Glasnost, accessed September 10, 2018, https://www.glasnostcommunications.com/case/a-creative-campaign-around-vodafones-new-positioning/.

4   Brenda Alvarez, "100 Brand Style Guides You Should See Before Designing Yours," Freelancer.com, April 26, 2016, https://www.freelancer.com/community/articles/one-hundred-style-guides-you-should-see-before-designing-yours.

5   Romita Majumdar, "Vodafone India Tunes in to a New Beat," *Business Standard*, November 14, 2017, https://www.business-standard.com/article/companies/vodafone-india-tunes-in-to-a-new-beat-117111401834_1.html.

6   NetImpact Solutions, "Vodafone's Iconic Tech Campaign in 2017," *Mint*, February 15, 2018, https://www.livemint.com/Opinion/GrPFkUmgaXwomMoCu5cTfI/Vodafones-iconic-tech-campaign-in-2017.html.

7   Michael Bailey, "Vodafone Taps Haystack, a Brisbane Startup, to Get Rid of Paper Business Cards," *Financial Review*, August 27, 2017, https://www.afr.com/business/vodafone-taps-haystack-a-brisbane-startup-to-get-rid-of-paper-business-cards-20170816-gxxuf8.

8   David Taylor and Jon Goldstone, "How to Reboot Brand Strategy for the Digital Age," *Campaign*, October 31, 2016, https://www.campaignlive.co.uk/article/reboot-brand-strategy-digital-age/1413429.

9   Danyl Bosomworth, "Brand Strategy—Core to Digital Strategy, but Often MIA," *Smart Insights*, March 9, 2017, https://www.smartinsights.com/online-brand-strategy/brand-development/brand-positioning-strategy/.

10 Darcy Schuller, "Brand Positioning in the Digital Age," Suvonni, accessed September 10, 2018, http://suvonni.com/brand-positioning-in-the-digital-age/.

11   George Musi, "The Downside of Digital's Explosive Growth? Too Many Marketers Are Failing to Think Long-Term," *Adweek*, March 22, 2017, https://www.adweek.com/brand-marketing/the-downside-of-digitals-explosive-growth-too-many-marketers-are-failing-to-think-long-term/.

12   Bosomworth, "Brand Strategy."

13   "How Brand Equity Matters in a Digital World," *Wedu* (blog), n.d., http://wedu.com/blog/brand-equity-in-a-digital-world/.

14   Tim Murphy (senior vice president of digital marketing, Chubb), in phone interview with the author, March 2018.

15   "Tito's Handmade Vodka Establishes Brand Loyalty with an Authentic Social Strategy," Sprout Social, accessed September 10, 2018, https://sproutsocial.com/insights/case-studies/titos/.

16   Peter Adams, Chantal Tode, and Natalie Koltun, "Campaign Trail: Netflix Says It's a Joke; KFC Records Road Trip Cassette; PB&J's Breakup Bombshell," *Marketing Dive*, September 22, 2017, https://www.marketingdive.com/news/campaign-trail-netflix-says-its-a-joke-kfc-records-road-trip-cassette-p/505572/.

17   Ace Hardware, "Ace Hardware Acquires E-Commerce Startup The Grommet," *Industrial Distribution*, October 3, 2017, https://www.inddist.com/news/2017/10/ace-hardware-acquires-e-commerce-startup-grommet.

18   Ace and The Grommet, "Ace Hardware Teams Up with Product Launch Platform the Grommet to Make 'Ace The Place' for Innovation," (The Grommet, November 29, 2016), https://assets.thegrommet.com/press logos & files/Press Releases/AceHardwareGrommetPressRelease.pdf.

19   Jarvis Bowers (vice president digital marketing, Holland America), in phone interview with the author, March 2018.

20   Ayaz Nanji, "How B2B and B2C Firms Approach Personalization Differently," *MarketingProfs*, May 10, 2018, https://www.marketingprofs.com/charts/2018/34737/how-b2b-and-b2c-firms-approach-personalization-differently.

21   Nicola Fumo, "The Psychology of Customization," *Racked*, June 1, 2016, https://www.racked.com/2016/6/1/11772798/customization-monogramming-personalization-pins.

22   Pacific Content, "Telling Stories Instead of Interviewing Experts—Zendesk Rethinks the Company Podcast," *Medium*, March 1, 2017, https://blog.pacific-content.com/telling-stories-instead-of-interviewing-experts-zendesk-rethinks-the-company-podcast-53cc8e8a6bca.

23   Schuller, "Brand Positioning in the Digital Age."

24   Rose Johnstone, "Brand Strategy in the Digital Age," *Innovation Enterprise*, accessed November 5, 2018, https://channels.theinnovationenterprise.com/articles/brand-strategy-in-the-digital-age.

25   Ben Grossman, *Content Creation Best Practices and the Problem with Editorial Calendars*, SlideShare, March 18, 2015, 68, https://www.slideshare.net/bengrossman/content-creation-best-practices-the-problem-with-editorial-calendars.

26   Kelly Services and EveryoneSocial, *Why Kelly Services Got Their Recruiters Active on Social Media*, April 2017, http://ellegriffin.com/wp-content/uploads/2017/04/Why-Kelly-Services-Got-Their-Recruiters-Active-On-Social-Media.pdf.

27   Peter Minnium, "The Definitive Guide to Digital Brand Lift," *Marketing Land*, January 6, 2016, https://marketingland.com/definitive-guide-digital-brand-lift-157764.

CHAPTER 10

1   Nick Blythe, "Are Organisations in the Marine Industry Exploiting the Power of Brand?" BLUE Communications, November 29, 2017, http://www.blue-comms.com/are-organisations-in-the-marine-industry-exploiting-the-power-of-brand/.

2   Jonathan Wichmann, "Being B2B Social: A Conversation with Maersk Line's Head of Social Media," interview by David Edelman, McKinsey & Company, May 2013, https://www.mckinsey.com/business-functions/marketing-and-sales/our-insights/being-b2b-social-a-conversation-with-maersk-lines-head-of-social-media.

3   Blythe, "Organisations in the Marine Industry."

4   Interbrand, "Best Global Brands 2017 Rankings," 2017, https://www.interbrand.com/best-brands/best-global-brands/2017/ranking/.

5   Paul Hague and Matthew Harrison, "Marketing Segmentation in B2B Markets," B2B International, accessed September 10, 2018, https://www.b2binternational.com/publications/b2b-segmentation-research/.

6   CEB, *From Promotion to Emotion: Connecting B2B Customers to Brands*, 2013, https://www.cebglobal.com/content/dam/cebglobal/us/EN/best-practices-decision-support/marketing-communications/pdfs/promotion-emotion-whitepaper-full.pdf.

7   Hague and Harrison, "Marketing Segmentation in B2B Markets."

8   FullSurge, *The Anatomy of a Growth Guru*, 2015, https://www.fullsurge.com/growth-guru-3.

9   Steve Wnuk (vice president of marketing, Quad/Graphics), in phone interview with the author, April 2018.

10 Ed Keller (chief marketing officer, Navigant), in phone interview with the author, May 2018.

11 Keller, interview.

12 Andrew Gross (executive vice president of marketing, Serta), in phone interview with the author, May 2018.

13 Ann Rubin (vice president of corporate marketing, IBM), in phone interview with the author, May 2018.

14 Wnuk, interview.

15 CEB, *From Promotion to Emotion*.

16 Martha Mathers, "B2B Buyers Are Full of Emotion. Is Your Branding?" CMO.com, August 28, 2017, https://www.cmo.com/opinion/articles/2017/8/9/b2b-buying-is-full-of-emotions-ptr-tlp.html.

17 CEB, *From Promotion to Emotion*.

18 Yvette Morrison (vice president of marketing, Snap-on), in phone interview with the author, May 2018.

19 Jess Pike, "7 B2B Brands Using Emotional Engagement to Enhance CX," *B2B Marketing* (blog), August 18, 2017, https://www.b2bmarketing.net/en/resources/blog/7-b2b-brands-using-emotional-engagement-enhance-cx.

20 Christine B. Whittenmore, "What Great Brands Do With Mission Statements: 27 Examples," *Flooring the Customer* (blog), Simple Marketing Now, October 10, 2017, https://www.simplemarketingnow.com/blog/flooring-the-consumer/bid/168520/what-great-brands-do-with-mission-statements-8-examples#airbnb.

CHAPTER 11

1   Ann Rubin (vice president of corporate marketing, IBM), in phone interview with the author, May 2018.

2   Rubin, interview.

3   John Marshall and Rick Wise, "The Resurgence of the Corporate Brand," *Ad Age*, April 17, 2013, https://adage.com/article/cmo-strategy/resurgence-corporate-brand/240855/.

4   "'A Family Company at Work for a Better World' Highlights SC Johnson's Global Impact," SC Johnson, April 23, 2018, https://www.scjohnson.com/en/press-releases/2018/april/a-family-company-at-work-for-a-better-world-highlights-sc-johnsons-global-impact.

5   E. J. Schultz, "Why Hershey Is Shifting to Masterbrand Approach," *Ad Age*, February 5, 2016, http://adage.com/article/cmo-strategy/hershey-shifting-masterbrand-approach/302551/.

6   E. J. Schultz, "Coca-Cola's Corporate Brand Campaign Moves Beyond Soda," *Ad Age*, September 17, 2017, http://adage.com/article/cmo-strategy/coca-cola-s-corporate-brand-campaign-moves-soda/310490/.

7   "IPO Branding," AIMListing, accessed September 10, 2018, https://www.aimlisting.co.uk/flotation/ipo-branding/.

8   "Brand Valuation," Intangible Business, accessed on September 10, 2018, https://www.intangiblebusiness.com/legal/brand-valuation.

9   Interbrand, "Best Global Brands 2017 Rankings," 2017, https://www.interbrand.com/best-brands/best-global-brands/2017/ranking/.

10 Karl Greenberg, "CoreBrand Says There's Value in Corporate Brand," *MediaPost*, January 2, 2014, https://www.mediapost.com/publications/article/216443/corebrand-says-theres-value-in-corporate-brand.html.

11 Rick Wise, "Taking Your Brand to the Next Level," *Wharton Blog Network* (blog), *Wharton Magazine*, September 20, 2013, http://whartonmagazine.com/blogs/taking-your-brand-to-the-next-level/.

12 Mike Rocha, "Brand Valuation: A Versatile Strategic Tool for Business," Interbrand, accessed on September 10, 2018, http://interbrand.com/views/brand-valuation-a-versatile-strategic-tool-for-business/.

13 Rebecca Messina (former chief marketing officer, Beam Suntory), in phone interview with the author, May 2018.

14 Simon Sinek, "How Great Leaders Inspire Action," TED, September 2009, https://www.ted.com/talks/simon_sinek_how_great_leaders_inspire_action?language=en.

15 Marshall and Wise, "Resurgence of the Corporate Brand."

16 "Patagonia's Mission Statement," Patagonia, accessed September 10, 2018, https://www.patagonia.com/company-info.html.

17 "About REI," REI, accessed September 10, 2018, https://www.rei.com/about-rei.

18 "Every Day Is Better When You #OptOutside," REI, accessed September 10, 2018, https://www.rei.com/opt-outside.

19 Howard Markel, "How the Tylenol Murders of 1982 Changed the Way We Consume Medication," *PBS NewsHour*, September 29, 2014, https://www.pbs.org/newshour/health/tylenol-murders-1982.

20 24/7 Wall St., "The 10 Companies Burned Worst by Bad Press," *The Atlantic*, June 14, 2011, https://www.theatlantic.com/business/archive/2011/06/the-10-companies-burned-worst-by-bad-press/240448/#slide10.

21 "Deepwater Horizon—BP Gulf of Mexico Oil Spill," US Environmental Protection Agency, updated April 19, 2017, https://www.epa.gov/enforcement/deepwater-horizon-bp-gulf-mexico-oil-spill.

22 Tony Jaques, "Lessons from an Oil Spill: How BP Gained—Then Lost—Our Trust," *The Conversation*, April 22, 2015, http://theconversation.com/lessons-from-an-oil-spill-how-bp-gained-then-lost-our-trust-40307.

23 Ron Bousso, "BP Deepwater Horizon Costs Balloon to $65 Billion," Reuters, January 26, 2018, https://www.reuters.com/article/us-bp-deepwaterhorizon/bp-deepwater-horizon-costs-balloon-to-65-billion-idUSKBN1F50NL.

24 Jackie Wattles, Ben Geier, Matt Egan, and Danielle Wiener-Bronner, "Well Fargo's 20-Month Nightmare," *CNN Money*, April 24, 2018, https://money.cnn.com/2018/04/24/news/companies/wells-fargo-timeline-shareholders/index.html.

25 Denise Lee Yohn, "Why Companies Are Advertising Their Master Brand," *Harvard Business Review*, March 28, 2016, https://hbr.org/2016/03/why-companies-are-advertising-their-master-brand.

26 Yohn, "Companies Are Advertising Their Master Brand."

27 Al Ries, "Focus Is the Difference between Your Company Brand and Apple's," *Ad Age*, September 12, 2012, http://adage.com/article/al-ries/focus-difference-company-brand-apple/237133/.

28 Wise, "Taking Your Brand to the Next Level."

29 Venture Capital Dispatch, "Zappos and Amazon Sitting in a Tree," *Venture Capital Dispatch* (blog), *Wall Street Journal*, July 22, 2009, https://blogs.wsj.com/venturecapital/2009/07/22/%E2%80%9Czappos-and-amazon-sitting-in-a-tree%E2%80%A6%E2%80%9D/.

30 Tony Hsieh, "Your Culture Is Your Brand," *HuffPost*, updated December 6, 2017, https://www.huffingtonpost.com/entry/zappos-founder-tony-hsieh_1_b_783333.html.

CHAPTER 12

1 Deloitte, "The Deloitte Greenhouse Experience: Corporate Innovation Labs," accessed September 10, 2018, https://www2.deloitte.com/us/en/pages/operations/solutions/deloitte-greenhouse-experience.html.

2 Jeff Suttle (client experience leader and the facilitator of the session, Deloitte University), in phone interview with the author, March 2018.

3 BusinessDictionary, s.v. "employee engagement," accessed September 10, 2018, http://www.businessdictionary.com/definition/employee-engagement.html.

4 William J. McEwen, "Your Brand Is in Their Hands: How Your Employees Can Make—or Break—a Brand Relationship," *Gallup Business Journal*, April 15, 2010, https://news.gallup.com/businessjournal/127340/brand-hands.aspx.

5 "5 Steps to Internal Brand Introduction," *BrandingBusiness* (blog), October 24, 2013, http://www.brandingbusiness.com/blogs/5-steps-to-internal-brand-introduction.

6 Gallup, "The Engaged Workplace," accessed September 10, 2018, https://www.gallup.com/services/190118/engaged-workplace.aspx.

7 Denise Lee Yohn, "Engaging Employees Starts with Remembering What Your Company Stands For," *Harvard Business Review*, March 13, 2018, https://hbr.org/2018/03/engaging-employees-starts-with-remembering-what-your-company-stands-for.

8 Kayla Ellman, "6 Lessons from the Best Employer Branding Case Studies," *The Muse*, n.d., https://www.themuse.com/advice/6-lessons-from-the-best-employer-branding-case-studies.

9 Weber Shandwick and KRC Research, *Employees Rising: Seizing the Opportunity in Employee Activism*, April 2014, https://www.webershandwick.com/uploads/news/files/employees-rising-seizing-the-opportunity-in-employee-activism.pdf.

10 Paul Barton, *Maximizing Internal Communication: Strategies to Turn Heads, Win Hearts, Engage Employees, and Get Results* (Lake Placid, NY: Aviva Publishing, 2014).

11 Ellman, "Best Employer Branding Case Studies."

12 CSD Staff, "Applauding the QT Culture," *Convenience Store Decisions*, April 11, 2007, https://cstoredecisions.com/2007/04/11/applauding-the-qt-culture/.

13 Neeli Bendapudi and Venkat Bendapudi, "Creating the Living Brand," *Harvard Business Review*, May 2005, https://hbr.org/2005/05/creating-the-living-brand.

14 Carla Johnson, "The 50/50 Split between External and Internal Branding," Type A Communications, 2013, http://typeacommunications.com/the-5050-split-between-external-and-internal-branding/.

15 Carla Johnson, "Why Human Resources Is Essential to the Brand Storytelling Equation," Content Marketing Institute, December 26, 2013, https://contentmarketinginstitute.com/2013/12/human-resources-essential-brand-storytelling/.

16 Fritz Grutzner, "Stories Companies Tell: How Internal Stories Build Your Brand," *Brand Quarterly*, n.d., http://www.brandquarterly.com/stories-companies-tell-how-internal-stories-build-your-brand.

17 Ambrosia Vertesi, "Inside #HootsuiteLife: Inside the Making of our Employer Brand Playbook," Hootsuite (blog), October 9, 2015, https://blog.hootsuite.com/hootsuitelife-employer-brand-playbook/.

18 Stephanie Overby, "MGM Resorts's Tomovich: There's No Substitute for Experience," CMO.com, March 6, 2017, https://www.cmo.com/interviews/articles/2017/1/30/the-cmocom-interview-lilian-tomovich-chief-experience-officer-mgm-resorts-.html#gs.aKgNu54.

19 Colin Mitchell, "Selling the Brand Inside," *Harvard Business Review*, January 2002, https://hbr.org/2002/01/selling-the-brand-inside.

CHAPTER 13

1 Xerox, *2017 Annual Report*, 2017, https://www.xerox.com/annual-report-2017/financial-highlights.html.

2 Interbrand, "Best Global Brands 2016 Rankings," 2016, https://www.interbrand.com/best-brands/best-global-brands/2016/ranking/.

3 Barbara Basney (vice president of global brand, advertising, and media; Xerox), in phone interview with the author, June 2018.

4 Jack Neff, E. J. Schultz, Lindsay Stein, and Jessica Wohl, "Lowdown: New Report: CMOs Have Half the Tenure of CEOs," *Ad Age*, February 15, 2017, http://adage.com/article/cmo-strategy/lowdown-report-cmos-half-tenure-ceos/307992/.

5 Forbes, *Marketing Accountability: A CEO Blueprint*, October 2017, https://cmo-practice.forbes.com/wp-content/uploads/2017/10/Forbes-Marketing-Accountability-Executive-Summary-10.2.17.pdf.

6 Jon Miller, "The Five Stages of Marketing Accountability," Marketo (blog), August 2007, https://blog.marketo.com/2007/08/the-five-stage.html.

7 Deloitte and CMO Council, *CMOs and the Spark to Drive Growth*, May 2018, https://cmo.deloitte.com/xc/en/pages/articles/cmo-council-report.html.

8 Michael Brenner, "Time for Marketing Leaders to Reinvent Themselves Again, Says Latest CMO Study," Marketing Insider Group, July 9, 2018, https://marketinginsidergroup.com/strategy/marketing-leaders-reinvent-themselves/.

9 OrbisResearch.com, "Global Predictive Analytics Market 2017 Statistics, Facts and Figures, Share, Segmentation, and Forecast by 2023," Reuters, October 10, 2017, https://www.reuters.com/brandfeatures/venture-capital/article?id=17937.

10 Visual IQ, *Branding Measurement in Today's Accountable World: A Tale of Two Marketers*, September 2015, https://www.visualiq.com/resource-center/research-study/form/branding-study.

11 Forbes, *Marketing Accountability*.

12 Michael Million, "Determining the Right Brand Metrics to Track Performance," FullSurge, accessed September 10, 2018, https://www.fullsurge.com/resources/determining-the-right-brand-metrics-to-track-performance.

13 Aaron Smith and Monica Anderson, *Online Shopping and E-Commerce* (Pew Research Center, December 19, 2016), 12, http://assets.pewresearch.org/wp-content/uploads/sites/14/2016/12/16113209/PI_2016.12.19_Online-Shopping_FINAL.pdf.

CHAPTER 14

1 The Hershey Company, *Our Shared Goodness Promise*, accessed September 10, 2018, https://www.thehersheycompany.com/content/dam/corporate-us/documents/pdf/shared-goodness-promise-infographic.pdf.

2   Todd Tillemans (president, The Hershey Company), in phone interview with the author, July 2018.

3   Bill Taylor, "The 10 Questions Every Change Agent Must Answer," *Harvard Business Review*, June 18, 2018, https://hbr.org/2009/06/the-10-questions-every-change.

4   Prophet, *Brand Relevance Index*, 2016, https://www.slideshare.net/ProphetBrandStrategy/the-brand-relevance-index-brands-consumers-cant-live-without.

5   "Defining Brand Relevance," Prophet, last modified 2017, https://www.prophet.com/relevantbrands-2017/defining-brand-relevance/.

6   Prophet, *Brand Relevance Index*, 2017, https://www.prophet.com/relevantbrands-2017/.

7   The Harris Poll, *Reputation Quotient*, 2018, https://theharrispoll.com/reputation-quotient/.

8   "These Are the Top 5 Companies Americans Can't Imagine Living without in 2018," The Harris Poll, last modified 2018, https://theharrispoll.com/these-are-the-top-5-companies-americans-cant-imagine-living-without/.

9   Gallup, *The Gallup CE3*, accessed September 10, 2018, https://www.gallup.com/services/169331/customer-engagement.aspx.

10 Net Promoter System, "How and Why Did You Develop the Net Promoter Score?" Bain & Company, last modified 2018, http://www.netpromotersystem.com/about/why-net-promoter.aspx.

11 "Net Promoter Score," Medallia, accessed September 10, 2018, https://www.medallia.com/net-promoter-score/.

12 NICE Satmetrix, *US Consumer 2018 Net Promoter Benchmarks*, 2018, http://info.nice.com/rs/338-EJP-431/images/NICE-Satmetrix-infographic-2018-b2c-nps-benchmarks-050418.pdf

Bibliography

Aaker, David. *Brand Portfolio Strategy*. New York: The Free Press, 2004.

Aaker, David. "Ries and Trout Were Wrong: Brand Extensions Work." *Harvard Business Review*, April 5, 2012. https://hbr.org/2012/04/ries-trout-were-wrong-brand-ex.

Aaker, David, and Erich Joachimsthaler. *Brand Leadership*. New York: The Free Press, 2009.

Adamska, Magda. "Brand Architecture Part 2: The Difference between Sub-Brands and Endorsed Brands." *BrandStruck* (blog), September 12, 2016. https://brandstruck.co/blog-post/brand-architecture-part-2-difference-sub-brands-endorsed-brands/.

Adobe and Econsultancy. *Digital Intelligence Briefing: Taking Advantage of the Mobile Opportunity*. July 2016. https://files.acrobat.com/a/preview/3aa69674-f9e9-4603-8dff-d0b0bb80749c.

Ansett, Dave. "Brand Extension and the Cannibal Effect." *Truly Deep* (blog), accessed September 10, 2018. http://www.trulydeeply.com.au/2015/01/brand-extension-and-the-canibal-effect-brand-strategy-melbourne/.

Barrier, Julie. "A Brand Is Just a Brand—Unless It Has a Purpose." *Forbes*, September 22, 2015. https://www.forbes.com/sites/sap/2015/09/22/a-brand-is-just-a-brand-unless-it-has-a-purpose/#31e83ab8672b.

Barton, Paul. *Maximizing Internal Communication: Strategies to Turn Heads, Win Hearts, Engage Employees, and Get Results*. Lake Placid, NY: Aviva Publishing, 2014.

Barwise, Patrick, and Seán Meehan. "Making Differentiation Make a Difference." *strategy + business*, November 30, 2004. https://www.strategy-business.com/article/04412?gko=aa86e.

Basney, Barbara. Phone interview with the author, June 2018.

Bendapudi, Neeli, and Venkat Bendapudi. "Creating the Living Brand." *Harvard Business Review*, May 2005. https://hbr.org/2005/05/creating-the-living-brand.

Blodgett, Carolyn Tisch. Phone interview with the author, June 2018.

Blythe, Nick. "Are Organisations in the Marine Industry Exploiting the Power of Brand?" BLUE Communications, November 29, 2017. http://www.blue-comms.com/are-organisations-in-the-marine-industry-exploiting-the-power-of-brand/.

Booker, Christopher. *The Seven Basic Plots: Why We Tell Stories*. London: Continuum, 2004.

Bosomworth, Danyl. "Brand Strategy—Core to Digital Strategy, but Often MIA." *Smart Insights*, March 9, 2017. https://www.smartinsights.com/online-brand-strategy/brand-development/brand-positioning-strategy/.

Bowers, Jarvis. Phone interview with the author, March 2018.

Brenner, Michael. "Time for Marketing Leaders to Reinvent Themselves Again, Says Latest CMO Study" Marketing Insider Group, July 9, 2018. https://marketinginsidergroup.com/strategy/marketing-leaders-reinvent-themselves/.

Bughin, Jacques, Jonathan Doogan, and Ole Jørgen Vetvik. "A New Way to Measure Word-of-Mouth Marketing." *McKinsey Quarterly*, April 2010. https://www.mckinsey.com/business-functions/marketing-and-sales/our-insights/a-new-way-to-measure-word-of-mouth-marketing.

CEB. *From Promotion to Emotion: Connecting B2B Customers to Brands*. 2013. https://www.cebglobal.com/content/dam/cebglobal/us/EN/best-practices-decision-support/marketing-communications/pdfs/promotion-emotion-whitepaper-full.pdf.

Chen, Yuyu. "84 Percent of Millennials Don't Trust Traditional Advertising." *ClickZ*, March 4, 2015. https://www.clickz.com/84-percent-of-millennials-dont-trust-traditional-advertising/27030/.

Chernev, Alexander. *The Psychology of Choice Overload: Implications for Retail Financial Services*. Filene Research Institute, 2011. https://pdfs.semanticscholar.org/5e47/70e194927ef20b4d389702a0d24429c894cd.pdf.

Ciarlone, Leonor. *Building a House of Brands: Whirlpool Corporation's Blueprint for Success*. The Gilbane Report, August 2005. https://gilbane.com/case_studies_pdf/CTW_Whirlpool_Final.pdf.

Clancy, Kevin, and Jack Trout. "Brand Confusion." *Harvard Business Review*, March 2002. https://hbr.org/2002/03/brand-confusion.

Clancy, Kevin, and Peter Krieg. *Your Gut Is Still Not Smarter Than Your Head: How Disciplined, Fact-Based Marketing Can Drive Extraordinary Growth and Profits*. Hoboken, NJ: Wiley, 2007. https://books.google.com/books?id=It-DJJSjMGIC.

Conroy, Pat, Anupam Narula, and Siddharth Ramalingam. "A Crisis of the Similar." Deloitte Insights, January 1, 2012. https://www2.deloitte.com/insights/us/en/industry/consumer-products/a-crisis-of-the-similar-innovation-in-the-consumer-products-industry.html.

Cupman, Julia. "How B2B Marketers Are Embracing Brand as the Top Driver of Growth." *MarketingProfs*, March 16, 2018. http://www.marketingprofs.com/articles/print/2018/33760/how-b2b-marketers-are-embracing-brand-as-the-top-driver-of-growth.

Dahm, Christine. Phone interview with the author, June 2018.

Deloitte. "The Deloitte Greenhouse Experience: Corporate Innovation Labs." Accessed September 10, 2018. https://www2.deloitte.com/us/en/pages/operations/solutions/deloitte-greenhouse-experience.html.

Deloitte. *Oil and Gas Reality Check 2015: A Look at the Top Issues Facing the Oil and Gas Sector*. 2015. https://www2.deloitte.com/content/dam/Deloitte/global/Documents/Energy-and-Resources/gx-er-oil-and-gas-reality-check-2015.pdf.

Deloitte and CMO Council. *CMOs and the Spark to Drive Growth*. May 2018. https://cmo.deloitte.com/xc/en/pages/articles/cmo-council-report.html.

Dominguez, Steven. Phone interview with the author, March 2018.

Donnelly, Tim. "How to Maintain Brand Consistency across Product Lines." *Inc.*, November 18, 2010. https://www.inc.com/guides/2010/11/how-to-maintain-brand-consistency-across-product-lines.html.

Dowd, James, and Digital Surgeons. *The Science of Story: How Brands Can Use Storytelling to Get More Customers*. SlideShare, April 13, 2017. https://www.slideshare.net/digitalsurgeons/the-science-of-story-understanding-how-stories-work-for-brands.

Dvorak, Nate, and Robert Gabsa. "Failed Brand Ambassadors." *Gallup Business Journal*, January 10, 2017. http://news.gallup.com/businessjournal/201692/companies-dont-have-effective-brand-ambassadors.aspx.

Fishburne, Tom. "Why Don Draper Types Can't Control Brand Content Anymore." *Content Marketing Institute*, September 15, 2013. http://contentmarketinginstitute.com/2013/09/draper-types-cant-control-brand-content/.

Forbes. *Marketing Accountability: A CEO Blueprint*. October 2017. https://cmo-practice.forbes.com/wp-content/uploads/2017/10/Forbes-Marketing-Accountability-Executive-Summary-10.2.17.pdf.

Forbes Agency Council. "Six Critical Elements That Make TED Talks Compelling." *Forbes*, July 25, 2016. https://www.forbes.com/sites/forbesagencycouncil/2016/07/25/six-critical-elements-that-make-ted-talks-compelling/#71709571768d.

FullSurge. *The Anatomy of a Growth Guru*. 2015. https://www.fullsurge.com/growth-guru-3.

Fumo, Nicola. "The Psychology of Customization." *Racked*, June 1, 2016. https://www.racked.com/2016/6/1/11772798/customization-monogramming-personalization-pins.

Fussner, Julie. Phone interview with the author, June 2018.

Gallup. "The Engaged Workplace." Accessed September 10, 2018. https://www.gallup.com/services/190118/engaged-workplace.aspx.

Gallup. *The Gallup CE³*. Accessed September 10, 2018. https://www.gallup.com/services/169331/customer-engagement.aspx.

Greenberg, Karl. "CoreBrand Says There's Value in Corporate Brand." *MediaPost*, January 2, 2014. https://www.mediapost.com/publications/article/216443/corebrand-says-theres-value-in-corporate-brand.html.

Greenwald, Michelle. "The Evolution of Brand Marketing Strategy from One To Infinity." *Forbes*, January 21, 2018. https://www.forbes.com/sites/michellegreenwald/2018/01/21/the-evolution-of-brand-marketing-strategy-from-one-to-infinity/#2d24e0ae4afa.

Gross, Andrew. Phone interview with the author, May 2018.

Grossman, Ben. *Content Creation Best Practices and the Problem with Editorial Calendars*. SlideShare, March 18, 2015. https://www.slideshare.net/bengrossman/content-creation-best-practices-the-problem-with-editorial-calendars.

Grutzner, Fritz. "Stories Companies Tell: How Internal Stories Build Your Brand." *Brand Quarterly*, n.d. http://www.brandquarterly.com/stories-companies-tell-how-internal-stories-build-your-brand.

Hagel, John III, John Seely Brown, Tamara Samoylova, Kasey M. Lobaugh, and Neha Goel. *The Retail Transformation: Cultivating Choice, Experience, and Trust*. Deloitte University Press, 2015. https://www2.deloitte.com/content/dam/Deloitte/za/Documents/consumer-business/ZA_RetailTrans_ConsumerBusiness_101515.pdf.

Hague, Paul, and Matthew Harrison. "Marketing Segmentation in B2B Markets." B2B International, accessed September 10, 2018. https://www.b2binternational.com/publications/b2b-segmentation-research/.

Harris Poll, The. *Reputation Quotient*. 2018. https://theharrispoll.com/reputation-quotient/.

Headstream. *The Power of Brand Storytelling: How Brand Storytelling Can Meet Marketing Objectives*. SlideShare, June 22, 2015. https://www.slideshare.net/Headstream/the-power-of-brand-storytelling.

Hollis, Nigel. "It Is Not a Choice: Brands Should Seek Differentiation and Distinctiveness." Millward Brown: Point of View, 2011. http://www.millwardbrown.com/docs/default-source/insight-documents/points-of-view/MillwardBrown_POV_Brand_Differentiation.pdf.

Hsieh, Tony. "Your Culture Is Your Brand." *HuffPost*, updated December 6, 2017. https://www.huffingtonpost.com/entry/zappos-founder-tony-hsieh_1_b_783333.html.

Interbrand. "Best Global Brands 2016 Rankings." 2016. https://www.interbrand.com/best-brands/best-global-brands/2016/ranking/.

Interbrand. "Best Global Brands 2017 Rankings." 2017. https://www.interbrand.com/best-brands/best-global-brands/2017/ranking/.

Johnson, Carla. "The 50/50 Split between External and Internal Branding." Type A Communications, 2013. http://typeacommunications.com/the-5050-split-between-external-and-internal-branding/.

Johnson, Carla. Phone interview with the author, July 2018.

Johnson, Carla. "Why Human Resources Is Essential to the Brand Storytelling Equation." *Content Marketing Institute*, December 26, 2013. https://contentmarketinginstitute.com/2013/12/human-resources-essential-brand-storytelling/.

Johnstone, Rose. "Brand Strategy in the Digital Age." *Innovation Enterprise*, accessed November 5, 2018. https://channels.theinnovationenterprise.com/articles/brand-strategy-in-the-digital-age.

Kantar Millward Brown. *2015 BrandZ Top 100 Global Brands*. 2015.

Keaney, Michelle. "Consumers Are Willing to Pay More for Purposeful Brands." *Marketing Week*, September 19, 2016. https://www.marketingweek.com/2016/09/19/consumers-are-willing-to-pay-58-more-for-purposeful-brands/.

Keller, Ed. Phone interview with the author, May 2018.

Keller, Ed, and Brad Fay. "Word-of-Mouth Advocacy: A New Key to Advertising Effectiveness." *Journal of Advertising Research* 52, no. 4 (December 2012): 459–64. https://doi.org/10.2501/JAR-52-4-459-464.

Kelly Services and EveryoneSocial. *Why Kelly Services Got Their Recruiters Active on Social Media*. April 2017. http://ellegriffin.com/wp-content/uploads/2017/04/Why-Kelly-Services-Got-Their-Recruiters-Active-On-Social-Media.pdf.

Kotler, Philip, and Kevin Lane Keller. *Marketing Management*. Boston: Prentice Hall, 2006.

Kumar, Nirmalya. "Kill a Brand, Keep a Customer." *Harvard Business Review*, December 2003. https://hbr.org/2003/12/kill-a-brand-keep-a-customer.

Light, Larry, and Joan Kiddon. *Six Rules for Brand Revitalization: Learn How Companies Like McDonald's Can Re-Energize Their Brands*. Upper Saddle River, NJ: Prentice Hall, 2009.

Marshall, John, and Rick Wise. "The Resurgence of the Corporate Brand." *Ad Age*, April 17, 2013. https://adage.com/article/cmo-strategy/resurgence-corporate-brand/240855/.

Mathers, Martha. "B2B Buyers Are Full of Emotion. Is Your Branding?" *CMO.com*, August 28, 2017. https://www.cmo.com/opinion/articles/2017/8/9/b2b-buying-is-full-of-emotions-ptr-tlp.html.

McCarron, Suzanne. Phone interview with the author, June 2018.

McEwen, William J. "Your Brand Is in Their Hands: How Your Employees Can Make—or Break—a Brand Relationship." *Gallup Business Journal*, April 15, 2010. https://news.gallup.com/businessjournal/127340/brand-hands.aspx.

Messina, Rebecca. Phone interview with the author, May 2018.

Miller, Jon. "The Five Stages of Marketing Accountability." Marketo (blog), August 2007. https://blog.marketo.com/2007/08/the-five-stage.html.

Million, Michael. "Determining the Right Brand Metrics to Track Performance." FullSurge, accessed September 10, 2018. https://www.fullsurge.com/resources/determining-the-right-brand-metrics-to-track-performance.

Million, Michael. "Perspectives on Orchestrating Customer Experience." http://cdn2.hubspot.net/hubfs/858343/Articles/Perspectives-on-Orchestrating-Customer-Experience.pdf?t=1462290037021.

Minnium, Peter. "The Definitive Guide to Digital Brand Lift." *Marketing Land*, January 6, 2016. https://marketingland.com/definitive-guide-digital-brand-lift-157764.

Mitchell, Colin. "Selling the Brand Inside." *Harvard Business Review*, January 2002. https://hbr.org/2002/01/selling-the-brand-inside.

Morrison, Yvette. Phone interview with the author, May 2018.

Murphy, Tim. Phone interview with the author, March 2018.

Musi, George. "The Downside of Digital's Explosive Growth? Too Many Marketers Are Failing to Think Long-Term." *Adweek*, March 22, 2017. https://www.adweek.com/brand-marketing/the-downside-of-digitals-explosive-growth-too-many-marketers-are-failing-to-think-long-term/.

Nanji, Ayaz. "How B2B and B2C Firms Approach Personalization Differently." *MarketingProfs*, May 10, 2018. https://www.marketingprofs.com/charts/2018/34737/how-b2b-and-b2c-firms-approach-personalization-differently.

Neff, Jack, E. J. Schultz, Lindsay Stein, and Jessica Wohl. "Lowdown: New Report: CMOs Have Half the Tenure of CEOs." *Ad Age*, February 15, 2017. http://adage.com/article/cmo-strategy/lowdown-report-cmos-half-tenure-ceos/307992/.

Net Promoter System. "How and Why Did You Develop the Net Promoter Score?" Bain & Company, last modified 2018. http://www.netpromotersystem.com/about/why-net-promoter.aspx.

NICE Satmetrix. *US Consumer 2018 Net Promoter Benchmarks*. 2018. http://info.nice.com/rs/338-EJP-431/images/NICE-Satmetrix-infographic-2018-b2c-nps-benchmarks-050418.pdf.

Nielsen. *Nurturing Innovation: How to Succeed in Years Two and Three*. June 2015. http://markedsforing.dk/sites/default/files/nielsen__sustaining_growth_report_0.pdf.

Nielsen. *The Sustainability Imperative*. October 2015. https://www.nielsen.com/us/en/insights/reports/2015/the-sustainability-imperative.html.

OrbisResearch.com. "Global Predictive Analytics Market 2017 Statistics, Facts and Figures, Share, Segmentation, and Forecast by 2023." *Reuters*, October 10, 2017. https://www.reuters.com/brandfeatures/venture-capital/article?id=17937.

Overby, Stephanie. "MGM Resorts's Tomovich: There's No Substitute for Experience." *CMO.com*, March 6, 2017. https://www.cmo.com/interviews/articles/2017/1/30/the-cmocom-interview-lilian-tomovich-chief-experience-officer-mgm-resorts-.html#gs.aKgNu54.

Pine, B. Joseph III, and James H. Gilmore. *The Experience Economy: Work Is Theatre and Every Business a Stage*. Boston: Harvard Business School Press, 1999.

Prophet. *Brand Relevance Index*. 2016. https://www.slideshare.net/ProphetBrandStrategy/the-brand-relevance-index-brands-consumers-cant-live-without.

Prophet. *Brand Relevance Index*. 2017. https://www.prophet.com/relevantbrands-2017/.

Radley Yeldar. *2016 Fit for Purpose Index*. 2016. http://ry.com/services/brand/fit-for-purpose-2016/.

Ries, Al. "Focus Is the Difference between Your Company Brand and Apple's." *Ad Age*, September 12, 2012. http://adage.com/article/al-ries/focus-difference-company-brand-apple/237133/.

Ries, Al, and Jack Trout. *Positioning: The Battle for Your Mind*. New York: McGraw-Hill, 1981.

Rocha, Mike. "Brand Valuation: A Versatile Strategic Tool for Business." Interbrand, accessed on September 10, 2018. http://interbrand.com/views/brand-valuation-a-versatile-strategic-tool-for-business/.

Rubin, Ann. Phone interview with the author, May 2018.

Schuller, Darcy. "Brand Positioning in the Digital Age." Suvonni, accessed September 10, 2018. http://suvonni.com/brand-positioning-in-the-digital-age/.

Sinek, Simon. "How Great Leaders Inspire Action." TED, September 2009. https://www.ted.com/talks/simon_sinek_how_great_leaders_inspire_action?language=en.

Smith, Aaron, and Monica Anderson. *Online Shopping and E-Commerce.* Pew Research Center, December 19, 2016. http://assets.pewresearch.org/wp-content/uploads/sites/14/2016/12/16113209/PI_2016.12.19_Online-Shopping_FINAL.pdf.

Staack, Volker, and Branton Cole. *Reinventing Innovation: Five Findings to Guide Strategy through Execution.* (PwC, 2017). https://www.pwc.com/us/en/advisory-services/business-innovation/assets/2017-innovation-benchmark-findings.pdf.

Stankeviciute, Rasa, and Jonas Hoffmann. "The Slippery Slope of Brand Expansion." *Marketing Management* 20, no. 4, (Winter 2011): 26–31. https://archive.ama.org/archive/ResourceLibrary/MarketingManagement/documents/Slippery Slope.pdf.

Suttle, Jeff. Phone interview with the author, March 2018.

Taylor, Bill. "The 10 Questions Every Change Agent Must Answer." *Harvard Business Review*, June 18, 2018. https://hbr.org/2009/06/the-10-questions-every-change-.

Taylor, David. *Brand Stretch: Why 1 in 2 Extensions Fail, and How to Beat the Odds.* Chichester, UK: Wiley, 2004.

Taylor, David, and Jon Goldstone. "How to Reboot Brand Strategy for the Digital Age." *Campaign*, October 31, 2016. https://www.campaignlive.co.uk/article/reboot-brand-strategy-digital-age/1413429.

Tillemans, Todd. Phone interview with the author, July 2018.

Trappe, Christoph. "7 Brand Storytelling Best Practices to Grow Your Audience." *Content Science Review*, April 26, 2017. https://review.content-science.com/2017/04/7-brand-storytelling-best-practices-to-grow-your-audience/.

Trout, Jack. "'Positioning' Is a Game People Play in Today's Me-Too Market Place." *Industrial Marketing* 54, no. 6 (June 1969): 51–55.

Tugend, Alina. "Too Many Choices: A Problem That Can Paralyze." *New York Times*, February 26, 2010. http://www.nytimes.com/2010/02/27/your-money/27shortcuts.html.

Visual IQ. *Branding Measurement in Today's Accountable World: A Tale of Two Marketers.* September 2015. https://www.visualiq.com/resource-center/research-study/form/branding-study.

Weber Shandwick and KRC Research. *Employees Rising: Seizing the Opportunity in Employee Activism.* April 2014. https://www.webershandwick.com/uploads/news/files/employees-rising-seizing-the-opportunity-in-employee-activism.pdf.

Wichmann, Jonathan. "Being B2B Social: A Conversation with Maersk Line's Head of Social Media." Interview by David Edelman. McKinsey & Company, May 2013. https://www.mckinsey.com/business-functions/marketing-and-sales/our-insights/being-b2b-social-a-conversation-with-maersk-lines-head-of-social-media.

Wise, Rick. "Taking Your Brand to the Next Level." *Wharton Blog Network* (blog). *Wharton Magazine*, September 20, 2013. http://whartonmagazine.com/blogs/taking-your-brand-to-the-next-level/.

Wnuk, Steve. Phone interview with the author, April 2018.

Wobben, Carolin. "Success Factors of Brand Extension in International Marketing." Master's thesis, University of Hamburg, 2006. https://www.grin.com/document/58639.

Yohn, Denise Lee. "Engaging Employees Starts with Remembering What Your Company Stands For." *Harvard Business Review*, March 13, 2018. https://hbr.org/2018/03/engaging-employees-starts-with-remembering-what-your-company-stands-for.

Yohn, Denise Lee. "Why Companies Are Advertising Their Master Brand." *Harvard Business Review*, March 28, 2016. https://hbr.org/2016/03/why-companies-are-advertising-their-master-brand.

Zhu, Yi, and Anthony Dukes. "When It's Smart to Copy Your Competitor's Brand Promise." *Harvard Business Review*, March 23, 2017. https://hbr.org/2017/03/when-its-smart-to-copy-your-competitors-brand-promise.

About the Author

MITCH DUCKLER is founder and managing partner of FullSurge (www.fullsurge.com), a brand and marketing strategy consultancy based in Chicago, Illinois. He has more than twenty-five years of brand management and management consulting experience.

Prior to FullSurge, Mitch was a senior partner at Vivaldi Partners Group and a partner in the Chicago office of Prophet, where he co-led the brand strategy practice area. His client base includes Fortune 500 companies and numerous world-class brands, such as Exxon Mobil, Deloitte, Kellogg's, Best Buy, American Family Insurance, NBCUniversal, Cox Communications, Alcon, The Home Depot, and General Electric.

Mitch began his career in brand management at Unilever, where he worked on category-leading personal care brands, including Suave and Degree. He also worked for The Coca-Cola Company, where he helped launch an in-house consulting group that provides consumer and brand marketing consulting services to many of the company's largest retail customers.

Mitch is a faculty member of the Association of National Advertisers (ANA) School of Marketing. He earned a BS in business from the University of Minnesota and an MBA from the University of Michigan.

Connect with me:
https://www.linkedin.com/in/mitchduckler/
https://twitter.com/MitchDuckler

A Word about FullSurge

Many of the concepts and perspectives presented throughout this book have been shaped and inspired by the collective work of the partners at FullSurge.

FullSurge is a brand and marketing strategy consulting firm that helps clients achieve enduring, demand-driven growth through brand strategy and development. Our service offerings span many of the topics detailed in this book, including brand positioning, portfolio strategy, architecture, experience, and extension and growth. Over the years, the firm has been privileged to work with some of the most prestigious and valuable brands in the world. Our clients include ExxonMobil, Deloitte, Hyatt Hotels, Blue Cross Blue Shield Association, Alcon, American Family Insurance, Cox Communications, and ManpowerGroup.

For more information on FullSurge and case studies detailing how we've helped clients build world-class brands and drive profitable growth, please visit us at www.fullsurge.com.

Made in the USA
Columbia, SC
29 July 2019